Flights of The Voyager

By

Matthew A. Nelson

If you purchase this book without a cover you should be aware that this book may have been stolen property and reported as "unsold and destroyed to the publisher. In such case neither the author nor the publisher has received any payment for this "stripped" book.

This book is about some of the flying adventures that Matthew A. Nelson has made over the years. All photographs, unless noted otherwise, were made by Matthew Nelson, and are copyrighted.

Copyrighted 2011 by Matthew A. Nelson

All rights reserved. Except as permitted under the U. S. Copyright Act of 1976, no part of this publication may be reproduced, distributed, or transmitted in any form or by any means, or stored in a database or retrieval system, without the express permission of the author. You may contact the author at matt.nelson@wildblue.net.

Flights of The Voyager, March 2011. ISBN 978-0-9834208-0-4

Forward

"Igor's son, Michael Sikorsky, once said "aviation is a pleasant mental disease". If ever there was an individual that embodied this concept it would be my friend and fellow adventurer Matt Nelson!

From the first time we met at an airshow in Alaska to our next horsepower driven sojourn, whatever, wherever, I know Matt will be there at the starting gate.
Ready. Set. Go!"

"This quote from my friend Douglas Fulton, who is part-owner of the Antonov An-2 pictured on the upper right photo of the front cover, is a good way to start this book." Photo credit goes to Ken Gray, a professional photographer.

The photo on the bottom left of the cover (J-3 Cub on floats) is by Mike Kincaid.

Every person has stories to tell; every pilot has had flights that have been memorable, exhilarating, and/or scary. Some flights have made the pilot feel closer to God when they see the beauty of His works; other times the pilots pray fervently to God to help them safely land the aircraft.

Most military, airline, commercial, general aviation, and bush pilots have stories to tell that would make my own flights look like I've been riding around in an airplane that's on a child's Merry-Go-Round. Many of these same pilots have flown through very adverse weather and over hazardous terrain hundreds of times, often under combat conditions. There is no way, nor is it my intent, to match my experiences with these people, for whom I have the utmost respect. That being said, I still have been privileged to fly in several planes as a pilot and/or as a crewmember.

My career hasn't been that of a pilot, but as an electronics technician and engineer working in the aerospace industry. While I was in the Army in the Sixties I was fortunate to be assigned to fly as a non-rated crewmember in the back of a Navy EA-3B jet, the Skywarrior, piloted by CDR Scott Beat. For three years I worked as a telemetry technician at Edwards AFB, where the Air Force conducts flight-testing on new aircraft. They were testing the F-15, the F-16, the B-1, and the A-10 when I was there during the mid-Seventies. Before my retirement in 2009, I spent another thirty-one years on NASA contracts, testing the

Space Shuttle and International Space Station communication systems, and tracking satellites in Antarctica. While working at the Johnson Space Center in Houston, I obtained my private pilot's license, and eventually bought my first airplane, a 1947 Stinson 108 Voyager. Three days later, I was in Alaska with the intention of picking up my seaplane rating. Most pilots who go for the seaplane rating receive it in about seven hours; it took me thirty-eight hours over a two-year period. While chasing this rating, I met Douglas Fulton and Neal Oppen, who own a Russian-designed and Polish-built An-2, the worlds biggest bi-plane. I flew a bunch of hours in that plane. In 2008, my friend Roger "Mzungu" Moore flew with me in Africa in a Cessna 182, and while there we both flew in an old DeHavilland Tiger Moth. For this book, I have chosen to write about some of my flights in the EA-3B, the Stinson 108, floatplanes, the An-2, and the African trip.

Over the years I have had an insatiable wanderlust, and have traveled on each of the seven continents, and through all fifty states. Since the name of my first plane was the Stinson 108 Voyager, I have also started calling myself "The Voyager"; hence, the name in the title.

This book is dedicated to my wife Karoline, our daughter Michelle and her husband Keith, our daughter Cheri and her husband John, and our two granddaughters, Camyrn and Cadie. I also dedicate this book the memories my parents John and Marjorie Nelson, my sister Cathy Nelson, to the many other relatives and friends who have also passed on, and to all the pilots and aircrews who have perished. I thank God for giving me the privilege and gift of flying over His wonderful creation.

Contents

1.	Flight to the Angels	1
2.	I was an Army Guy Flying in a Navy EA-3B Skywarrior	23
3.	The Voyager Flies the Voyager	33
4.	There Ain't No Better Flying Than Floatplane Flying!	71
5.	A Vagabond's Story of Hopping a Freight Plane, the Antonov An-2	155
6.	African Flying Safari	247
7.	Airplanes of Friends	295

Flight To The Angels
March 1992

Young lady, why do you say, "How are we today?" Don't
You know how you are? How do you expect me to answer?
As a prisoner in a nursing home, victim of a stroke, my
Means of communication is very limited. All I can do is
Lay here in quiet embarrassment, while you give me a bath.

Powdered eggs are not my favorite blah breakfast. Like sawdust,
They dribble down my chin, and mix with my spit, which
Nobody seems to care about, nor wants to clean. Zombie,
You call me. What do you know? You are young and pretty,
Full of life, and cannot visualize yourself, old and gray.

You say that I look like I am ready to board the Flight
To the Angles. What a paradox, that Death is called
"Flight to the Angles", considering nearly a century of
Flight has been my life. Under your breath, you say,
"*Pops, you smell more like Hogan's goat than clover honey!*"

Girl, you don't know what bad smells like until you have
Walked behind a mule all day. Growing up on Granddad's
Farm, I can remember dreaming of flight. Occasionally, a
Bi-plane would fly over, and I knew that someday I would
Be at the controls of one. Did you say honey?

Grandma made the best homemade bread. Hot, fresh out of
The oven, with melting butter, fingers sticky with honey
From Granddad's bees. Images of smoked ham, fresh sweet
Corn, and homemade chocolate ice cream for desert bring
Me back to those favorite memories of childhood.

Great Grandfather Charles Brewster Hubbell and his son
John Elbert Hubbell both served with the NY 153rd Regiment
During the Civil War. Daughters change their names when
They marry; as a result, my Granddad's name is Ernest Gremel,
Who was the son of a Great Lakes Sea Captain.

Stinging my face, the sands at Kitty Hawk made me cry
On that cold, windy, December day. Granddad said history
Was in the making, but at age five, all I wanted to was
Go home. My tears dried as I stood in awe, fascinated
By the first flight of the Wright Brothers.

In my teens, I worked for free as a mechanic to learn to fly.
Then, at twenty, I flew a SPAD VII in France, in the same
Squadron that flew against Baron Manfred von Richthofen.
Exhilarating as the hope of having the Red Baron in our
Gun sights, gut wrenching was the fear we would be in his.

Upon firing my guns, and seeing the Fokker D.VII react
Violently to the bullets in its fuselage, I flew close
Enough to the German pilot to verify my first kill. I
Had a fleeting glance into blue eyes agonizing that
There would be no more talk about "After the war..."

As if waltzing with its invisible partner Gravity,
The Fokker augured into the ground, without exploding.
From the air I could see the crash site was near our
Aerodrome. I landed my plane and everyone cheered.
We immediately drove to the smoldering wreckage.

Jumping off of the truck before it stopped, I ran to
The pilot. "Call the Doctor" I yelled. Bleeding, and
Unconscious, he died in my arms. A one-month old
Photograph of him, his pretty wife, and a young son
About two years old stuck to his blood-soaked pocket.

Gremel is a German name. My granddad immigrated from
Munich in 1850 at age ten. This pilot and I could have
Been friends, could have both fought on the same side.
What have I done? My friend WWI Ace Eddie Rickenbacker
Handed me a saw, and I cut off the propeller at the spinner.

Beer flowed that night. Everyone wanted to shake my
Hand, buy me a drink, and caress the cut off prop,
Which was the conversation piece of the evening.
Blaming beer as the cause of me getting sick was less
Honest than blaming memories of a German pilot's eyes.

Somona, the cleaning lady asks, "Mr. Gremel, why do you
Have tears in your eyes? I wish you could talk to me."
This lady brings me home made tacos that the nurses don't
Know about, places a fresh flower in a vase everyday,
Gives me picture calendars, and always talks to me.

My mother died during childbirth. Devastated, my dad
Vanished into the Alaskan goldfields, leaving me with
Granddad. Inspired by his salty sea captain stories, I
Chose to sail around the world, taking my discharge in
France, after the signing of the Armistice.

Tramp steamers to Rome, Venice, Athens, Constantinople,
And a place nobody ever heard of called Sinop, on the South
Black Sea coast. There, broken Greek marble columns
Silently spoke of the triumphs and tragedies of ancient
Warriors, ignored by men riding in solid wheel ox-carts.

In Jerusalem, I picked up as a souvenir a square-cut
Stone the size of a dice out of a Roman road. Did
Christ's feet touch this stone as He walked from the
Garden of Gethsemane on His way to the cross? Perhaps
The time is near when I will be able to ask Him myself.

Rough Turkish cigarettes parched my throat as the hot
Sun reflecting off of sands near the Pyramids burnt my
Face. River of Moses, Riddle of the Sphinx, Tombs of the
Pharaohs, so exhilarating, so enchanting. Riding a camel
In Egypt cured me of any romantic Bedouin notions I had.

Africa. The day I finally hiked to the top of Mount
Kilimanjaro left me puffing and wheezing like a Stanley
Steamer. Proud Black hunters led me on safaris. While
Eating gazelle steak, I worried about lions. Elephants
With ivory tusks and giraffes roamed the Plains of Kenya.

"Magnificent" inadequately describes the beauty of the
Taj Mahal. How can such a rich luxury exist in India,
The Land of the Sacred Cows, while so many are starving?
Stepping around crippled beggars, wallowing in their own
Stench, I felt guilty as I averted my eyes from theirs.

To tell of my experiences on this Round-the-World
Trip, I would have to write a book. I can't even hold
My hands still. Kathmandu to see Mt. Everest, then to
Bangkok, to Borneo, on to Australia. There, I drank
Beer with an Aussie pilot, who gave me a kangaroo pin.

Those lads from Australia and New Zealand were the
Bravest of all. Little did they expect to see me when
They told me back in France to look them up if I ever
Travelled to their countries. Many beers cloaked many
Tears; men couldn't cry while toasting those who died.

Exotic, beautiful birds sang in the rain forest near
Cairns, Australia. The best diving in my life occurred
In the Great Barrier Reef. Clam shells two feet in
Diameter, royal blue starfish, and fish of every color
All lived in coral reefs, guarded by reef sharks.

To experience the exquisite colors of Ayers Rock, in the
Northern Territory, one must view it at sunrise. Fire
Opals, Aborigine handmade boomerangs, and graceful,
Bouncing kangaroos are dominant in my memory of the
Land called Down Under.

Mt. Cook, the crown of the Southern Alps on the South
Island, Franz Josef and Fox Glaciers, fjords such as
Milford Sound, the extinct snow-covered volcano of Mt.
Egmont on the North Island, and Maori cultural influence
Leads one to believe New Zealand is paradise found.

Finally, after several months of roaming in New Zealand,
I obtained a deckhand job working on a supply ship going
To the states, via Papeete, Tahiti. Imagine my surprise
While walking around that island, of seeing a young lady
Without a top to her dress, as if in a Gauguin painting!

Long after mountains of Tahiti disappeared over the
Horizon, images of that girl lingered in my mind, as did
Upside-down coconut trees playing ping-pong with a full
Moon on Pacific Ocean reflections...Farm boy, combat
Veteran, pilot, world traveller, now a man of twenty-one.

Home from the War. Ecstatic to be in the land of the
Free, alive. Proud, somewhat arrogant, a well-travelled
Pilot, with a jet black bushy beard; and no visible
Wounds. Clickity-clack, America from a boxcar: Arizona
Cactus, West Texas, Gatlinburg, north to Michigan.

Nothing had changed but me. Civil War vets interrupted their
Checker games, feebly shook my hand, welcomed me home.
With eyes staring into the past, they ask me how Fly Boys
Could know anything about war, flying those inferno
Machines, high above the smell of blood, guts, and death.

Infected by disease called travelitis, I realized the
Restlessness in my soul guided my inner being to search
For a direction not marked on my compass - up. Ambling
Down the path called Destiny, I came across a 1918 Curtiss
JN-4D Jenny. Prior to owning a car, I flew my own plane.

Honing my flying skills, I soon joined the fraternity of
Veteran pilots, barnstorming county fairs. Introducing
Other to the marvels of flight, we entertained them
With their first rides in Flying Machines. Within a few
Months, my Jenny and I landed in Jackson Hole, Wyoming.

Every bit as spectacular as the Swiss Alps, and Mt. Cook
In New Zealand, America's Alps are the Tetons. My Jenny
Flew with her twin sister in mirrored formation over the
Calm waters of Jenny Lake, intruding on the solitude of
Twice imaged snow-capped peaks, pink from an ebbing sun.

Herds of majestic elk live near the Tetons. In autumn,
When they are in rut, their bulging is heard for miles.
Golden leaves of Aspen contrast in a harmonious balance
Of nature with royal blue skies, tall green pine trees,
Branches heavy with diamond dust of early snowfall.

Time for Physical Therapy. Robert is OK. He tells me
About his girlfriends, and his plans to enroll in medical
School. Like Somona, he talks to me as if he knows I can
Hear. But brother, at my age, some of the exercises he
Puts me through would make a man half my age wince.

Hard up for cash, and winter coming on, I decided to try
Doing some honest labor, instead of flying youngsters
In my Jenny around the Tetons and calling it work. Fence
Mending and rounding up strays didn't sound too difficult.
Nobody said anything about Wyoming winds at forty below!

Only in his piercing bluish-gray eyes did Arrowhead Andy
Resemble a TV cowboy. Short and bald, his tobacco-
Stained toothy grin disarmed me into thinking that I
Only signed on to ride his brand until Spring. My plan:
Rope, brand, forget the old coot, and fly my Jenny away.

As if describing Arrowhead Andy, an unknown poet wrote,
"...Bronc buster, wild Indian fighter, Grizzly bear
Hunter, pretty good windmill mechanic, too." One crisp,
Cold, winter night, air scented by burning pine logs,
Between bites of elk steak, I asked him about his name.

He spat out his chew, grinned, took a swig of "White
Lighting", and with firelight flickering in his eyes, he
Told of balding early. Wounded by a arrow in his right
Shoulder in an 1875 Indian skirmish, he tricked a scalp-
Hunter by smearing blood on his head and playing dead.

War souvenirs - an arrowhead mounted on a belt buckle, a
Sawed-off German propeller. Bound by a bond of shedding
Blood of admirable adversaries, my plan of forgetting an
Old coot disappeared in the melting snow. My heart had
Been roped and branded by his beautiful daughter, Ella.

Red-hair, green eyes, high-spirited, Love of my Life. We
Clashed in the beginning. I was nothing but a restless
Pilot, living in the bunkhouse with the other hands. She
Rode a horse better than any man, and immensely enjoyed
Embarrassing me as the greenhorn from Michigan.

Loosing a horse race to Ella actually appealed to me. If
She won, I had an obligation to teach her to fly. As she
Stepped into the cockpit of my Jenny, her eyes sparkled
When she said, "Greenhorn, let's see what this bucket of
Bolts will do." Fortunately, Jenny didn't hold a grudge.

Oh, how we soared through the clouds and through the
Passes of the Tetons that day. The ecstasy I felt that
Day surpassed that of my first plane ride. Impressed her on
My smooth landing techniques.. bumpity, bump. "Greenhorn,
You fly like you ride a horse." Then, she kissed me!

Intensifying my amnesia of a single man's life, Ella soon
Wore my ring of gold. Our vows were exchanged at
The Church of The Transfiguration, which is the little
Church with the pine Cross in the front of the picture
Window overlooking the incredibly beautiful Tetons.

Insatiable passions, cold winter nights, and God's gift
Of Life to us caused Ella's stomach to swell. Old Doc
Porter congratulated me on the birth of my son, but I had
The feeling he had seen the miracles of life before. God,
Please help me, I don't know anything about being a daddy.

Wearing a yellow robe, a radiance glowing from her face,
Ella's beauty as she quietly pondered little toes and a
Little nose is as vivid today as the day my son entered
Our hearts. One year later, I again had the privilege of
Seeing that lovely look; God blessed us with a daughter.

Family man, family responsibilities. What future did a
Pilot working as a cowboy have in the wonderful country
Of Wyoming? Dreams of aviation and improving airplanes.
Aeronautical Engineer program - Montana State University
In Bozeman. How could this farm boy pass mathematics?

My Jenny and I flew to Bozeman, Ella drove an old Model T
Truck with Bud and Marjorie. Fortunately, we could afford
Tuition. Somehow we made it, and Ella taught me to ski.
In 1926 I graduated with a Bachelor of Science Degree and
Thought I knew enough about airplanes to become famous.

I received a job offer from Ryan Airlines in San Diego.
Ella and I flew out in my Jenny, sightseeing through the
Grand Canyon. We rode a train to Wyoming for the kids.
Having hoboed in boxcars, paying for Pullman tickets
Disgusted me, but Ella thought I should act respectable.

Adjusting to San Diego, I started my Engineering career.
In February, 1927, Ryan contracted with businessmen
From St. Louis to build a plane for Charles Lindbergh.
Proud to have participated in its design, part of me flew
In the Spirit of St. Louis, across the Atlantic to Paris.

Prohibition and the Depression. Everything changed, and
My career disappeared for a couple of years. Odd jobs fed
Ella, Bud, and Marjorie, but my heart broke when I had to
Sell my beloved Jenny to pay the rent. When one is broke,
Fifty dollars is like winning the Irish Sweepstakes.

Lockheed Aircraft in Burbank, California established itself
By building Jack Northrop's designed Vega, the plane
Amelia Earhart flew solo across both the United States
And the Atlantic in 1932. I hired on in time to work on
The Electra, the plane she last flew in 1937.

Finally, its eleven o'clock; time for lunch! Too bad
Grandma can't replace these institutional cooks.
Now, I have the chance to climb into the cockpit of my
Wheelchair, taxi past the rose garden, concentrate on
Clearing the trees, and if I'm lucky, see a plane fly.

In 1936, Ella's father died and left a small inheritance.
Wanting to escape the pain, we decided to go Europe. In
Munich, we found Granddad's boyhood home. Upon telling
The lady of the house we were Gremels, she smiled and
Invited us in, she then showed us the room of his birth.

Memories of Granddad engulfed me; tears threatened to
Embarrass me. So I forced myself to think of something
Funny, and thought of Great Grandfather's Civil War letter.
Goldbricking was probably invented by a foot soldier in
Caesar's Army, but Granddad perfected it into a fine art:

"My health is much better than it has been for years. I have tolerated easy times as I do about as I please and you may be sure I do not please to do much this hot weather. I do not drill nor attend dress parade or in fact do nothing except picket guard where it suits my convenience which is about every three days always provided the weather is fair and when they try to push me beyond this I just walk to the hospital and get excused from all duty for forty-eight hours. I expect to be transferred to the invalid corps next month and do guard duty in some forts."

Grandpa John Hubbell told stories of seeing the Union Army
Fly balloons for spying. German newspapers praised the
Hindenburg's flight to Rio de Janeiro in March. Fate once
Again favored us; we were able to exchange our steamship
Tickets for the last available tickets to Lakehurst, N. J.

A chance to cross the Atlantic in LZ129 (the Hindenburg)
Overrode our disturbed feelings of seeing the NAZI emblem
On its tail. The Hindenburg departed Friedrichshafen-
Lowerthal May 6 1936 on her maiden flight to Lakehurst.
Across Germany, Holland, England, northwest to America.

Flying as a passenger on this gigantic airship thrilled
This middle-aged pilot. To be allowed to take the controls
For an hour was a cherished gift from Captain Lehmann. He
Knew by my incessant questions that whatever made me tick
Required I be separated from earth by a blanket of clouds.

Relaxing over the middle of the Atlantic Ocean, chatting
With fellow passengers, the familiar face of one well-
Dressed lady bothered me. Where had I seen her before?
As she stood up from a lounge chair, she knocked her
Purse over; my face pained as I picked it up for her.

A tattered photograph of a young and proud German pilot
Standing next to his pretty wife, and a young son about
Two years old made my blood run cold. Rushing to my
Cabin, eighteen years of bitter tears flooded out. Ella
Always knew I had held something back about the war.

With thirty hours remaining in flight, how could I
Face this lady? Sitting quietly by myself, she asked if
She may join me. "By the expression on your face, I knew
You were the one who shot my husband down. Right? For
Years I hated you so much. This isn't easy to talk about."

"Have you seen me visiting with my friend, Father Schulte,
The Priest on board this flight? During the War he was a
German pilot. Now, he flies as a missionary. He helped me
Realize that in combat, there is only a split second
Difference of who lives and who dies. You were faster."

"You did what you had to do. It was either him or you.
I'm sure he would have shot you down. I can't call myself
A Christian and be full of hate at the same time. Herr
Gremel, you are forgiven. Now, you must learn to forgive
Yourself." I slept better that night than I had for years.

After landing in Lakehurst, we flew in a Ford Tri-Motor to
Wyoming, where we camped in the mountains. Springtime in
The Rockies. Wildflowers were in bloom, the streams full
From melting snow, and the night sky so clear one could
Touch the Milky Way. Deer watched us from safe distances.

Ella sacrificed her love of the Wyoming ranch so I could
Design airplanes in California. We bought a few acres
Between Burbank and Palmdale. Painting the canvass of the
Mojave Desert, God contrasted the pinks and oranges of
Early sunrises against twisted and gnarled Joshua trees.

In those years prior to World War II, many thousands of
People out of work migrated to California. We had felt
The pangs of the Depression in the early Thirties, but
Counted our blessings that I had managed to hire on with
Lockheed. Nobody who lived through those times forgets.

Our house must have appeared in the Hobo Directory as the
Place to eat the best home-cooked wheat rolls. Ella never
Turned anyone away, and more wood usually needed to be
Cut, or a fence might need mending. Hungry, honest men
Do not hurt children, and each had his own story to tell.

Johnny, the man who later became our son-in-law, rode the
Rails for a few weeks. He said he drank the best coffee in his
Life from a tin can while in a hobo camp. Once, he loaded
Watermelons for four hours, then received fifteen cents.
He told the boss to keep it, if he needed money that badly.

Marjorie didn't marry Johnny Nelson until after World War II
Started. Diogenes, the ancient Greek, roamed the world
Carrying a lantern seeking an honest man. His journey
Would have ended had he found this fine man from Alabama.
As a child of nine, Johnny hawked roasted golden peanuts:

"Double-jointed, humped-back, California, knock-kneed, bow-legged, pigeon toed, hammered down, sawed off PEANUTS! Grown in the shade, parched in the sun. If you don't have a nickel you can't get none! They're so hot they'll warm your teeth and curl you hair, make you think you're a millionaire! Get em now and get em cheap; get em now, get a heap, while they last, selling two bags for a nickel! Not only good, sweet as honey, and the best you can buy for the money. They'll do you good and help you, too; make the old feel young and the young feel new. Guaranteed not to rip, rear, run down the hill, get hot and smell between your toes in hot weather. Get em while they last. Good all the time! How about some, Mister?"

News of Pearl Harbor didn't reach me until that Sunday night.
I had been prospecting out in the Mojave Desert. Old men
Smoking cigars stuck wall maps with thumbtacks: Our ships,
Planes, regiments, territories, defenses; their armies,
Navies, weaknesses. Didn't talk of young men who will die.

Bud wanted to enlist the next day, but I said he had to
Finish high school. In June of 1942 he joined the Army-
Air Corps to fly. He didn't make it as a pilot, but was
Selected to be a Bombardier-Navigator on a B-17.
He married Mabel, and fathered three fine sons.

Marjorie, my most precious daughter, always cared for
Other people, gave of herself, and shared such a deep
Faith in God with her new husband Johnny. They drove
"If-it", a 1929 Model A, to Tacoma, where he worked in
Shipyards on aircraft carriers, and her asthma cleared.

Ella packed parachutes to help in the war effort, and I
Designed warplanes at Lockheed. One of the sharpest
Designers in aviation history, Kelly Johnson, asked me to
Join his engineering team on the P-38. I felt honored,
For even then, his reputation preceded him.

The country cheered when Jimmy Doolittle bombed Tokyo,
With B-25's flown off a carrier deck a few months after
Pearl Harbor. Our airplanes and our pilots had to be better
Than those of our enemies. We had a war to win. Eventually
We did, but not without paying a very high price.

"We regret to inform you..." said the dreaded yellow
Telegram. No! Not my son, my little boy. Surely, there
Must be some mistake. What a terrible coincidence, shot
Down in a raid over Germany. Is this how nature balances
Her books: A son's father; a father's son?

"The War to end all wars" concluded on Armistice Day. The
War to end all wars started in Hiroshima. One hundred
Thousand Japanese wiped out by one bomb; twelve million
Jews and undesirables gassed by the orders of one madman.
Assyrians eliminated thousands in ancient cities.

Those were other people's mothers, fathers, daughters,
Sons. They were statistics in newspapers.. 'Yes, I'll have
More lemonade"... Those millions did not release my hand
When taking their first steps. They did not look up at me
With a dirty face, grin, and say, "Daddy, I love you!"

Ella never fully recovered, and I'm not sure I did
Either. It seemed as though the gashes in our hearts
Would bleed incessantly. Gradually, a skin called time
Allowed the shirt of life to cover naked wounds, creating
Illusions that to be dressed was to be healed.

Knowing that our hearts were breaking, God once again
Replenished the loss of a loved one with new life.
Laughter and squeals of delight from six grandchildren,
As they gleefully discovered their own world, lightened
Our burden; smiles returned, our tears were those of joy.

"It is time to listen to the fifth grade choir sing to us, Mr.
Gremel." Oh Good! We can move out of our rooms again,
And socialize. We all sit in our wheelchairs, propped up
By pillows. The kids are delightful, and often, funny.
After that will be BINGO, but I would rather play chess.

After World War II, those of us in aviation shared the
Pleasure and challenge of Chuck Yeager breaking the sound
Barrier. It mattered not that his Bell X-1 had been built
By a competing company. Those years of flight-testing
At what is now Edwards Air Force Base are fond memories.

Mostly fond memories. Too many good test pilots died.
They knew the risks involved flying airplanes to the
Envelope, keeping America on the forefront of air power.
But they flew anyway. And the rest of us drank to them
At Pancho Barnes's Happy Bottom Riding Club.

Or we drank toasts to those that broke the records, like to
Scott Crossfield for becoming the first to fly at Mach 2,
And to Bob Hoover, for his many exploits as a test pilot,
And his precision flying in a P-51 Mustang that thrilled
Millions of people at air shows around the country.

Along came the jet age, and with that, the Korean War.
Some called it a "Police Action", but those dodging
Bullets and Bombs share a different view, as did the
Pilots who flew F-86's in MiG Alley. The surviving airmen,
Soldiers, sailors, and marines eventually came back home.

Ex-military pilots found themselves buying Cessnas,
Pipers, and Beechcraft. They might not be flying high
Performance airplanes, but they could not stay out of
The air. Neither could thousands of other men and women,
For whom learning to fly became an obsession.

Ella and I flew with two of our grandchildren to Devil's
Tower, Mt. Rushmore, and Yellowstone in our Stinson
Voyager 108-1, and on up through Canada to Alaska.
Whales, salmon, bald eagles, caribou, grizzlies, and
Denali dazzled me; I even learned to fly a floatplane!

Sputnik electrified the country, and Kelly Johnson's
Skunk Works developed the U-2 and the Blackbird. Long
Working hours didn't leave much of a home life, but Ella
Knew not to ask me about what projects I worked on. That
Wonderful lady had been my strength for so many years.

Traveling to Antarctica had enticed me since Admiral
Byrd flew over the South Pole. Recognizing that I needed
A respite from classified work, Lockheed sent me there
In the early Sixties to check out the use of Hercules
Aircraft landing on the ice at McMurdo and the South Pole.

Observing whales, penguins, and seals in their natural
Environment, and seeing the multi-colors of bluish-green
Glacier ice, contrasted against the pure white volcano of
Mt. Erebus, made me feel thankful that God had shown me
More evidence of how awesome His Creation really is.

There's a place called Ob Hill that overlooks McMurdo
Sound. On top of Ob hill is a cross, placed eighty years
Ago as a memorial to Robert Scott, who perished on his
Fateful trip from the South Pole. As I struggled to climb
Ob Hill, words from "The Old Rugged Cross" guided me up.

For some reason, that Hymn reminds me of what disturbs me
Most about people. The Lord's Prayer says, "... Hallowed
Be Thy Name..."; One of the Ten Commandments says not to
Take the Lord Thy God's name in vain. God's last name is
Not Damn; the "H" in Jesus H. Christ means, to me, Holy.

Spending Christmas in McMurdo and lonely for my family,
I wallowed in self-pity, almost failing to enjoy glistening
Snow off of distant glaciers, a crystal blue sky enhancing
The beauty of Mt. Erebus, and the meaning of Christmas
Reflected in the eyes of those at the candlelight service.

To fly to and from McMurdo, one must travel through New
Zealand. Over thirty years had passed since I had visited
Kiwi war buddies. My pilot friends were now grandfathers;
It seemed as though that I was talking to the fathers of
The young men I had flown with - did I look old to them?

In February of the next year, Ella and I flew to Japan,
To be awed by spectacular ice and snow carvings at the
Snow Festival in Sapporo. Once again, though, God's
Artistic talent reigned superior to man's as we viewed
A crimson sunset on the snow-capped volcano of Mt. Fuji.

That reminds me of 1968, when as a guest of Naval
Squadron VQ-1 and the Army Security Agency's 1st SAD,
I was given a lifetime thrill: CDR Scott Beat performed a
Barrel roll over Mt. Fuji in a Douglas EA-3B jet, perfectly
Timing it so that we were upside down over the crater.

As guests of the Imperial Hotel in Tokyo, Ella and I had the
Privilege of seeing Frank Lloyd Wright's design which
Blended simple, but eloquent, Japanese culture with
Functional aspects of American architecture. This hotel
Survived an earthquake the same week we married.

Ladies dressed in pink kimonos smiled shyly at our
Awkward attempts to speak Japanese. Occasionally, Shinto
Shrines with roofs curled at the corners like elf shoes
Would delightfully appear as we toured the narrow city
Streets in taxi cabs driven by laughing Kamikaze pilots.

By the time we mastered the art of eating rice with
Chopsticks, and learned that Saki gave bad hangovers, it
Was time to leave. We sailed from Yokohama as passengers
On a cruise liner; the memory lingers on of sailing into
San Francisco at midnight under the Golden Gate Bridge.

For me, that bridge is symbolic of the Golden Age of Flight,
From which men first flew airplanes, and now fly spaceships.
Alan Shepherd, Gus Grissom, John Glenn, Scott Carpenter,
Wally Schirra, Gordon Cooper, and Deke Slayton are the
Mercury astronauts who crossed that ethereal bridge.

Those were exciting days. Just before Alan Shepherd
Lifted off in Mercury 7, the Russians surprised us all by
Launching Yuri Gagarin. Although he lived in the Soviet
Union, the pilot in us all admired his bravery. Man had gone
From flying airplanes to spacecraft within fifty-eight years.

Until then, my career focused on aircraft design. Just prior
To my retirement, I was given the chance to participate
In the Lockheed design of the Agena spacecraft for the
Gemini program, the two-man predecessor to the most
Famous event of all mankind: The Apollo Program.

One day, the plant had a visit by one of the Gemini
Astronauts, Mr. Neal Armstrong. While shaking hands with
An astronaut tends to lift ones spirits, my pride of
Humble contributions to the space program just about
Burst the day he became the first man to walk on the moon.

After retiring in the mid-sixties, I often walked the
Beaches, listened to the pounding surf, quietly enchanted
By the golden sunsets bouncing off thundering waves,
Crushing onto rocks. Once, I had no money in my pocket,
But went home with a starfish and a sand dollar richer.

During those years, it was incredulous how those young
People dressed. Hippies wore their hair long, and many
Chose to go to Canada to avoid the draft. How can one
Not fight for their country? Perhaps Viet Nam awoke this
Country into thinking that actions of war may be immoral.

An often-heard motto then was to "Do your own thing".
John Stuart Mill wrote in his Essay "On Liberty" about a
Hundred years earlier that people should have the right
To do what they wanted to do, as long as they didn't hurt
Others, and took responsibility for own actions.

My four grandsons all joined the military, and three of
The four went to Viet Nam. They all came back alive. But
During that time frame, Tragedy twice again struck its
Uncaring head, taking my granddaughter Cathy in a car
Wreck, and my grandson Eddie in a propane accident. Why?

Here I am Lord, I am an old man, and have lived a full
Life. You could have taken me, and not these young
Adults. Doesn't this cycle of old men living and young
People dying ever end? I must bear not only my own pain,
But watch my children endure the agony of children lost.

One more time, we picked up the pieces of shattered
Hopes. The world continued to turn, and exploration of
Space began to excite me, while Ella gradually became
More withdrawn. Fortunately, we had friends and family
Who cared, and now we had great-grandchildren to love.

In the early Seventies, I visited a friend at the Jet
Propulsion Laboratory, and my timing was just right.
Employees were signing their names to the Voyager 1
Spacecraft, and I was invited to do so. My signature is
Now travelling past the boundaries of this solar system.

By the Eighties, my grandchildren were grandparents. My
Grandson works at NASA, and he took me to the first Space
Shuttle launch. He has desires to travel into space, and
Is confident that sometime he will actually escape the
Bounds of gravity, to view the world without borders.

One grandson cleans up the environment, one lives in
The state of South Carolina, and my beautiful grand-
Daughter lives in Illinois, working as a paralegal. Both
Marjorie and Johnny have retired to a farm in Missouri.
Although they have had hard times, their faith is strong.

Ella succumbed to a heart attack about five years ago. She bravely endured the pain, and minimized it so others Wouldn't be uncomfortable around her. What a remarkable Woman that God gave me for a partner to share life with! For her, death came as a blessing, and her pain is gone.

Just before she died, she said, "Greenhorn, I have a Confession to make - I cheated on you once." Oh no, that Can't be true! I was always faithful to you. Then, with The same sparkle in her eye, she said, "On the day we had Our race, I made sure that I had my father's fastest horse."

Alone again, after sixty-five years of marriage. How would I ever make it without her? But I talked to her, and I Know she listened. Gradually, the one-day-at-a-time Approach worked. I fell asleep at night with visions of Her beauty, hearing her laughter, and feeling her love.

Until my stroke, I lived by myself, self-reliant and Independent of my family. Placing me in an old folks' Home to receive constant care probably seemed the right Thing to do for me, and the decision to do so a difficult One to make. These facts I understand.

But, my good family, if you so concerned about my Welfare, why is it that no one visits me anymore, as you Did in the early months? Even though I could not focus My eyes, and I acted unresponsive, I always knew you were Here, and my heart leapt for joy when you entered my room.

Although I do not communicate very well, you can still Talk to me about your problems and your happiness. I Listen well. Now, the staff here at the home and my Memories are all that keep me company. Had I never Travelled, nor raised a family, what would my memories be?

In my life I have witnessed flight from Kitty Hawk to the
Rings of Saturn. As the fourth man to walk on the moon,
Apollo XII astronaut Alan Bean paints about humanity on a
Celestial body in "Helping Hands"; "To Beautiful To Have
Happened By Accident" recognizes God as The Creator.

Once, I saw a painting of three men walking to a space
Shuttle, with an image of Christ in the stars. They were
Soviet Cosmonauts; the painting was entitled, "Go With
God". Isn't it wonderful, for the nation that wouldn't
Acknowledge the Presence of God, to have such an artist?

In this world there are many religions. For me, the right
One is Christianity. I have sinned, but feel forgiveness
By accepting Jesus. I cannot accept that God does not
Exist. One who can make a seashell have the same
Mathematical spiral as distant galaxies does exist.

Jesus said that in His Father's house are many mansions.
One may be called space travel. Perhaps I will be able to
Travel to those distant galaxies in the form of conscious
Energy. That would be quite a journey for a boy who used
To walk behind a mule, dreaming of becoming a pilot.

Life has been beautiful, and painful. Do not pity me
Because I am old. Old age is the price paid for living.
Instead, pray for me to recover, because I still hope to
Ride the Trans-Siberian Railroad, visit the Patagonia
Mountains, walk the Great Wall of China,

Go back to Alaska to take another ride in a floatplane,
See the Midnight Fire Dance of the Aurora Borealis,
Hold more grandkids in my arms,
And watch people landing on Mars,
Before I board my Flight to the Angels.

I was an Army guy flying in a Navy EA-3B

EA-3B flying over Mt. Fuji

"Butch,

You are always in my mind when I remember our first PR-9 mission together. I will always remember how wide your eyes got when I had you stand next to me when I did a barrel-roll over Mount Fuji in Japan and no coffee spilled out of my cup, sitting on the pilot's console! – What fun! Scott Beat"
(Author, So Many Ways To Die – Surviving As A Spy In The Sky)

Flying in the EA-3B Skywarrior

Common to other kids of my day, my first flight was in a J-3 Cub. Mr. Jones, one of my teachers, took up students one at a time around the city of Casper, Wyoming. I was twelve years old. I knew then that someday I would learn to fly. While in high school, I joined the Civil Air Patrol with the hope of learning to fly. It did not happen then, but one summer I did go to Cheyenne with the CAP for a two-week camp, and we all traveled in a C-47. Enroute to Cheyenne, I was given the opportunity to sit in the left seat of the C-47. The pilot told me to keep this horizontal bar centered. Well, when the bar went down, I was told to pull back on the yoke, and when the bar was high, I was told to push the yoke forward. Simple enough. But the passengers in the back weren't too thrilled with the roller-coaster ride that I gave them, even though I didn't feel that sensation. On the return flight I was not allowed back in the cockpit!

My first commercial flight was either on Western or Frontier Airlines, on a round trip between Casper and Billings, Montana, once again, while I was in high school. Frontier flew the Convair 580's, and Western used DC-6 airplanes. By the time I enlisted in the army in February 1965, I had several commercial flights under my belt. Just before I joined the army, I flew to Denver on a morning Western Airlines flight, had an interview at the recruiter's office, and was back in Casper for a 1 PM class at Casper College. It gave me bragging rights to my classmates.

The army had a way of letting me know I was not as sophisticated as I thought. I flew to Denver to enlist on February 16, 1965, rode a train to Kansas City, and was bussed to Ft. Leonard Wood, Mo. There, the sergeants had methods of stripping me of all my dignity. They always asked someone else: "Shape up soldier; do you want to be like Nelson?" Finally, I graduated from Basic Training, and ended up at Tulsa airport on a Braniff Airlines flight on my way home to Casper, where I met Rev. George Gilmour and his wife Sarah. The Gilmours are long time friends from Casper, and my friend Roger and I had visited them the previous year when we drove a Volkswagen to New York, via Alabama. Twenty-five years later, I passed though Tulsa airport, and showed my daughters Michelle and Cheri a section of airport terminal where I saw the Gilmours. My daughters still wonder how I can remember an airport terminal after twenty-five years but not remember everyday things. Just the power of aviation, I guess.

I spent the next couple of weeks in Casper, after which I left on a TWA wonderful flight from Denver to Boston, to attend an Army Security Agency school at Ft. Devens, which is about 40 miles from Boston. I think the TWA flight stopped in Chicago; it doesn't matter. What did matter is that there were about 50 new stewardesses on board heading to their assignments in Boston and New York. I was young, single, and in uniform, and they were young and single, and they smiled a lot, and I didn't leave with any names nor phone numbers, but that was OK, because at the time I had a girl friend in Casper. But it sure beat being on a flight filled with a bunch of bald-headed old guys!

Four months later, my mom and dad scraped together enough money to buy me a $100 ticket home, so they could see me before I went to Turkey for almost a year. That is the only airline ticket my parent's bought me, and I am forever grateful for that one, because I didn't have enough money to go home on my own. What I remember most about that trip is that my sister Cathy was crying when I was at the Casper airport waiting to go back to Boston, and that was next to the last time that I saw her alive.

A couple of days after arriving back at Ft. Devens, on August 25, 1965, I boarded Pan Am Flight 1, a Boeing 707 jet that went from New York to New York on a round-the-world trip that left daily. One of my regrets in life is that I never had the opportunity to fly that complete route, but even so, I was on a flying carpet ride to places only imagined before: London, Paris, Rome, Istanbul, and Ankara, Turkey. I never left the airports, but it was still fun knowing I had landed in England, France, Italy, and Turkey. The flight to Ankara may have been on a Turkish Airlines plane, but I don't remember.

From Ankara, I flew to Sinop, on Turkey's northern Black Sea coast, in a twin-engine Beechcraft that was piloted by an army officer. The pilot buzzed the army buildings, letting everyone know that we had mail with us. One of my future plans is to write more details about army life and that year in Sinop, but at the rate I do things, that may not happen for many more years. There, I met lifelong friends like Jerry Capps and John Brandenburg. Sinop was considered an isolated duty station, so it was always a treat to leave. I managed two trips while there, once to Ankara on R & R, and the other to the Holy Lands with a tour arranged by the chapel people in Sinop. When I went to the Holy Lands, three or four of us hired a taxi for $10 to go to Adana from Ankara, a distance of about 150 miles or so. The Air Force had a base at Adana. I was able to ride a C-130 for the first time, on a flight going to Beirut. Beirut had not been decimated by war then, and it was a very beautiful city, and it was enjoyable walking along the beaches lined with palm trees. British Eastern Airlines took me from Beirut to Damascus on a VC-10 jet, where I started the Holy Land tour.

One day in Sinop two US Navy jets flew low over the army base, heading to their home base at Adana (I think, but they may have been based at Rota, Spain). Somebody told me that army guys were flying in the back end of the jets, and that those guys had the same Military Occupation Specialty (MOS) that I had. That made my heart pound and gave me an inspiration to become a crewmember on one of those planes. It didn't happen right away, nor did it happen there, but eventually, before I left the army, I was a crewmember on an EA-3B, at Atsugi, Japan.

However, it took another couple of years before I started flying on the EA-3B. My next duty station after Sinop was in Chitose, Japan, which is located on the northern island of Hokkaido. I don't know the military designation, but the civilian version of the planes that flew from Tokyo (Tachikawa and Yakota AFB) to Chitose is the DC-4. I had several flights on these planes during the sixteen months that I was stationed in Chitose. One trip was to Korea for four days. I wish I could find the photograph that I took on board that flight, because it was near sunset, and the red glow around the rear of the two starboard turboprop engines closely matched the color of the sunset. About a year into my tour at Chitose, two friends from Ft. Devens and Sinop knocked on my door one day. Jim Pierce and Carl Jarvis were in Chitose for training, but were stationed at the Atsugi Naval Air Station, as crewmembers on the EA-3B. They were assigned to the 1st Special Activities Detachment (1st SAD), attached to naval squadron VQ-1.

I found out what I needed to do to be assigned to the 1st SAD, put in an official transfer request, met all the required qualifications after a trip to Okinawa for a high-altitude chamber ride and ejection seat training conducted by the Air Force, and on January 7, 1968 departed Chitose for Atsugi. That began the best year of the four that I spent in the army.

But it wasn't all good. Shortly after joining the 1st SAD, the North Koreans captured the USS Pueblo. And my sister Cathy was killed as a result of a car wreck. Major Craig Loe, the commanding officer of the 1st SAD, loaned me $50.00 to help me go home on emergency leave, and Jim Pierce drove me to Tachikawa AFB for a flight home. As a side note, I had orders to report to McCord AFB, which is near Tacoma, for the return flight to Japan, a couple of weeks later. I was born in Tacoma, and my parents named me after Dr. Matthew Havalina, the physician who delivered me. On the way back to Japan I looked him up, and finally met the man whose name I carry. I like to say that I was named after the person who gave me my first spanking!

Within a few days of arriving back at Atsugi, I had the distinct pleasure and memory of going on my first flight of PR-9, the EA-3B, Navy Bureau number 146449. The Douglas Aircraft Company built this aircraft; the Air Force equivalent was called the B-66. Normally, the plane was called an A-3 (and nicknamed the "Whale"), and was initially designed as a bomber, but the bomb bay was modified and an electronics compartment substituted in its place, hence, the first letter, "E". PR-9 had a crew of seven, which consisted of the Pilot, Navigator-Bombardier, a Navy enlisted man who was the plane captain, and four army guys who flew in the back manning the electronics equipment. Later on, Carl Jarvis died, but I have remained friends for many, many years with Jim Pierce, Frank Lovell, Joe Hodder, and Major Loe. (He was later promoted to Lt. Colonel, and is a now a civilian, but I have a hard time calling him by his first name.)

Commander Scott Beat piloted the plane on my first flight. Near the end of our four-hour mission, CDR Beat called me to the cockpit and gave me a briefing. Then he performed a barrel roll over Mt. Fuji. He timed it so that I was standing upside down looking directly into the crater of Mt. Fuji. That was one of the best plane rides of my life! Thanks, Commander Beat.

Most of the time our missions were classified, but one Sunday CDR Beat told us to bring our cameras, as we were going to go to Hokkaido to find out the squawks of the plane, since it was due to go back to the States for scheduled maintenance. Somebody loaned me an 8 MM movie camera, and for part of the mission I was able to be in the Navigator's seat, which was actually a co-pilot's seat. Hokkaido is about an hour's flight from Atsugi, so we made it a fun day, at least it was from my standpoint. The U.S military has a camp near Lake Shikoskhu, which we flew over. Our plane didn't have any markings except for the Stars and Bars. Some Air Force guy reported that an F-4 flew low over the lake, obviously a man whom did not know much about airplanes. After that, I asked CDR Beat if we could fly over the site that I used to work at in Chitose. He told me to spot it, which I finally did. While I was sitting in the right seat, we flew very low and fast over the site. Now, that jet plane had two J-57 engines on it, and we were probably thundering along at about 600 miles an hour. After the low pass, we went back to Atsugi.

My nickname is Butch, and that's what CDR Beat called me. The next day, he came up to me and said, quite unhappily I might add, "Butch, don't you ever ask me to fly over that place again!" Afterwards, I managed to find out bits and pieces. The Air Force reported seeing the F-4 at the lake; when we did our pass over the site, an army MP was going to shoot it down with his .45 pistol; he told a sergeant who came running out of the building that an unidentified Russian MiG with no markings had flown over. I met one of the MP's I knew from Chitose a few weeks later, and he asked me if I had been on that flight. When I said yes, he told me that he had never done so much typing is all his life. Our site had a direct teletype link (this was 1968, remember) to a particular Department of Defense facility in Washington, D. C., and for three hours the wires burned with questions about the MiG. Finally, someone had the sense to ask the Japanese Self Defense Forces if they had any intrusions of their air space. They said the only aircraft flying at the time in question was the Navy A-3 from Atsugi. In 2001, CDR Beat was at the second reunion of the 1st SAD. I asked him what he had been told by the powers-to-be, and he said, "No comment". I wish he had not been chewed out, but I don't think there was a person at the reunion that would not fly with him in another A-3 or any other aircraft at a moment's notice. As far as I am concerned, CDR Scott Beat is one of the best aviators that the Navy ever produced.

There was another flight involving MiG's that wasn't near as funny. Once, we had a couple MiG's intercept and fly near us. CDR Beat told us not to even look at them, and not to wave or anything. Since we were unarmed, he asked, "What can I do, throw my cigar at them?" What made it a more tense situation for us is that on a previous mission, before I joined the 1st SAD, there was another intercept, and it was said that the Russian pilots were begging their ground control people for permission to shoot down our plane.

As previously mentioned, the mission was highly classified, which means that the Pentagon knew about Project Seabrine, the code name. The year before I joined the unit, the plane and aircrew deployed to Shemya, Alaska. As I understand it, the Air Force sent a C-141 to carry the maintenance vans and other associated equipment of the 1st SAD and personnel to Shemya. Almost all the 1st SAD personnel were qualified aircrew, used to wearing flight suits and survival vests and sometimes not being very comfortable. The Air Force loadmaster insisted that the 1st SAD gang would have to wait until a "Comfort Pallet" could be located so all the deploying personnel could have a kitchen and airline seats. Lt. Mercer, the navigator, used a phone to call somebody at Pacific Headquarters in Hawaii about the problem. Within a few minutes, a message came out of the office of the Joint Chiefs of Staff, saying that all the men and equipment of the 1st SAD would be on the C-141, even if the Air Force had to dump the C-141 pilot!

I was fortunate not to have gone to Viet Nam, while other men my age did go and over 50,000 came home in body bags. Their mothers did not want them going to war and my mother did not want me to go to war. But sometimes, military men died without going to Viet Nam, as there were other places hostilities existed. As I mentioned earlier, the North Koreans captured the USS Pueblo in 1968. Then, in April 1969, they shot down an EC-121 plane, killing all on board. That plane was in VQ-1, the same squadron that the 1st SAD was attached to. I knew some of those people – they lived in the same barracks that I did. Although I was discharged from the army in February 1969, I stayed in Japan for a couple of months, and then worked my way back to the States on a cargo ship. The very first newspaper I saw after docking in San Francisco had headlines of the shooting down of the EC-121. On April 1, 2001, there were more headlines involving a VQ-1 aircraft: The Chinese rammed one of their fighters into an EP-3E, causing severe damage to the EP-3, and death to the Chinese pilot.

While I did not go to Viet Nam, I feel proud that I was able to serve my country as a member of the US Army Security Agency, and especially honored that I was chosen to fly with the 1st SAD, attached to Navy Squadron VQ-1. The details of our work are still classified as far as I am concerned, but I would like to include an e-mail from Bill Crane, another army person who flew with the 1st SAD:

1 Nov 2002

"Carolyn and I attended the A3D Skywarrior Association's reenactment of the 50th anniversary of the first flight of an A3D last weekend in Van Nuys, California. It was a very special occasion for me and the other 540 people who attended.

I wanted to report to you some comments made at the formal dinner by the guest speaker. The speaker was Rich Haver who is Special Asst. to the Sec. of Defense (Donald Rumsfield) for Intelligence. He was on a very tight schedule and arrived from Washington 10 minutes before his address and left to return to Washington 10 minutes after his address. He spoke for about 20-30 minutes about the importance and impact that the A3D Skywarrior and those who flew it have had on American history. At the end, the Skywarrior Association president, Mr. Al Rankin presented him with a beautiful model of an A3D Skywarrior. The model selected was one with the phased array antennas. Mr. Haver had been a VQ-1 pilot in the early 60's and recognized it for what it was.

In accepting the model, Mr. Haver commented that this was particularly representative of cooperation between the Army and the Navy. He then went of to tell the Navy about the Army's work and its impact on national defense. He had been Navel attaché' to Germany and also was involved with disarmament negotiations with the Soviet Union. He said as a result of the Army's intelligence gathered by their VQ-1 and VQ-2 projects, he as a negotiator had more information on Russian ICBM capability than the Russian negotiators.

There were only three Army (men) present. Needless to say, we let them know that we were there with a loud yelp. It was the first time that anyone had formally recognized our work. By far, most of the Navy had no idea what we were doing. After the dinner, we were treated with real respect by all."

July 13, 2004

On Monday, July 12th, I flew to Baltimore on a Southwest Airlines flight to attend the dedication ceremony of an EA-3B Skywarrior aircraft at Ft. Meade. This dedication was held at the National Vigilance Park, in front of the National Security Agency, to honor the men and women who served in VQ-1 and VQ-2 for their special and unique roles and service to the NSA, and therefore, the United States of America, during the Cold War. Like I wrote earlier, the plane that I flew on when I was stationed with the VQ-1 Squadron at Atsugi, Japan had been issued Navy Bureau Number (BuNo) 146449 and was called *"PR-9";* the one dedicated on this date of July 13th flew out of Rota Spain with the VQ-2 Squadron, and its BuNo is 146448. It was painted like BuNo 146450, a VQ-2 plane named *"Ranger 12"* lost in an accident on the USS Nimitz in 1987, killing all seven crewmembers on board. Families of the crewmembers of Ranger 12 were at the dedication.

EA-3B at the National Security Agency's National Vigilance Park in Ft. Meade, MD

My friend Hawks Abbott had called to tell me about the ceremony and something stirred within me that I knew I would be disappointed if I did not attend. As I heard the various speakers talk during the ceremony, I had a feeling of pride surge through me for being one of the people who served the good old USA flying as crewmembers on the EA-3Bs. My contribution to end the Cold War may have been small, but I feel like I still made a difference. The year I spent with VQ-1 certainly made a difference in my life. In late June of this year, I was in California, where I visited CDR Beat. He was working on a book and researching information about the Pueblo Incident in 1968. At Ft. Meade, I met two of the army people with whom I had served, Major Loe, and SFC Jack Clodfelter. All of these three people have been positive influences on my life. Thank you. [Post note, July, 2005: Three members of the 1st SAD, MSGT Woody Black, SFC Jack Clodfelter, and SP5 Carl Jarvis have all passed on. They are missed. After SFC died in January of this year, I have started calling him my Guardian Angel.]

Sept. 23, 2007

Today, the mailman brought me So Many Ways To Die – Surviving As A Spy In The Sky written by CDR R. Scott Beat. He wrote in my copy of his book the words on the first page of this story about our flight over Mt. Fuji. He is a fascinating man for whom I have the utmost respect! I would have bought this book anyway, but what made it even more special is that CDR Beat quoted me in the beginning of his book from one of the stories I had written and sent him, and then later in the book he mentioned my name one more time. Not only did he end his aviation career by having flown 18,000 hours, he distinguished himself even further by flying the legendary U-2 for a few years just before he retired after 27 years in the Navy. Thank you, CDR Beat, for your courageous and extraordinary service to our country. Thank you God, for giving me opportunity to fly with him, and to flown as a crewmember on the wonderful EA-3B. Adios, Amigo-sans! Viya con Dios!

The Voyager Flies the Voyager

Stinson 108-1 Voyager, owned by Tom Jenkins and Matt Nelson

Flying to Columbus, MT. Photo by Teresa Voorhees

Windsor, AZ

My First Plane, a 1947 Stinson 108 Voyager

Even before I started flying I had wanted to own my own airplane It took me a while, but I finally bought a 1947 Stinson 108 Voyager, nineteen years after I started flying. My first flight lesson occurred on March 9, 1983 at Houston Gulf Airport. Dave Henderson gave it to me in a Cessna 152. It took almost two years and 98.6 hours before I earned my Private Pilot's License on March 2, 1985. Actually, I had taken a check ride the previous December, but failed miserably, so had to go out and practice some more. The man who gave me the exam had also given Dr. Sally Ride, the first American woman in space, her check ride. I bet she passed it the first time. Oh, well! Sometimes I would be flying Cessnas and Pipers and enjoying my time alone in the cockpit while there were shuttle missions flying, thinking that while I was having fun, I imagined the astronauts wouldn't trade me places.

Early in my flying years, I heard a couple of stories that I still think of often. When B.G. Smith, one of my co-workers, heard of a pilot with over 30,000 hours crashing into a mountain, he said, "Well, that goes to show you that the mountain had more time in the air than the pilot." The second story goes something like this: Two young pilots saw an old man pre-flighting an airplane. Very methodically, he moved his greasy thumbnail down every line item on the checklist, holding it there until he completed the specific task listed. The pilots joked that the old man would probably die before he reached the end of the checklist. One of the men working at the airport overheard the pilots, and told them he would like to introduce them to the old man, so they walked over to him. "Boys," said the workman, "I'd like you to meet my friend, Charles Lindbergh"!

About 1984 or so, Houston Gulf airport held a local air show with planes like those that fly in the Reno Air Races competing. I saw this gray-hair old man wearing a flight uniform with the Eighth Air Force patch from World War II on his shoulder, dragging behind him one of the racers. The plane looked like it only had a wingspan of twenty feet. As the old man walked closer, I realized that he was Deke Slayton, one of the original Mercury Seven astronauts.

During the same period, my friend Jim Gardner was trying to round up eight buyers for a World War II Stearman. At the time, I didn't even know what one looked like, but liked the idea of learning to fly an open-cockpit bi-plane. Tom Jenkins, one of my good friends and elk hunting buddy, and I tried to take a Cessna 172 to San Antonio in April of 2002 to fly a Stearman, but we encountered bad weather enroute and came back to Houston. Then, over Memorial Day weekend, I drove to Kingsbury Aerodrome to see some World War I vintage airplanes one day, and to fly the Stearman the next day at San Antonio. Ed Gunter gave me my first ride in a Stearman, and I have been hooked ever since. For me, they are too expensive to own, but I sure enjoy flying them. Later during the year I went to St. Louis twice and flew in Bob Kraemers's Stearman. He was named in an article in the November, 2002 issue of AOPA Pilot. That's his Stearman named "Alice" on the bottom right photo of the book cover. I call it "Alice in Wonderland"!

Matt Nelson & Tom Jenkins, proud new owners of the Stinson 108-1, June 9, 2002, and grinning like a mule eating burrs!

While walking around Kingsbury Aerodrome, I spotted the Stinson 108 Voyager with a "For Sale" sign in the window. That evening I called the owner, and the next day, after I flew the Stearman, I had a short flight in the Stinson. Like the Stearman, I really wasn't familiar with a Stinson. The fabric fuselage had been replaced with aluminum and the original 150 HP Franklin engine had been replaced with a Lycoming 0435-C, a 190 HP military engine made when the dinosaurs had wings, with a Hartzell two-bladed prop attached to it. There were no radios installed, but boy, did that plane one year younger than me have a lot of power, and the owner made it fly so easily.

When I came back to Houston, I told Tom about it. Tom was working on his pilot's license, and wanted to buy a tail dragger. So two weeks after I saw the plane, on June 8, 2002, Tom and I, Carl Nepute, and Don Cooper flew a Cessna 182 to Zuehl airport, near San Antonio, to pick up the Stinson. I had been looking at buying an airplane for a while, but was thinking more of a Cessna 172 or a Beechcraft Musketeer or Sundowner. Next thing I know is that I have an airplane I don't even know how to fly, or at least take off and land. Tom and I put a radio with a built-in GPS receiver and a transponder in it, and we were good to go.

I started learning to fly the Stinson with CFI Don Cooper, and then later started flying with Carl Nepute, another CFI. Carl knows every grass strip around, and we buzzed some of 'em. He used to own a Stearman, and now Don has part ownership of another one. I have learned a lot from these two guys, as well as from Jim Gardner. Jim bought a Cessna-120 about the same time Tom and I bought the Stinson, so I have had some time flying it, as well. Sometimes there were maintenance problems in the Stinson, such as the time the prop started slinging oil on the windshield right after take-off, and the cylinders had to be rebuilt – welcome to the world of airplane ownership - and once, Carl took over the controls of a Champ we were flying and we ended up stuck in the mud and had to have an ATV give us a tow! We both laugh about that one. But I finally learned to take-off and land a taildragger!

I flew it as often as possible. A few months after buying the plane I took it to Beaumont for it's annual inspection. An air traffic controller told me that the Stinson's encoding altimeter / transponder read 3300 feet, although the altimeter inside the plane said I was at 5500 feet. After the inspection was complete, Tom, Jim Gardner, and I flew to Beaumont in a Cessna-172 to pick up the Stinson, and Tom and Jim brought it back to Houston. That same day my ground speed on the GPS receiver said I was traveling over 900 knots! The man at the avionics shop in Galveston said the encoder read minus 2000 feet below sea level. I have often heard it said to trust your instruments, but somehow, flying Mach 1 at 2000 feet below the surface sounds like the Stinson is a rocket mole!

NEWS FLASH MARCH 21, 2003.

TODAY, ANOTHER NEW POTENTIAL PILOT CAME INTO THIS WORLD. *Karoline and I now have a new granddaughter, Camyrn Dawn Larson. Camyrn is the daughter of our daughter Cheri and her husband John Larson. Ever notice how much the word daughter looks like laughter? So granddaughter must mean a lot of good laughter coming up. Wow! This is even a greater story than me flying the Stinson solo, which I did again today to celebrate. I told Cheri that I will have to take Camyrn flying, and she told me that she could just see me having to feed and change her every two hours. The Stinson uses a lot of fuel and has small gas tanks, so I usually try to fuel about every two hours. My personal useful range is also about two hours, so while the plane is being fueled I can fuel Camyrn. Cheri says I have to wait, perhaps until Camyrn turns 21! Oh, well, you can't blame a new proud grandpa from trying to take his granddaughter flying.*

Now, back to the rest of the story!

On the last weekend of April 2003, I flew the Stinson to Dallas for a meeting of The Explorers Club. I can become quite accustomed to this kind of lifestyle. When I landed at Redbird Airport, I taxied to one of the aviation outfits, where a line boy directed me to park to plane next to the double doors of the lobby. I had previously reserved a rental car; five minutes after engine shutdown I drove away. Once back in Houston, I taxied to my hangar, opened the doors, and drove my red Ford F-250 pickup out so I could park the plane. What a way to travel!

From March 10, 2003, the date I first soloed the Stinson, until took it to Galveston in April of 2004 for its annual inspection, I flew it solo for 96 hours. During the 13-month period that I flew those hours, sometimes Tom and I, or my son-in-law John Larson and I would go to Brazoria County Airport (LBX) near Angleton, Texas and eat lunch at the Windsock Café, located right on the airport grounds. We would taxi up to the café and sit back and enjoy the looks that the restaurant patrons gave the Stinson. I also flew on several trips to towns that are one or two hours away from my home base of Pearland Regional Airport (LVJ), such as Beaumont to the East, and Burnet, Pleasanton, and Fredericksburg to the West. There is a Commemorative (old name was Confederate, which I liked better) Air Force museum at Burnet, which is a town near Lake Buchanan, where I have received a couple hours floatplane training in a Cessna 172.

When I flew to Fredericksburg in September 2003, I left the plane overnight at the airport and drove to a ranch near Johnson City, where The Explorers Club was having another meeting. On the evening I arrived, we went out to a cave and watched bats emerge. One of the attendees was Astronaut Charles Duke, who walked on the moon during the Apollo 16 mission. In my mind I will always remember one photograph I wish I had taken but it would have been inappropriate. As the bats flew out of the cave near twilight, Mr. Duke stood silently and watched, with a bright crescent-moon softly illuminating his face. Here is this guy that has walked on the moon and the moon hangs over his head sort of like a halo. The next day we were given a tour of the ranch, where some African antelope reside, and a dinosaur footprint remains. Our guest speaker that day was Dr. Jane Goodall. While flying the Stinson home the next day I couldn't help but marvel about the accomplishments of General Duke and Dr. Goodall.

My friend, Astronaut Joe Tanner, took me flying with him in a Stearman in November 2003. It's a bright yellow one that he has access to, and is kept in a hangar at the old Ellington Air Force Base. We flew for an hour, and he let me fly it for much of the time. In years past Joe instructed other astronauts in the Shuttle Training Aircraft and in the T-38s before he became an astronaut himself, and has 80 hours flying the Guppy. During this same year I had also flown with Bob Kraemer in his Stearman, flying over the Mississippi River, wondering about the barge pilots and the things they had seen over the years and wondering about the kind of cargo and the destination of the cargo. There's nothing like stick and rudder flying in an open cockpit airplane and grinning ear-to-ear with a big bugs-in-the-teeth smile!

For Thanksgiving of 2003, I took off in the Stinson to go see my mother and my sister Karen and her family who all live in Aledo, Illinois. My first fuel stop was in Longview, Texas. Last February and March, during the search for the debris from the space shuttle Columbia burn up, many search crews operated from this airport. Inside the lobby were several items such as patches from the STS-107 mission that were given by NASA to these great Americans. Because I hadn't taken off until about noon from the Pearland Airport, it was nearly dark when I arrived in Ft. Smith, Arkansas. I found a motel and settled in for the night, wondering if the weather would ground me the next morning. It did. If I had my instrument rating, or if I had had more experience, I might have given it a try, but I decided against flying in low visibility and ended up renting a car and driving to Illinois. On the way I passed through Lebanon, Missouri, and decided to go see the house where Mom and Dad lived for sixteen years until his death in 1996. I'm glad that I stopped; his name was still on the mailbox. Either nobody was home, or nobody lived there anymore, but the house seemed like it was in better shape than when my folks lived there. Mixed emotions! In 1995 I had bought airline tickets a couple months prior to Thanksgiving while I was living and working in Wallops Island, Virginia in preparation for my trip to Antarctica in 1996, the year I Wintered-over. My boss and I had had a disagreement prior to me visiting my folks, and he had threatened to fire me over a misunderstanding, but I am glad that I insisted that I would be going to Missouri before my trip to the ice. It was at this house in Lebanon that I last saw my dad alive, just prior to my departure to the ice on the day after Thanksgiving, 1995. The ironic part about it all is that I was driving to this same house on December 23, 1996 to take my folks to the St. Louis airport so they could spend Christmas with us. I had bought my new F-250 after coming home from the ice, and had planned on starting back working with Lockheed Martin before Christmas, but they told me to wait until January 1997. So my plan was to drive to Missouri, take my folks to St. Louis, fly with them to Houston, spend Christmas at home, then go back with my folks to Lebanon, and continue driving around the country for a week or so. My folks had taken their dogs to a kennel and were driving home on I-44 when the fan belt broke. My dad was walking to Wal-Mart about a mile away to buy another fan belt and collapsed as he was nearing the exit ramp. He was probably dead by the time he hit the road; if not, he perished within a few minutes. At that time I was only four hours away, and I have to admit, even as strong as my faith is in God, when I die I hope to ask God why couldn't He wait to take Dad a few hours later, because it had been over a year since I had seen him and I was so close. I'm sure God has His reasons, but I sure don't understand them now. What breaks my heart even further is that the night before I had talked to Mom on the phone but I didn't talk to Dad. Time to move on.

In May 2004, the Experimenters Aircraft Association (EAA) held a fly-in at New Braunfels, Texas. My son-in-law John and I drove there to see it. Bruce Bohannon had his Exxon-sponsored "Flying Tiger" on the ramp. He is still trying to fly his plane to 50,000 feet. He has come close, but hasn't made it yet. One of these days he will. Once or twice he had to dead-stick the plane onto the runway at Brazoria County Airport. But he is a superb pilot, and managed to do that unnerving task very skillfully. My main flight instructor, Carl Nepute, taught Bruce to fly gliders many years ago; while giving me training in the Stinson, we landed once and did a fly-by at Bruce's Flying Tiger grass strip.

So why did John and I drive to New Braunfels when I own a Stinson and the weather was good? Well, the Stinson was in its annual inspection at Galveston. As I previously mentioned, I had flown it there on April 28, 2004. With the exception of two weeks in February of 2005, the Stinson stayed in Galveston for almost an entire year. I finally flew it back to its home airport of Pearland, Texas on April 20, 2005 (that day would have been my dad's 85th birthday). It's a long story why it had been down for so long, but part of the time the cylinders were being rebuilt. They had been rebuilt a year earlier, but the workmanship from another mechanic was poor, so when I took the plane to Bill Wynn, a top-notch mechanic with a sterling reputation for craftsmanship and integrity, he performed a compression check and gave me the bad news. Five of the six cylinders on the World War II Lycoming O-435-C engine were salvageable; but we had to scrounge the country to find the sixth one. Ouch! Jim Gardner flew with me in January to break in the engine, but then I did a hard landing and had to have the shock absorbers replaced in the plane. In February the magnetos had to be reworked due to an excessive drop of RPM in the right one, and the air speed indicator and altimeter weren't reading right. We figured out later that the air speed indicator probably gave me an erroneous reading of 80 MPH, when it was probably much less, causing me to stall about 20 feet above the runway, giving me the hard landing in January. In February, when I took the plane back to Galveston to have the magnetos repaired, while crossing over the threshold during landing, my altimeter read 500-feet, when in actuality

I was only about 30-feet above the runway. Bill purged the pitot lines and hooked up the static line to the instruments, which he found disconnected. I had properly set the altimeter prior to the flight.

With good compressions, the engine just barked, sounding almost like a Harley-Davidson. Between April 20th and May 14th, I flew the plane eight times. One of those times Tom went with me to grab a hamburger at the Windsock Café at the Brazoria County Airport (LBX). On that particular day the local EAA chapter was hosting a fly-in and serving bar-b-que, so Tom and I changed our minds about having a hamburger at the Windsock. But any other time, if you want a good hamburger, go to the Windsock.

Camyrn at age 2 (2005) with "Pop" in front of the Stinson! Photo by Michelle Nettles

On May 1, 2005, I took my older daughter Michelle's fiancé Keith Nettles flying. Karoline's parents were in Texas from Wyoming and I wanted them and Camyrn, whose was two years old, to see the Stinson, "Pop's airplane". After Keith and I landed, we taxied to the area where everyone was parked and Michelle took some photos. Well, I would be doing Camyrn an injustice if I failed to include the photo of me holding her, and I don't want that to happen. She sat quietly in her dad's lap while we taxied to the hangar. I kind of wanted to take her flying, but her mom said 'No!"

Broken Crankshaft

Typical day in May in South East Texas. Light ocean breeze, somewhat muggy, but not as bad as those dreaded July and August hot humid days. Not quite like flying in an open cockpit Stearman, but those sliding windows on the Stinson gives the breeze a place to hang out while passing through the cockpit, to rest for a few minutes before embarking on its journey around the world. Grateful for the brief chance of hitchhiking in the cockpit, the wind normally gracefully cools the pilot momentary, before it too is funneled back into the sky, guided by forces even stronger than itself. Today something is different with the pilot, who watches the lazily windmilling prop with a look of horror and intense concentration on his face, oblivious to the wind's effort to cool him. And something is different with the plane. No longer does the neighing of 190 horses drown out the wind's soothing sound. So the wind listens, because there is a change in the plane and in the pilot, and the wind goes silent and hears the pilot praying out loud to God, and the wind lingers long enough in the cockpit to say, "Godspeed, Matthew!" and God speeds up and directs the new guardian angel, Jack Clodfelter, to take care of Matthew. Upon exiting the window, the wind looks back and says, "Good luck, Kid", and God gives the kid good luck and the wind slacks off and God and Matthew safely land the plane together, although the engine has stopped completely. Saying that Matthew lands the plane without power is not quite accurate, because he lands under God's Power. Matthew steps out of the plane and gives many thanks to God, and tells the wind, "Via con Dios, adios amigo!"

"And he rode upon a cherub, and did fly: yea, he did fly upon the wings of the wind." *Psalms 18:10*

"The wind goeth toward the south, and turneth about unto the north; it whirleth about continually, and the wind returneth again according to his circuits." *Ecc 1:6*

"The wind bloweth where it listeth, and thou hearest the sound thereof, but canst not tell whence it cometh, and whither it goeth: so is every one that is born of the Spirit." *John 3:8*

On May 14, 2005, while flying my Stinson, I had the opportunity to perform one of those engine out, emergency landing procedures that all pilots endure sooner or later when the instructor pulls back the throttle and tells the pilot, "You just lost an engine, where are you going to land?" Only this time, there was no instructor with me, and the engine wasn't turning at 500 or 600 rpm. It wasn't running at all. Fortunately, I was near Brazoria County Airport (LBX) near Angleton, Texas where I had just entered the downwind traffic pattern for runway 17 when the engine just died, shattering my eardrums with the silence, which was only broken with me continuing my prayers of asking God for His help. Boy, that deafening roar of silence opened the adrenaline floodgates! Those prayers had started just a few minutes earlier after I departed LBX on runway 17. About four miles away, over the town of Lake Jackson, I suddenly experienced a rough engine and/or prop vibration at an altitude of 1500 feet. The engine quit momentary, so I switched from my right nearly full tank to the full left gas tank (although I had earlier checked for water in the fuel) and headed back to LBX. Although the vibration never left, the plane flew well enough that I thought I could safely land on runway 17. Although my direction of flight was opposite of the normal runway traffic, when the engine quit I turned towards runway 35 at a 45° degree angle, pushed the nose forward to hold a constant speed of 80 mph, and surprised myself how calmly I made my radio call: "Brazoria County traffic, Stinson 8706 Kilo has an engine out and I'm coming in on (runway) 35." A hovering helo pilot asked my position, and I said, "Abeam the numbers on the South, about 1000 feet to the West." He responded, "I'll watch out for you." I radioed a quick "Thanks" and tried to do an engine restart. No luck. All I knew for sure was that I was coming down and was going to have to use every bit of piloting skill I had ever learned. Once over runway 35, I banked left, my left wing tip was about thirty feet above the grass, then I rolled back to the right directly over the center line, landed, did a slight bounce, and settled the plane down, and then had enough momentum to continue to roll about three hundred feet to a turn off between the runway and the taxi way, made the turn and came to a safe stop about halfway between the runway and taxi way. I made sure everything was off, stepped out of the plane while the helo pilot continued to hover nearby. I was shook up, but OK. My hands started shaking when I stepped out of the plane.

I figure I had about twelve seconds from the time the engine stopped until I landed. Now, on future astronaut applications, I can now apply to be a shuttle pilot in addition to being a mission specialist, since I now have experience with dead-stick landings. A power-off landing doesn't sound quite as ominous as using the words "dead-stick landing". The guys at the airport said I was now in the same league as Bruce Bohannon, but somehow I can't help but think that he is a much better pilot than I am.

When I called Karoline to tell her I needed a ride home, I told her that I was OK and the plane was OK, but I had just done an emergency landing when the engine quit. It took a second or so before the words sunk in – "You had to land with no power?" she exclaimed! One of the commercials on TV at the time of this incident had a guy pushing his motorcycle and his wife drives up, "Daddy just had to have a motorcycle, didn't he?" After she picked me up, Karoline said, "Daddy just had to have an airplane, didn't he?" My friend Joe Cavazos celebrated his 40th birthday that evening – I went to his party, but Brian Collier recalls that my hands were still shaking. While this definitely shook me up, in no way does it compares to what happens often to Alaska bush pilots. Charles M. Thomas Jr. wrote a book called "Wings over Wilderness" about his friend Paul Shanahan. Paul had at least three crankshafts break on him while flying in Alaska, and on one occasion the prop went spinning off into the Brooks Range, with no paved runway within 1000 feet of him!

Broken crankshaft from the Stinson's Lycoming O-435 engine.
Photo by Bob Canup

Post landing revealed no water in the fuel, but Bill Wynn found both mags had sheared at their hard rubber couplers, and the starter drive shaft had broken. Without going into all the bolt-by-bolt details, eventually, the six cylinder Lycoming O-435 engine was shipped to Omaha for repair by Central Cylinder Service, Inc. After they received the engine I had a call from one of the mechanics telling me that the engine had a broken crankshaft. I guess a crankshaft snapping into two pieces is a good enough reason to experience those sudden and unusual vibrations. Look Mom, I now have a twin-engine airplane, one with four cylinders and one with two cylinders! God was sure watching over me that day. SFC Jack Clodfelter, my old army sergeant, who died in early 2005, had his first chance to become my guardian angel that day. I wasn't figuring on breaking him in for his new role as guardian angel until July when I had planned on flying the Stinson to Alaska.

"bravo! aviate, navigate, communicate (if you get at chance.) glad you were proficient and took immediate action, had you hesitated you might have a re-build on your hands. well done, sir. too bad about Alaska, but worrying about a sick engine up there doesn't offer quite the same recovery options... Reads" (Astronaut Bill Readdy) - This was from an e-mail I received from him.

One unique thing about the Stinson story is that while the airplane was at the Brazoria County Airport, it was kept in the same hangar with the Sikorsky S-43, previously owned by Howard Hughes, which he used as a test plane in preparation for his anticipated flight around the world in the Spruce Goose. Phillip Zwahr, my mechanic there, had the office manager of Tri-City Aviation took the next photo.

Howard Hughes S-43 and my Stinson. Photo by Lorraine Garcia

Lorraine Garcia, the Customer Service Representative for Brazoria County Airport, designed a brochure for the S-43. Quoting directly from the brochure, here are a few facts about the S-43 Sikorsky:

CHRONOLOGY

1935 – The S-43 had its first flight.

1937 – Howard Hughes purchased the Sikorsky for the purpose of a record setting flight around the world. He began flying at the tender age of 14.

World War II – There is strong evidence that the S-43 was used for secret missions – This information is classified to date.

May 17, 1943 – With Hughes at the controls, the plane crashed at Lake Mead, Nevada, with two casualties and three survivors.

1947 – After an expensive and lengthy restoration from the 1943 crash, Hughes used the Sikorsky for extensive design testing and to sharpen his flying skills. Hughes made over 200 take-offs and landing from water to prepare for this one time flight. [His flight around the world]

1952 – For reasons known only to him, Hughes orders his favorite plane – the Sikorsky, to be kept under 24-hour guard in a hangar at Hobby Airport in Houston, Texas.

April 5, 1976 – Howard R. Hughes died. Howard Robard Hughes, Jr. (1905 – 1976), aviator, movie producer, and billionaire was born in Houston, Texas.

1977 – The Sikorsky was purchased by a collector named Ronald Van Kregten, and Restoration of the Sikorsky aircraft began.

October 6, 1990 – The first flight of the Sikorsky since 1952 was ferried from a maintenance base in Manvel, Texas to Ellington Airport with Captain Jesse E. Bootenhoff at the controls."

Back in the Air

March 14, 2006

Finally, ten months to the day when the crankshaft broke, I finally flew the Stinson. Carl and I flew a Cessna 172 to Brazoria County Airport, and then flew around the local area in my own (and Tom's) airplane. What a great feeling! To top it off, I absolutely greased the two-point landing. Carl brought the Stinson back and I flew the 172. A week or so later my friend Ron Caswell came in from Florida to support the upcoming STS-121 mission. He wanted to see the plane, so after work we went out to the hangar and I started it up. The plane, not the hangar!

June 10 – 11, 2006

Well, flying the Stinson 40% of the time and having it in maintenance the other 60% of the time is still about right. Well, it ain't right, but that's how it has been over the four years Tom and I have owned the plane. Generator problems and prop problems were the latest reasons. Oh well, the mechanics have families to feed and bills to pay, too. I just wish they would generate their income from somebody else's generator!

But today, on June 10th, I filed a flight plan, topped off the fuel tanks, borrowed Bob Simle's external antenna for my handheld GPS receiver, waved to him while he videotaped me pre-flighting the Stinson, and took off to San Antonio's Stinson Field. Yep, Stinson Field, named after the same Stinson family that designed and built my Stinson. The Explorer's Club was having a dinner in San Antonio. Actually, going there was out of the way for my planned flight to Kentucky, Illinois, Minnesota, Nebraska and places in-between, but it just gave me an excuse to fly longer. Westward we headed, me and my Stinson flying machine, first at 4500 feet, then at 2500 feet, because I wanted to be able to see the ground and blue sky between the clouds, instead of maybe having to illegally fly through the inside of gray clouds with no visibility. The GPS receivers did their thing, my thumb on the chart kept me honest, the plane, and newly rebuilt engine with a single piece crankshaft from my Alaskan friend Shane Horton and my recently overhauled prop all did their thing, and between sips of water my grin did its thing of tickling my ears. There is Eagle Lake, home of my very first cross-country destination; over there is Shiner, home of a Texan beer and one of those old grandeur 19th century downtowns; look, there is the Gonzales water tower that Tom Jenkins and I remember very well from a flight several years ago that gave us the name of the town when we had drifted off course. Actually we had already passed the Gonzales water tower on that previous attempt to go to Stinson Field to fly in a Stearman, but five miles west of the town a wall of clouds that looked like Moses parting the Red Sea in the movie *The Ten Commandments* encouraged us to turn around. San Antonio approach asks my destination; they tell me to contact Stinson Tower and the man in the tower clears me in for the landing. One more time I ask God's help on the landing; one more time He gives it. Taxi to the parking area in front of the tower, tie down the plane, and go into Check-Six Aviation. Good people there, and they operate like they know pilots generally don't fly the kind of combination vehicles that are planes in the air and convert to cars on the ground. Seems like their 1980s vintage loaner car was free or cost only around $10.

So I use it to drive to the luncheon hosted by Catherine Nixon Cooke, a former director of The Explorers Club. One of the people I met there is Dan Bennett, the newly elected president of the club. Recently Catherine came out with a book about her uncle called <u>Tom Slick, Mystery Hunter</u>. He was interested in flying, Yeti hunting, and other things that make all my travels look like I have been staying home in a rocking chair. He also founded the Southwest Research Institute, where high-speed photography was performed by NASA photographers during the investigation of the high-energy impacts of the foam that came off three years ago causing the STS-107 Columbia disastrous breakup. This evening (June 10th) the dinner was held in the remodeled livery stables of the old Pearl Brewery. George Jackson Jr. was the guest speaker and his talk was called *"Magic in Mexico"*. His gave a slide presentation showing the handmade jaguar masks the people make for an annual fiesta in Guerrero. Two contestants wearing the colorful masks fight each other brutally, then drink beer afterwards. In the past they often fought until one person died, but that has changed. It was an interesting evening, as all The Explorers Club dinners have been.

By 7:30 or so the next morning, I'm back at the airport, and can't pass up the photo-op of my Stinson parked in front of Stinson Tower. Using my portable radio, I called them up and asked permission to take the photo, which they pleasantly gave. No matter how well my friend the Stinson flies, we have a an agreement – as long as I keep fuel in the tanks it will fly; but if I forget to give my friend some liquid nourishment, it will stubbornly stop, and it doesn't care whether or not I am safe on the ground or whether or not we are in the air. The guys in the tower gave me permission to taxi to the fuel pumps, the pump eagerly extorted money out of my credit card, the Stinson was happy, and I was cleared for take-off. Once airborne, the tower guy gave me a heading and I had flight-following all the way to Georgetown, TX (perhaps an hour's flight).

Parked at Stinson Field in San Antonio

Pump gas, chit-chat with Scott, the guy in the terminal whom I met in March, give former An-2 pilot Simon Diver a call, and it's time to jump into the plane, hit the starter button a couple of times and head on out to Jonesboro, Arkansas (the same town that Roger Tresler and I had the 1960 Volkswagen engine replaced on our trip after high school graduation in 1964). Wrong! That poor Stinson hadn't fully recovered from major surgery. It wanted to start again and go airborne, but the starter was covered with oil and maybe the generator wasn't feeling well. Scott gave me the phone number of Don Dison, owner of Aim Aviation Services, and Don just happened to be at the airport with his son working on a motorcycle. From the moment I first met Don I liked him. When he drove up with his son in a golf-cart, chomping on an unlit cigar, the first words out of his mouth were, "That's a beautiful looking bird", or words to that effect. Within an hour of being towed to his hangar, I once again hit the starter button, and the prop turned many thousands of revolutions as it gave the Stinson enough lift to fly all the way back to Pearland Airport. Don charged me a fair price and did excellent work. It was tempting and would have been easy for me to try to continue my journey to Minnesota, but I couldn't go on a trip like that with a questionable starter and/or generator. During the next couple of weeks I made three or four more local flights in the Stinson, but it was queen of the hangar all during the month of July and much of August waiting for the generator to be repaired and a couple of oil leaks to be stopped. A piece of the generator had to be hand-made because nobody seems to have the proper seals available for the generator.

NEWS FLASH! July 27, 2006 ONCE AGAIN, A NEW PILOT IS BORN! *Parents John and Cheri Larson announced the birth of their second daughter Cadie Lynn Larson, while happy grandparents, aunts and uncles, as well as older sister Camyrn stood by. Cadie, age 1 hour, seemed more concerned about eating than she did flying in her grandfather's Stinson ancient flying machine, according to others, but to me her cry sounded more like, "IWANNAGOFLYING!" There is another new pilot that Pop can take flying when her Mom let's her go. Now, I have two granddaughters!*

October 27, 2007

Famed aviator Steve Fossett departed in a single-engine airplane from the upscale Flying-M Ranch in Nevada sometime in October and just flat disappeared. It took about a year to find him at his crash site. He had jillions of hours and had set all kinds of aviation records. It's kind of scary knowing that pilot's with all kinds of time can still die in aviation accidents. Closer to home, there is another Flying-M Ranch in North East Texas near the town of Reklaw that isn't quite as well known as the first one. There is a good chance I will never be invited to the ranch in Nevada, but it wouldn't bother me too much to go back to the REKLAW Fly-In, which occurs annually on the last weekend of October. My friend Dave Moore had flown in with his friend who owns a Cessna 170, so he was there taking photos of me and my Stinson machine when we landed there. Lots of taildaggers, and lots of good bar-b-que. While I was waiting to take-off, this huge shadow passed over me – Whoa! What was that? – Dave managed to capture the photo of me taking off while another An-2 that is home-based here in Texas was taxiing back. On the flight back, my GPS receiver showed me clipping right along with a ground speed of 149 MPH. Good tail wind!

May 27, 2008

Six years ago, on May 25th, I flew my good old red F250 pick'em up truck at low altitudes to Kingsbury Aerodrome, and that is where I first spotted the Stinson. Each year on the Saturday of Memorial Day weekend and Veteran's Day weekend I have wanted to fly it back to see the air show, but never made it. After traveling over there a couple months ago, I sort of kept Saturday, May 24th open as a good day to fly the Stinson machine over there this year. So I did! The Stinson honed over there just as naturally as the swallows return to San Juan Capistrano. I no more had touched down on the grass strip and parked the aircraft when Dan Dirks walked up to me. He is the person from whom Tom Jenkins and I bought the Stinson. I didn't go into all the details of the Stinson's biography since we purchased it, but did tell him of some of the major aches and pains. He was glad to see his old plane again, but declined an offer of a ride. Maybe he didn't trust it!

Stearman coming in for a landing, with the Stinson machine watching.

When I started making plans to fly to Kingsbury, I contacted Alan Crawford to see about flying his Cessna 172 seaplane around Lake Buchanan, and fly the Stinson to Llano, which is fairly close to where Alan lives. Nope, Llano is in the Texas hill country, where people who live in Austin, Dallas, San Antonio, and Houston go to leave the big city and take up all the available motel rooms. There was no room at the inn at Llano, but Burnet had expensive rooms available at one of the major chain motels, and one that was not expensive at all. I called the Sundown Motel and didn't quite trust the non-American who was from out of town. He was too willing to make my plastic money card go through the chunk-a-chunk machine. After I read a review over the big Al Gore electronic network, I felt I made a wise decision declining to give out my card number. The best thing the person who wrote about the motel said the shower didn't work, and it went downhill from there. So I figured that I could stay in Lampasas at a motel owned by the same outfit that owned the expensive one in Burnet, only for $50 less, and then fly the thirty miles down to Llano on Sunday morning. Sounded good in theory.

Like a camel, the old Stinson could fill up on some liquid refreshment, and then wander on out into the hills. We have an understanding – as long as I take it to the local pub, it will do it's best to fly, but it's an ornery beast - if I fail to buy it drinks, there is some point where it will just stop, whether we are flying or not. In some ways it is cold hearted and fearless – it loves to fly, but isn't afraid to auger in, either. I try and keep it contented. There is no public airplane bar at Kingsbury Aerodrome that I know of, so I told the Stinson we could go to San Marcos and I would buy a round or two. It agreed, and off to San Marcos we went. With full tanks, Lampasas became our next destination.

They don't call me Captain Kangaroo without good reason. Listening on the radio to the automatic weather station at the Lampasas airport, I figured I could handle the wind, which was right down runway 16, 12 knots, gusting to 20. As I lined up on final, I noticed that the orange windsock indicated the wind was right across the runway, blowing from the West. OK, I have to make a crosswind landing, not my favorite, but I can handle it. But I wasn't prepared for the runway that sloped downward in my direction of travel. OK, set it up, aileron right, left rudder, do a slight bounce, didn't like the tilt of the runway –

worried about a prop strike, so I gave it full throttle to do a go around, but had a bunch of runway left, so I thought I would try again, and then WHAM, the plane hit hard from about five feet. I managed to control it without a ground loop or a prop strike, stayed on the runway until the turnoff, taxied to a tie-down, shut everything off, took a long drink of water, stepped out of the plane and checked for damage. It looked like the only thing damaged was my pride. It doesn't matter how many good landings you make, there is always that one lurking in the shadows of complacency.

I have often thought about flying the Stinson to the West Texas town of Alpine. Initially, I had planned on refueling at Sonora, but then I saw in my book on Texas airports that it had the same down slope as the one in Lampasas (yep, that book even showed the slope at Lampasas but I was now a bit more educated). Ozona airport didn't have sloping runway and it was still within range of my avgas-to-noise converter Stinson flying machine. Estimated flying time to Alpine was four hours, I told the Lockheed Martin (my old company) Flight Service (not my old company) weather briefer, and that I would be stopping in Ozona for fuel. He advised me of wildfires 12 miles East of Alpine. After filing my flight plan, I bought another drink for the old Stinson Voyager, and off we went into the wild gray yonder. Hazy, man was it ever hazy! And bumpy! By the time 1 landed at Ozona, I had already eaten my sandwich, just to settle my stomach. By that time I was beginning to wonder if not going to Alpine would be the smarter idea. God sent SFC Jack Clodfelter or one of my other Guardian Angels to help me land the plane gracefully. Actually, in Lampasas, they kept me safe when I was doing my audition for Captain Kangaroo. The self-service gasoline pump at this airport didn't even have a credit card reader, which I didn't mind at all. Greenback dollars were cheerfully accepted by the older white-haired lady who told me about the West Texas winds reaching 40 MPH or higher. (I can attest to that when I was with Douglas and Neal two years ago flying the An-2 from La Porte to Phoenix.) Fortunately, they weren't that high at Ozona, but inside the terminal six or seven professional firefighters were on standby to fly their helicopters and Beech Barons to fight the Alpine fires. They told me that the winds were so strong in Alpine that professional pilots/firefighters were grounded. That was good enough information for me to not pursue my long-time goal of flying to Alpine.

These firefighters were from Montana and Washington. One had several hatpins on his baseball cap, among of which were the STS-107 mission pin and one of the space station. He told me he had helped with the search in East Texas after the Columbia disaster. Another guy had a DVD of the firefighters in action in the mountains of Idaho that was quite interesting; a lady helicopter pilot played it on her laptop. All of these people are very good and very proud of their role as aviator firefighters; they have a right to be proud. I wish my piloting skills were half as good as theirs.

Time to hit the road. Make that time to go airborne. Once more, just the Voyager and me, on our own voyage. It was still bumpy, but not as bad as it had been an hour earlier. I was able to climb to 5500 feet. On the way to Ozona I had to stay low, because of the low clouds. Over the mesquite trees and old oil well drilling patches we did fly, somewhat parallel to I-10, other times it was just me and the Stinson and the cactus and mesquite trees. I thought about landing in Fredricksburg, and staying overnight at the Hangar Hotel, which is right on the airport and a nice place to stay, but there were 60° crosswinds, gusting past 20 knots, and I didn't want a repeat performance of my Lampasas landing; besides, if I went on to the La Porte airport I could use the money it would have cost to stay at the Hangar Hotel to buy more avgas for the Stinson. A couple hours after leaving Ozona I did a straight in approach to runway 13 in San Marcos, bought another round of drinks for the Stinson, and headed on back to Houston town. This time I stayed at 3500 feet, and used the new Nikon several times on the way home. There are some really neat fields and I learned how to improve my aerial photography. As I came closer to La Porte airport, I flew over Clear Lake, and had a good view of Johnson Space Center and Building 44, where I go to support the American space program and to receive a paycheck so I can keep the Stinson's thirst quenched so the two of us can go airborne. Instead of me staying at the Hangar Hotel, and tying the plane to the ramp, the Stinson rested in its own hangar, I drove to T-Bone Tom's for a steak, and I slept in my own bed.

On Memorial Day, I debated for a while whether or not to wrestle with 20 knot crosswinds again, but the winds came down more to my liking, so I drove back to the airport and took a friend to go pick his truck up at a crop duster's field just a little East of Nome. Nope, not the well known Nome, that is far West of Houston, Alaska, but the not so well known Nome that is a short distance East from Houston, Texas. I've been to Houston, Alaska and to Nome, Texas, and I would rather be in Houston or Nome, Alaska! Coda Rieley flew his Cordon II experimental plane from Nome, and needed a ride back to pickup his pickup. Once more, the Stinson Voyager Camel demanded that I buy another round of drinks, and then we were airborne all over again. We dodged some clouds, flew around one of those tall dragon radio towers that like to eat airplanes for lunch, and Coda showed me the grass strip. I didn't doubt my ability to land on the short strip, but some nasty telephone poles sprouted just in front and to the left of me as I was on final, so I landed using an upside-down question mark approach. Coda complimented me, asking if I was sure that I didn't work as a crop duster. Sometimes, you are lucky; other times, they call you Captain Kangaroo! Not too long afterwards, I managed another lucky landing at the La Porte airport, and was able to log 11.5 hours for the weekend. Thank you God, for keeping me safe and for allowing me to fly.

May 18, 2009

Today I had my retirement luncheon at Mamacita's, a good place to go for Mexican food. Heading for Montana. Several people showed up, and some even said some nice things about me! My boss, Jeff Sugano, spoke first, followed by Dr. Phil Hopkins, the man who hired me in 1978 spoke. My friend Hawks Abbott came down from Nebraska and told about the projects I had worked on when he and I served in the Reserve Unit of the Naval Space Command. B. G. Smith, the senior NASA test director for ESTL, then came forward. He and Pat Patrick and I had worked as a small team together for many years. My long time friend of 42 years, Buck Buchanan, spoke, and Ned Robinson, the NASA manager for ESTL closed it out. Before the luncheon, Hawks and I went up in my old Stinson flying machine, flying over the Baytown Bridge, the Kemah Bridge, and NASA.

Texas To Montana, 2009

Voyager Log Flight Day 1 - Saturday, July 4th

Happy Birthday America! I celebrated by enjoying and exercising my freedom to fly. The time had come to fly my 1947 Stinson 108-1 Voyager to its new home in Townsend, Montana. Karoline and I had retired and moved there at the end of May.

Yesterday, Gil Johnson and I flew on Frontier Airlines from Bozeman, Montana to Houston, Texas, where my daughter Michelle and her husband Keith picked up us at the big airport. It had only been slightly more than a month since Karoline and I had moved to Townsend, but enough time had passed that I felt trapped in the concrete jungle and mountains of oil refineries, chemical plants, freeway overpasses, and kazillion cars. Already, I was missing the mountains of Montana and the much cooler temperatures and lower humidity. I miss Michelle and Keith, working on the space program, and my friends, but that's about all. Oh, ya! I miss the good Mexican restaurants in the Clear Lake area, and I was glad that Michelle drove us to Estabans in League City, because we have been going there for several years. There is a difference between Tex-Mex food and Montana-Mex food. I love Montana, but I like Tex-Mex food much better than Montana-Mex food.

Gil is an instructor pilot whom I had flown with three times in Montana. Since he knows how to fly in mountains and has a ton of experience, I had asked him to help me bring the Stinson from La Porte, Texas to Townsend.

Michelle and Keith drove us out to the La Porte airport (T41) at 8:30 AM, and shortly afterwards several friends came out to see me, which I really appreciated. Hopefully, I haven't forgotten to mention anyone; if I have I am sorry. Bob Simle was there with his nearly two-year old son Kaden; Buck Buchanan, Joe Cavazos, Jim Fox, Lance Borden, Dave Moore, Gideon and Jan Jones, Bob Wagstaff and his wife Nancy also came out. My 63rd birthday party this year was held at Bob's big maintenance hangar for K&W Aviation.

Gil and I pre-flighted and loaded the plane; out came the digital cameras, hugs and handshakes; at 10 AM I yelled "Clear Prop!" and started the engine on the old Stinson flying machine. Check - Oil pressure in the green, tach at 1000 RPM, make final waves, release the brakes, and we are taxiing to Runway 23. After take-off, from where I sat in the pilot's seat, I couldn't see the hangars or anyone on the ground, but I waggled my wings to those good people as we flew overhead.

After flying off and on for over twenty-five years in the Clear Lake area, I didn't need a chart to point the plane towards the Johnson Space Center. I showed Gil Building 44, where I had spent many years of my life supporting the space program. Our first stop was at Clover Field (LVJ), which is now called Pearland Regional Airport. I wanted to say hello to my long time friend and flight instructor, Carl Nepute. He and I have flown many hours in the Stinson; before I went to Africa last year he brought me up to speed in a Cessna 182. Israel Vences, a good friend and co-worker since 1982, was with Carl when we taxied up to the terminal. Israel and I had worked together for many years and countless hours on the space shuttle's Ku-Band system. Wayne Messenger, one of the guys who work at the airport, came up to shake my hand. I met him about the same time as when I bought the Stinson, in 2002. Ten minutes later, we were airborne again.

Our next stop was at Brazoria County Airport (LBX), to buy cheaper fuel and to see my friend Tom Jenkins. He was my partner when we bought the Stinson, and even though I eventually bought him out, a man could not ask for a better or more honest partner than Tom. Except for Buck, of all the friends I saw, I have known Tom the longest. While we were fueling the plane, J. D. Rhodes came up. He is a mechanic that had replaced the ancient wheels and brakes when the left main wheel exploded earlier this year when I landed at LBX. Another honest man. Tom brought Gil and me a hamburger while we were at J. D's hangar. As a side note, it was at this airport where I safely landed with God's help four years ago when the Stinson's crankshaft broke.

Right around noon once again I yelled "Clear Prop!" and soon afterwards we were airborne again. We headed towards Eagle Lake, crossed over I-10, and landed at San Marcos (HYI) for fuel. Our taxi in was normal until we turned to go to the fuel pumps – two guys in a red bi-plane (think it was a Pitts, but not sure) who were taxing out didn't see us, and it looked like they were going to run into us. They should have been making "S" turns to see what was in front of them, but they weren't. I didn't have much room to maneuver, Gil was yelling at me and at the people in the bi-plane and swearing on the radio, all at the same time. It wasn't until later I realized his precarious position, because the spinning prop of the bi-plane was heading straight for Gil's door, but I was worried that if I applied right brake (there are only brake pedals on the pilot's side) like he told me that the two planes would be going nose-to-nose with two props going round-and-round. I yelled "Watch-Out!" on the radio and the other plane finally stopped, about 25 feet away. By this time, Gil had unbuckled and jumped out of the Stinson. He made sure the other guys knew we were there, and then climbed back into my plane. They were just as shook up as we were, because it took them three tries to restart their plane. Gil told them to put the mixture in, and after that the bi-plane started, and slowly taxied around us. All four of us were making sure that there was adequate clearance between the wings of the two planes. During the entire episode, we never heard one word from these guys, not an apology, not anything. It wasn't until we were closer to the fuel pumps that I heard a radio call from them, and then it was only an announcement that they were taking off and joining a flight of five bi-planes. One more time, my guardian angel SFC Jack Clodfelter kept me safe. Thank you Jack, and thank you, God, for sending him.

    Once the Stinson's thirst was quenched, Gil and I chilled a bit in the terminal area. With two GPS receivers on board, and Gil keeping close tabs on the chart, it was pretty easy for us to find Sonora (SOA), our next stop. Besides, it is close to I-10! The fuel hoses were kept underground, and it took a phone call to someone whose phone number was posted on the FBO door to find out where they were. After refueling, we went inside and used the floor to plot our next leg to Alpine, as we munched on a sandwich.

    For the past several years I have wanted to fly the Stinson machine to Alpine. Last year, I came as close as I ever had to going there, but when I stopped at Ozona I decided not to when helicopter firefighters who had been fighting fires in Alpine were grounded in Ozona due to the strong winds in Alpine. Ozona is further West than Sonora, and the furthest West I had ever taken the Stinson. This year, the winds were light after leaving Sonora, so there was no problem flying the last segment of the day. Finally, I was able to see West Texas from the air! It is desolate, and I probably should be spelling that word with a capital "D". I didn't see any scenery that appealed to me until we crossed over the mountainous region just East of Alpine. It didn't hurt my feelings at all that the winds were light enough that I could have used either runway 1 or 19 at Alpine-Casparis Airport (E38). I chose runway 1, because the terminal was near the North end of the runway. My landing there was the smoothest of the entire trip; I just greased the plane onto they runway. I had called a car rental place a few days before, so we had a car waiting for us. After 6.7 hours of flight time, I was ready for a good steak dinner, which I found in the Buffalo Rose restaurant, across the street from our motel. I don't see it happening, especially after living in Montana, but should I ever decide to move back to Texas, it would be in the Alpine area. The whole idea of this flight is to take the Stinson out of Texas and into Montana. But still, I had had a good day overall, and besides seeing Michelle and Keith, I saw several friends, flew across more of Texas than I ever had before in the Stinson, and finally had landed at Alpine. Not bad for the first day of flight in the Stinson Voyager from Texas to Montana.

Voyager Log, no flight day - Sunday, July 5th

Weather made it a no flight day, but that didn't mean we couldn't eat some more good Mexican food. And we did! Gil needed a battery for his cell phone, so later in the morning we drove to the True Value Hardware store. Pretty impressive! It is owned by Bob Ward, the brother of Dennis Ward, who is the step-dad of my son-in-law John. But Bob wasn't working that day, so I didn't have the chance to tell him that I am a friend of his brother. Just before we left the store, we met a husband and wife team who had flown their expensive plane into Marfa, about 25 miles away. The lady had a diamond on her hand that looks like it is the child of the Hope Diamond. They are big into Arabian horses, and travel over the U.S. of A. and Canada showing their horses. Gil and I had lunch at a restaurant – you guessed it – a Mexican restaurant! Our waitress was a cheerful college girl whose goal was to teach history of the Big Bend Area. If she teaches with the same enthusiasm that she shows as a waitress, her students are going to have a tremendous teacher. That afternoon we drove around the surrounding area; Gil bought us a pizza dinner at a local pizza place, and then I drove to Ft. Davis by myself after dinner.

Voyager Log Flight Day 2 - Monday, July 6th

Rain! One more time. But by eleven o'clock it had cleared enough that we took off, only on a different route than what we had planned. Initially, I thought we would fuel up at Las Cruses, New Mexico, and then go the Show Low, Arizona, with a final stop at the Grand Canyon Airport. Part of the reason to go to Show Low was to see my friend Norm Kalat, who was my first instructor when I learned to fly seaplanes, and whom I had flown across the Grand Canyon in a Cessna two years ago. The best laid plans.... So, when we departed Runway 1, we flew fairly straight North to the Roswell International Airport (ROW). It might have been a more interesting trip to write about had we encountered any flight crews from flying saucers, but we didn't, perhaps because they don't have much interest in 1947 Stinsons and/or their elderly flight crews. I was surprised to see all the derelict aircraft from major airlines and some now defunct airlines and cargo haulers, planes such as L-1011s painted with the TWA logo, and 747s whose glorious days of flight were over now stood silent, almost as if they knew they were now in an airplane hospice, living out their last days hoping that the guys with the cutting torches would pass them by.

Our weather briefer told us about two major thunderstorms that were showing blotches on his radar screen, but said if we took off soon we could probably avoid them. We had some bumps, but the storms were about twenty miles apart, and we managed to fly through the imaginary line centered between them, and still stay out of Military Operational Areas (MOAs). Once clear, we changed course and headed to the Grants-Milan Airport (GNT), which is located on the Western side of New Mexico. Albuquerque Approach Control vectored us to the South of their fine city, and I regret not dragging out my camera to photograph some of the countryside from the great American Southwest that we saw a few miles to the West.

After refueling at the Grants airport, we spent about a half an hour relaxing and flight planning to the Grand Canyon Airport (GCN), via Winslow, AZ. When we took off straight to the West, the nearby mountains were daunting to me, but they didn't bother Gil at all. He taught me to fly over rocks, because you can take advantage from the heat generated from the rocks to obtain lift. Gil is an old glider pilot, and knows how and where to look for thermals. I have had about 12 hours in gliders, but never became very proficient in them.

As we flew Westward towards Winslow, the oil that the prop started slinging towards the window gave a coating that became difficult to see through, especially as the sun came closer to setting. While I could have continued flying the plane, Gil cheerfully took over, and I finally took my camera out of the bag and started using it a bit. Partially because I wanted to observe Gil's landing technique, I suggested that he do the landing at the Winslow Lindbergh Regional Airport (INW).

Like I wrote earlier, the Stinson only has brake pedals on the pilot's side, so after Gil landed, it was up to me to use the brakes, and I had no problem doing so. But, when I tried using the right brake to turn the plane, I couldn't do it. Gil stepped out of the plane to take a look and discovered that the piece of chain holding the right tail wheel spring had broken. I shut down the plane and stepped out to see for myself. We didn't have much choice but to push the plane off the active runway and over to the terminal/FBO. I did have to use my camera for a photo of the moon over the Stinson when we tied it down. Nobody was around but there was a phone number of the manager. I tried calling him, but only heard his recorded voice message. We gave consideration of taking one of the "S" hooks off the end of a tie down chain to use on the plane (I would have left money for it at the FBO), but couldn't take it off easily.

I left a note with my name and cell phone number on the back door of the FBO, and Gil and I threw in our gear in a courtesy car, with a bumper sticker of the Grizzlies, the team for the University of Montana in Missoula. There wasn't even a key in the ignition but to start it all you had to do was to turn the ignition switch. I felt uneasy with us driving it, but called the manager of the FBO again and left a message that we had it. As we were looking for a place to stay, we passed by the La Posta Inn, where I had had lunch a year ago with the Explorers Club. I knew that even if rooms were available, they would be very expensive; right across the street from it was another motel that definitely would have been cheaper, but when we drove into the parking lot I told Gil we needed to leave. It looked like a haven for dope dealers, and Gil readily agreed when he saw how sleazy both the people hanging around open doorways and the place looked. We left immediately, and wandered around town until we came to a Motel 6 that looked like a five-star hotel after what we had just seen. Yep, they had a non-smoking room with two beds. While we were eating dinner at a nearby Denny's my cell phone rang. The caller was the owner of the FBO, and was calling from Mexico. He said the maintenance shop was closed, but did say we could take one of the "S" hooks and could use tools from the shop. It was OK with him that we had the car.

Voyager Log Flight Day 3 - Tuesday, July 7th

In the seven years I have owned the Stinson flying machine, I don't recall fixing a problem for as cheaply as I did today. Gil and I drove to a local hardware store and I bought a segment of chain and four carabineers for a total of $5.50. Just before we stopped at the hardware store, my cell phone rang and the lady who operated the FBO was calling to see when we would be returning the car, because somebody had made plans on using it. Within about 15 minutes we were back at the airport and two couples who had flown in from Sedona in their Beechcraft were waiting for us. Once again, I saw another lady with a ring on her finger that probably cost as much as my house. But the people were nice and said they had flown in for breakfast, and that they would be done using the car in an hour or so. It took longer to take the tools out of the plane than it did to fix it. The actual carabineer I used cost $1.25 before tax.

With a clean windshield, both tanks full of go juice, and a working tail wheel, we soon departed Winslow for Valle Airport (40G), located about 20 miles South of the Grand Canyon. Enroute we passed to the North of Meteor Crater, and I almost said, "Let's fly over the crater", but didn't, and now regret it. Last year I had hiked around the rim. What's even worse, I let my camera stay in the bag. Dumb me. Near Flagstaff is Humphrey's Peak, a 12,633-ft. mountain that we avoided by going to the North of it, which put us on a direct course to the Valle airport. It was a good decision to go there and fuel up instead of the Grand Canyon Airport, because fuel was about $2.00 per gallon cheaper, and there is a landing fee charged at the Grand Canyon Airport. I had driven into Valle Airport last year, but it's a lot more fun to fly there. There have a great aircraft museum there, and we were given a special tour of the Ford Tri-motor aircraft that used to fly people over the Grand Canyon. Inside the museum there is also a Stinson Detroiter, which was the first commercial plane to carry passengers over the canyon. I didn't use my camera here this year, because I had done so last year.

To fly a private plane over the Grand Canyon heading North, you have to be at 11,500 feet and only fly through designated corridors. We chose the Dragon Corridor. I was glad we had departed from Valle Airport so we could use the 20-mile distance to climb up high enough to be legal. Gil made one radio call to the tower at the Grand Canyon airport, and after giving our location, was told to proceed on course, and that we were out of their airspace. That was the last communication we had with the tower people. My friend Norm Kalat told me that his former boss had made over 6000 flights across the "Ditch"; I was happy to be on my second one. I think flying with Norm two years ago was a bit more special, because it was the first time I had flown across the canyon as a pilot. But for a long time I had wanted to fly the Stinson across it – in fact this is why I chose this route, as opposed to just flying straight from Houston to Montana, which would have been several hundred miles shorter. Actually, Gil did most of the flying across the canyon, and I did all of the photography. With the Stinson's sliding door window open, I didn't have to worry about a dirty glass or glare; all I did was go into shutter priority mode, which I set for $1/1000^{th}$ of a second, and I had the auto-focus turned on. We had a good flight across the canyon, although it seemed much too short. I would rather have crossed it in the early morning light, but it was closer to noon when we did. I never tire of seeing God's majestic beauty we humans call the Grand Canyon. Makes me wonder what wonders He has in store for us when we all make that journey across the boundary between life and death (as we know it here on Earth).

Our next fuel stop was at Page, AZ. This is an interesting airport, very busy, located on the Southwest side of Lake Powell. The airport at Jackson, Wyoming is one of the prettiest airports I have ever been to, with a background of the Tetons, but the Page Airport (PGA) has its own beauty. Once again, because I wanted to fly my camera, I gave Gil the controls of the Voyager, especially after leaving Page for Moab, Utah. Flying along Lake Powell ranks very high on the list of scenic routes, every bit as high as flying across the Canyon. There was one mountain that looked like were going to fly into it, but Gil was flying then and I didn't think he wanted to die anymore than I did, so I just relaxed and photographed the mountain before Gil maneuvered around it.

Prior to leaving Montana, I had hoped to fly across Monument Valley, but figured later that it would be too far out of the way. But after flying the Lake Powell segment, and having a good idea of fuel consumption, when I saw the rocks of Monument Valley off to the East, I told Gil I would like to fly over them. We slowly took the Stinson flying machine up to 15,000 feet, the highest I have even been in it. I photographed the altimeter when we were at 13,000 feet, but this altimeter doesn't show any indication of passing through 10,000 feet. At 13,000 feet the altimeter displays 3,000 feet. Later, Lance Borden commented that my photo looked like I was only flying at 3,000 feet. I told him that an analog clock could be reading 3 o'clock in the afternoon, or it might be 1500. Had we actually been at 3,000 feet instead of 13,000 feet, we would have been close to two miles underground. Except for one time in an airliner at umpteen thousand feet, I had never seen Monument Valley from the air. It is impressive from the ground, and it is beautiful from the air.

After flying over Monument Valley, we turned North, and flew across Utah's Canyonland. This is another part of the country where the landscape is harsh, rugged, and has a stark beauty of its own. I was surprised to see how much oil was all over the pane when we landed at Moab (CNY). Quite sobering, knowing that we had flown across the Grand Canyon only a few hours earlier. Had we lost our oil, and the engine froze, we might have had quite a time picking a place to land. But we both knew that, and took a calculated risk. However, had we had as much oil spread across the plane when we landed in Winslow as we did in Moab, we probably would not have flown across the canyon. We checked the oil each day, and surprising enough, there was not much consumption, even with the prop slinging oil. We added a quart in Winslow, but even then we probably didn't need to. In fact, it was by adding this oil that we probably had so much oil slinging.

When we landed at Moab, it was after everybody had shut down and left. We didn't know where we would be staying, the airport is several miles away from town, there was no courtesy car, and the people who had business cards advertising taxi service wanted between $50 and $80 to take us to town. We called a couple motels to see if they had airport delivery, and were told no. While we were mulling things over, a guy came out driving a small bus. We asked him if he could drop us off at a motel. He thought about it and gave his boss a call. Not only did Lee take us into town, he picked us up at the motel in the morning and gave us a ride back to the airport. I did give him some money for his efforts. We had to wait for about an hour for some planes to come in that were bringing back a group of excited river rafters, but it was well worth the wait. Near the motel where we stayed was another Denny's; by the time we finished dinner the motel had no vacancy. One more day did God take care of me, like He has done everyday of my life! What a glorious day of flying we had, past Meteor Crater, across the Grand Canyon, up Lake Powell, and over Monument Valley. Thank you, God.

Voyager Log Flight Day 4 - Tuesday, July 8th

While we waited for Lee to pick up us and take us back to the airport, Gil told me about intricacies involved in dancing the Tango. I guess he is quite good at it, and he has a passion about it that shows. I have to admit, while I have never tried it, nor expect that I ever will, I do like watching Tango dancers, especially those from Argentina. They are always so graceful.

My original idea when flight planning the entire trip was to fly up the Western side of Wyoming after departing Moab, stopping at Kemmerer and Jackson for fuel, and then fly over the Tetons and Yellowstone, cut across to Bozeman, and then meander on up to Townsend. Weather has a way of changing a pilot's mind.

New designation: Salt Lake City. But not the big SLC airport where the heavy iron flies in and out of, but Salt Lake City 2 Airport (U42), located a few miles South of the big one. Turbulence can be wicked going there, but it wasn't bad today. I never have figured out why there are different colored segments of water on Salt Lake, but they are interesting to see. We landed about two hours after leaving Moab, taxied up to the fuel area, and went inside the FBO to do more flight planning, ate a sandwich, and were soon airborne again. Our flight path took us over the big lake, and we could easily see the runways of the other airport, but we had to stay clear of their Class B airspace. As we flew towards Idaho, we could see plenty of mountains, but nothing stood out as being intimidating. We had clear skies and a fairly smooth flight, but the winds had picked up by the time we landed at McCarley Airport (U02) in Blackfoot, Idaho.

When we stopped for fuel, we would always look over the charts again, and make minor tweaks if necessary. Somehow, our Salt Lake City sectional disappeared out of the plane. Probably the wind stole it, but we never saw it again. I hated to spend $9.00 to buy another one, but we still had about 100 miles to cover on this chart, before we would need the Great Falls sectional. Both Gil and I are firm believers of using paper charts, even in these days of GPS receivers. The wind might steal a chart, but the batteries don't go dead on paper.

From Blackfoot, we had planned on flying direct to Townsend, but after talking to the weather guys and hearing about some nasty storms in Montana, we made the decision to land at Idaho Falls Airport (IDA) and wait it out. This was only about 20 miles from Blackfoot, but we didn't want to go any further without more information. Gil did the landing and I handled the brake work. I was hoping we wouldn't be stuck there, especially since we were only about two hours away from Townsend. In the pilot lounge I kept track of the weather while Gil took a nap. Two globs of heavy rain located of Missoula and Bozeman were slowly moving Eastward. About 5 PM we decided the globs had dissipated enough for us to give it a try.

Once airborne, we headed towards Dillon, MT for a checkpoint, as we stayed fairly close to I-15. The mountains underneath us looked like they were covered in green velvet. I bet elk live in those mountains. Yesterday's flights across the Grand Canyon, Lake Powell, and Monument Valley were spectacular, but this mountainous scenery was totally different and every bit as beautiful. At one point we briefly passed through a hailstorm. I had never seen this from the air; it looked like the opening scene of Star Wars, with all the galaxies coming right at you at light speed. South of the Canadian Border, North of someplace, we crossed I-90 East of Butte and West of Three Forks, where the Madison, Gallatin, and Jefferson Rivers come together to form the headwaters of the Missouri River. Soon, we could see the town of Townsend and Canyon Ferry Lake, which the Missouri flows into, a couple of miles from my house. I descended from ten thousand feet, lined up for the downwind of runway 16, turned left base, and did a fairly decent landing at the Townsend airport (8U8). After taxiing to the tie down area (the hangar I had leased a few days earlier wasn't ready to use) and shutting down the plane, I shook Gil's hand, and said, "We made it!". Surprisingly, there wasn't much oil on the windshield or the rest of the plane. We secured the Stinson, unloaded it, and in a few minutes Karoline picked us up. Our total flight time was 24.6 hours. Thank you God for keeping us safe. Now that I have flown the Stinson from Houston to Townsend, I'm halfway to Alaska from Texas!

Hopefully, this time next year I will be writing about taking the good old Stinson flying machine "North to Alaska"! The voyage of the Voyager continues. Maybe one of these days my granddaughters Camyrn (age 6 in 2009) and Cadie (age 3) will be flying in the Voyager with me. Here we all are at the Townsend Airport!

Camyrn, Cadie, and "Pop" and the Stinson flying machine at Townsend Airport

Thy righteousness is like the great mountain;
thy judgments are a great deep:
O Lord, thou preservest man and beast. PSALMS 65:6

The Accident - June 14, 2010

There won't be a trip to Alaska this year. Today, I wrecked the Stinson. Russ Voorhees, my mechanic, had repaired an oil leak, and then told me to take the plane up around the pattern and bring it back to his hangar to verify the leak was fixed. My landing was good, but when I applied the brakes the plane veered off the runway and I ground-looped it, causing the plane to go straight down on its prop. At that time I saw a small amount of fuel leaking out of the vent on the right gas tank, and then the plane settled back onto its tail wheel, in the normal ground configuration. I shut off the fuel, the magnetos, and the master switch, and probably looked like a clown as I made a fast exit. Not a good day in Dodge. But once again, the good Lord watched over me, and my guardian angel Jack Clodfelter came to protect me. I can't say that I didn't have a scratch, because I had one on my left arm.

June 25th

The FAA sent out two inspectors on Monday to look at the Stinson. Today I received a Certified Letter telling me that I had to do a check ride with one of their inspectors in a tail wheel airplane, or they would start proceedings to yank my pilot's license. Not good. I also received notice that the insurance company totaled the Stinson, and is going to pay me the full amount for which it was insured. That part is good. Actually, loosing the Stinson was a blessing in disguise. In the eight years I had it, I managed to custom design the prop blades by putting the nose of the plane onto the ground, rebuilt or replaced a total of seventeen cylinders on a six-cylinder engine, had a crankshaft break in flight, a wheel exploded while landing one time, several times oil splattered all over the windshield where it was difficult to see, and it cost a lot of money to keep it flying. Because of an unusual prop / engine design going back to World War II, parts were expensive and difficult to obtain, and a new prop would have cost over $25,000. Not $2,500, but $25,000! This doesn't sound right, and it wasn't, but that's the way it was. The Stinson wasn't insured as much as what a new prop costs! God has always watched over me and kept me safe.

July 2nd

Today I started flying a 2003 Citabria with Ben Walton, owner of Summit Aviation in Bozeman. I was initially nervous about going up, but once airborne I acted like a pilot and not a guy who had wrecked an airplane. I'm not used to flying a plane that so new and nice.

August 27th

After several hours of flying the Citabria, I took my check ride with Derek Amos, a very good FAA inspector. All I had to do was to make three take-offs and landings. Sounds simple enough, but it took me several flights with instructors Ben Walton, Scott Erwin, and Stephan Robinson before I was ready. When I flew with Derek, my skill level and confidence was high enough that I easily passed. A few days earlier I had talked with Derek, because I didn't feel I was ready. He asked me what the problem was, and I told him I had a tendency to bounce on landings. He laughed, and said, "Welcome to the world of flying taildraggers!" He told me to relax, and after that I started making decent landings. Of course, God helped.

September 15, 2010

The Stinson is now history, but life goes on. I flew my new-to-me 1958 Cessna 172! The insurance money arrived two weeks after my accident in the Stinson. So I'm back in the air flying my own plane again! Life is Good. God is Good! Since it has a skunk on its tail, and I worked for Lockheed for 25 years and they had the Skunk Works, although I did not work on that program, I have started calling my new plane the "Cessna Skunk Works!"

My new-to-me 1958 Cessna 172. I call it the Cessna Skunk Works!

Townsend Airport (8U8)

At every airport, there are a group of pilots who hang out together, swap stories, solve the world's problems if only the world and its politicians would listen, have friendly discussions of the merits of taildraggers versus nose-wheels, Cessnas versus Pipers, etc, and are always ready to give a helping hand. At Houston's Ellington Field, Jim Gardner and Lance Borden hang out. In La Porte, TX, Gideon Jones was a WWII B-24 pilot who once was a POW, and is one of the nicest men in the world. He and his wife Jan always had a hot cup of coffee ready to give away. Bill Wynn at Galveston, J. D. Rhodes at Brazoria County Airport, and Carl Nepute and Wayne Messenger at Pearland Regional Airport fall in the same category. Tom Jenkins and Bob Simle are two more pilots that are good friends. These are but a sample of the good people whom I have met that speak Pilotese, and are on my good people list.

Townsend Airport is no different. Every morning at 10 AM there is a "Union Coffee Break" held in Russ Voorhees's hangar. I look forward to going there, and Karoline likes for me to go, since I'm out of her hair for at least an hour. She calls me, "The Old and the Restless!" Mike Ferguson normally brings chocolate chip cookies that his wife Jeanne bakes; he flies a Bonanza. For 27 years he was director of the Montana Aeronautics Division. Russ or Ernie Carlson flies the MiG Killer or Brand-X (see photos in the back of the book). Steve Palinkos has a Cessna 180 on wheels and the Cessna 185 on amphibs. Bryan Carroll has a beautiful RV-7 that he built himself. Al Irvin flies a Cherokee 140, as does Chuck Carver, from whom I bought the Cessna Skunk Works. Neil Salmi owns a Rans, which falls into the Light Sport category. Tony Sylvester is a retired airline pilot and has flown taildraggers, floatplanes, business jets, 767s, and Twin Commanders over forest fires. Douglas Cairns teaches at Montana State University and comes up in his Cessna 180. Barry Wilson is a helicopter pilot, owns a Cessna 140 and is restoring a Pitts with Russ. Chris Maxcy has built a home-built called a STOL King, which is like a big Cub that he hopes to fly in Alaska where he is a commercial fisherman. Phil Olson brings his Navion up from Three Forks. Several other pilots stop by on occasion. Each July 4th there is a Fly-In at the airport – fly on up and enjoy the beauty of Montana, and perhaps do a bit of hangar flying!

There ain't no better flying than floatplane flying!

Photo by Mike Kincaid

It Only Took Me Two Years to Earn My Seaplane Rating

Tom Jenkins and I bought the Stinson on June 8, 2002; on June 11th I took off on Continental Airlines for Anchorage for the wonderful world of floatplane flying.

Having flown as a passenger in floatplanes, and seeing others fly them, I finally decided that this summer was time for me to learn to fly floats. For months I had corresponded with Vern and Laura Kingsford, owners of Scenic Mountain Air / Alaska Float Ratings (www.alaskfloatratings.com) in Moose Pass, Alaska. Located between Anchorage and Seward, Moose Pass is a don't-blink-as-you-drive-through-it place, but a great scenic town. Surrounded by lakes, it is even more beautiful from the air. The Kingsfords have five planes, four of which are on floats. I flew the two Super Cubs for my training, doing most of it in N7862P, although I did fly Vern's plane N917VK twice. For one week I stayed at Moose pass, trying to earn and learn my Single Engine Sea (SES) rating. Instructors Norm Kalat and Will taught me the basics, such as normal water, rough water, and calm water take-offs and landings, step taxi and turns, plow taxi and turns, beaching and docking. My flying techniques weren't the best, but I enjoyed every exhilarating minute of my training. Typically, most pilots pick up their SES ratings in about 6–7 hours, but I have never done anything in a typical manner!

Alaska Float Ratings two Super Cubs, Moose Pass, Alaska

We flew on and off Trail Lake, Grant Lake, Kenai Lake, Johnson Lake, and a couple of others. Emerald green water abounded; moose grazed near the edge of Trail Lake; the train between Seward and Anchorage rumbled across a bridge over the lake daily. They don't call it Moose Pass for nothing. One evening while I sat in the pilot's lounge, a mama moose and her calf ambled in front. One day Norm and I went to the Kenai and / or Harding Ice Fields, and it was as if I were flying over Antarctica again. I met other pilots taking the course, including a farmer in South Dakota, a dentist who lived in Anchorage, another man who made his living flying bush planes, and a few airline pilots that were also military officers whom had flown in Afghanistan a month after September 11th. The September, 2002 issue of AOPA Pilot has a story about Alaska Float Ratings.

Look at the grin on the guy sitting in the front seat

One night while training I flew to Johnson Lake (I think that's the name of it) with Norm, he took off, and I camped by myself. Catching and cooking one fish for supper erased for me the memory of another Alaska fishing trip. (In 1999, my friends Bob Simle, Brian Collier, and Hawks Abbott had gone to Alaska and flown out to Lake Bulchitna in a DCH-2 Beaver, dreaming of catching some king salmon, but not a single one of us even had a single nibble, nor ever lived it down!) I was absolutely alone, enjoying the serenity and solitude. About 2 AM I awoke from the sound of a beaver slapping his tail and building his (or her) den near my campsite. Another day, Phil Thibodeau, one of Vern's instructors, and I flew a C172 to Talkeetna, and then flew to 10,000-feet on the Southern side of Denali. That was some spectacular flying! Phil hadn't been there himself. On the return trip, we refueled at Talkeetna, and somebody asked us if we were the pilots who didn't seem to know where they were going. It happens!

Taylorcraft owned by Arctic Flyers at Lake Hood

After flying with Alaska Float Ratings for a few days, and not being as proficient as I needed to be to pass the check ride for the SES rating, Vern suggested that I continue with my plans to fly elsewhere in Alaska, and then come back a week or so later. I had made arrangements to fly with Heidi or Richard Ruess, owners of Arctic Flyers at Anchorage's Lake Hood. Mr. Ruess told me the day I arrived that the water was too rough for my level of flying floats, and suggested I come back that evening. I guess he ought to know, since he had over 35,000 hours of flight experience. Once again that evening, the winds were too strong, so I came back the next day. They were booked at the time, but in the mean time, I had made arrangements to fly a new Maule-7 on a demonstration ride. I don't remember the pilot's name, but he allowed me to take the controls after we took off from the land airfield bordering Lake Hood. That afternoon, I drove to Merrill Field, and practiced touch-and-goes in a Cessna-172, then drove back to Lake Hood, and flew with the son of the Maule-7 pilot in an Aeronica on floats. We flew across Cook Inlet, and went to some lake where we practiced rough water landings and takeoffs (splash-and-dashes). This was the first time I had even done any landings flying from the right seat. Finally, the next morning I flew with Heidi Ruess in her husband's F-19 Taylorcraft. For some reason, her own T-Craft wasn't ready to fly. Flying on-and-off of busy Lake Hood is quite different than flying off the low traffic lakes that Vern uses. Heidi, like other instructors, told me that I really needed to learn to use the rudders better, especially since I showed them a photo of the Stinson.

Mike Vivion's Cessna 170B in Fairbanks

After flying with Heidi, I drove to Fairbanks, sleeping in a rented van about thirty miles out. The following day I flew on and off the Tanana River with Mike Vivion in his Cessna 170B on floats. River landings and take-offs give a whole new perspective on flying floats, especially doing step turns on a curving river. Mike was Alaska's first Master Certified Flight Instructor. After leaving Mike, I immediately drove across the field and flew in a Maule-5 on wheels. I'm not sure about a fabric airplane, but from what I understand, the material used these days is quite good. That doesn't detract from the fun I have of flying a Maule or a Citabria or a Champ (which I had flown in Houston before I came to Alaska).

That night, I drove to an area near Denali and camped again in the van. I had thought about regular camping but my mosquito spray was about as effective as one tank fighting the Chinese army – they just keep on coming. The next morning, on a spur-of-the-moment decision, I flew as a passenger with ERA Helicopters on a tour of Denali. It turns out that the pilot had worked for Vern Kingsford a year or two earlier. That was another breathtaking ride, and besides seeing the highest mountain on the North American continent, we also saw a few grizzly bears.

Back in Anchorage, I just couldn't resist going on another floatplane fishing trip. The kings were running, so I had to at least try. I signed up for a one-day trip with Regal Air and flew in the co-pilots seat of a DeHavilland DCH-2 Beaver. That just emphasized that sooner or later I would fly one. We flew to Lake Creek, about a mile from where Brian, Bob, Hawks, and I had been three years earlier. And I had the same kind of luck. When we landed, there were people waiting to take their king salmon back on the return flight. After all day with a guide, and no luck, when the plane came back at 4 PM, people in the next boat over started catching kings. But we couldn't wait, so we motored back to the waiting plane empty handed. To the king salmon with my name on it, perhaps not even hatched yet, one year you will be in my photographs and freezer until my friends and family and I make a meal of you!

The following day I drove back to Moose Pass, to take another lesson flying the Super Cubs. After waiting around all day, I finally had a chance to fly with Vern. I had wanted a chance to fly with him before I went for the Seaplane check ride, just to have an idea what he would have me do when he gave the actual check ride. For the second time, I sat in the front seat of Super Cub N917VK. We took off and headed to the same area that I had camped a week earlier. Vern started putting me through the paces, and I managed to show him that I had learned the basics of floatplane flying. But I messed up slightly when it came to docking, so as a result I didn't fly with him or his instructors anymore, and left without my SES rating. Oh, well! But I hold no grudges, and for several months wore a blue ball cap with the name of "Alaska Float Ratings" and embroidery of Super Cub N917VK on the front of it.

I left Moose Pass a few minutes later and drove to Anchorage, where I stayed in a hotel room at Ace Hangars on Merrill Field. One of the best rooms I have ever stayed, with a view right over the airport! The next day, before I caught my flight back to Houston, I had a demonstration ride in a Husky on amphibians, in which we landed both on water and back on the concrete at Merrill Field. Then I flew with Marc Paine in a fairly new Cessna 172 for about an hour-and-a-half around the Anchorage area. Had I earned my seaplane rating, I could have had a lesson or two in a Widgeon, and this is something I had hoped for. Perhaps, another day!

For two weeks having been airborne one way or another every day of my trip, after piloting two Super Cubs, one Aeronica, one Taylorcraft, and one Cessna 170B, all on floats, plus three Cessna-172s, a Maule-5 and a Maule-7, receiving a demonstration ride in a Husky, and riding as a passenger on a DCH-2 Beaver and a helicopter, it was time to head back to Houston. I logged twenty-seven hours during this wonder period of my life, enjoyed the flying and beautiful scenery, caught me a fish, saw friends like Dave, Jean, and Rachael Bieganski, and ate with Dawn and Bill Caswell, where I had me a caribou roast.

On July 20, 2002, the thirty-third anniversary of the first manned lunar landing, I drove to Lake Palestine, Texas, and flew with Danny Duggan in his Cessna-170B on floats. He had a hangar near the lake, and had one of the best setups for planes that I have ever seen. I would have taken the Stinson, but wasn't good enough to go solo in it. I never had a chance to fly with Danny again, because he died of cancer a few months later.

1946 Stinson, Seattle Seaplanes, 2003

The urge to fly a DCH-2 Beaver on floats never left, so in November, I flew to Seattle and took a lesson from Kenmore Air that lasted over an hour in one of these planes. This is one of the best and easiest planes I have ever flown. I love flying my Stinson, but I could sure enjoy making my living flying the DCH-2. While I was in Seattle, I also flew a 1946 Stinson with Jim Chrysler, owner of Seattle Seaplanes.

Matt and DCH-2 Beaver, Kenmore Air, Seattle, 2003 – love that plane!

July 1, 2003

Once again, I was back in Alaska. Julia Tripp was the flight instructor that gave me another ride in a floatplane. The night before I had checked around at the Talkeetna Airport for somebody to give me a floatplane lesson and was told to call Alaska Floats and Skis and ask for her. We made arrangements to meet and I followed her to Christiansen Lake, East of Talkeetna, where we flew for an hour in a Taylorcraft BC-12 D. The weather wasn't all that great, but I had fun anyway. She and Jim Chrysler told me that it wouldn't take much for me to finish my seaplane rating. Someday…

Alaska Floats and Skis Taylorcraft BC-12 D at Lake Christiansen

April 16-18, 2004

Déjà vu all over again. I went back to Seattle and flew the same two planes I had flown with Kenmore Air and Seattle Seaplanes. Since I own a Stinson 108, it would be good to earn my SES rating in Jim Chrysler's Stinson 108. Jim is a great guy to fly with.

May 30, 2004

Memorial Day. One of these days I might just finish my rating, but today was just another boring day flying floatplanes. Ho, Hum! Ya, right! Alan Crawford makes his living as a pilot for Southwest Airlines, but lives along the shore of Lake Buchanan near Austin, Texas. And, he has his own Cessna 172 on floats. Well, the wanderer and the seaplane wanna-be pilot in me decided that flying with Alan today would be a good way to spend the three-day weekend. I would have flown over to Burnet in my Stinson flying machine, but in reality it was a Stinson non-flying machine, in the shop in Galveston for its second go-around of cylinder replacements. Once again, my Ford F250 and I flew in very low earth orbit and made our way over to Lake Buchanan, even without the aid of a GPS receiver! Ancient, these mariners!

Lake Buchanan is fed by the Colorado River. The river starts as the Green River in Wyoming, somewhere along the way turns into the

Colorado River, flows through the Grand Canyon, and through some twist of fate, winds up in Texas. Bet you believe that one, don't you? Mike Vivion and Alan are the only people with whom I have flown where we landed on a river. Karoline and I have been on a boat trip up the Canyon of the Eagles, starting at Lake Buchanan and riding the boats into the Colorado River. This time, Alan and I did our splash and dashes on the river a few times, and then a few more times on the lake. Terrible way to spend a holiday weekend!

July 2004

Karoline, Michelle, Cheri, John, and Camyrn drove to Wyoming. Prior to their trip, I had planned on flying my Stinson there, but it was still in the shop. Since I hadn't spent much time in Idaho, I decided to fly on Southwest to Boise and meet them in Wyoming. From Boise, I drove to Wyoming first. At Jackson Hole Aviation, I picked up some more mountain-flying instruction in a Cessna 172 that I had flown on another trip with Hawks Abbott. The Cessna seemed out of place with all the corporate jets, but I probably had more enjoyment flying it than the corporate pilots who quickly climb to altitude and engage the autopilot. On this nearly cloudless morning with the sky the deep-blue color for which Wyoming is famous, we flew parallel to the Tetons off our left wing, followed the Snake River, climbed to over 13,000 feet, crossed over a mountain range to the north, and just enjoyed the view for 1.2 hours. Too soon, we had to go back. I have told Karoline that when I am an old man (older than now), sitting in my rocking chair, waiting to board the Flight to the Angels, it would please me immensely to be passing my last days on earth looking at the Tetons, and it would probably much cheaper than throwing my money away in a nursing home.

As always, looking at these mountains brought to the surface the nagging question of why did I ever leave Wyoming? Of course, back in 1978, the opportunity to work on the space shuttle program might have had something to do with it. As much as I love the West, Wyoming couldn't give me that chance. So I traded the mountains and elk and mule deer and antelope and the Indian Medicine Wheel in the Big Horns and the geology of the Tetons and Yellowstone and Devil's Tower and the Wind River Canyon and Garden Creek Falls on Casper Mountain and being able to drive in wide-open spaces with few other vehicles to work on the space program. Did I make a good choice? Yes and no. It has been a thrill to work on equipment that has flown in space. Had I stayed in Wyoming I would have had the regret of not working with the space stuff, and the different trips and adventures that have come my way may not have. In terms of having a job, I don't know what else I would have done, but it won't bother me when it comes time to leave the heat and humidity and flat lands and jillions of people and traffic jams of the Houston area behind me.

July 7th

My destination today was McCall, Idaho, where I had a Cessna 172 reserved the next day for a couple of hours with McCall Mountain/Canyon Flying Seminars, LLC. I could easily live in McCall, with its nearby mountains and lakes. Until a week or so before I left Houston, I had no idea that my work on the space program had any connection with anyone in that town. The day I called to see about flying with this company, I had a conversation with an answering machine. A little while later, my phone rang at work, Paige Walker, the lady calling, said, "Hi Matt, you work at the Johnson Space Center." I must admit, that statement caught me by surprise, but then she went to explain that she recognized the first three digits of my phone number, because she used to work there. Turns out, she knew some of the same people I have worked with, and additionally, her husband, Dave Walker, had been an astronaut, but had died three years earlier of cancer. She asked where I worked, and I told her Building 44, where I worked on the space shuttle and space station communications systems. It's a small world stuff: Paige had previously worked as a co-op in the same building as I do, and at one time or another, had worked on the Electronic Still Camera, which was a project I had also worked on as a civilian and also when I was attached to the Naval Space Command as a reservist. The connection goes even further.

Dave Walker flew on four shuttle missions. One was STS-30, and one of the astronauts that flew on that mission was Dr. Mary Cleave. My friend Nora Van Burgh had once heard Dr. Cleave talk, and then talked to her afterwards. So I once went to Dr. Cleave's office and requested that she sign two photos of herself for me to give to Nora. Dr. Cleave said, "I remember talking to her!" When I told this to Paige, she said that it was Dr. Cleave who introduced her to Dave Walker. Paige rented from Dr. Cleave. When I gave Nora the photos of Dr. Cleave, I also gave her another one of the shuttle's Ku-Band system, which I have spent many years of my life working on. On my wall at home I have a collage of photos that was signed by the crew of STS-53 for my support of the Electronic Still Camera effort. Dave was the commander of that mission. Then, while I was in Alaska in 1995 for training before I went to Winter-over in Antarctica, STS-69 flew. Dave Walker was also the commander for this mission. On the road to Poker Flat, which is outside of Fairbanks, there is a place that is a bar and a restaurant. I left an STS-69 decal at the bar, because Ken Cockrell was flying as the pilot on the same mission. I knew him through my association with the Naval Space Command. Additionally, Barbara Morgan, who was backup to Christa McAulife, the teacher that perished in the Challenger, is now an astronaut herself, (although I don't know her) and is from McCall.

July 8th

At 6:30 AM, I met Paige Walker and Marti Wegner, an excellent flight instructor who works for McCall Mountain/Canyon Flying Seminars, LLC. Marti started the 1958 Cessna 172A by pulling an old "T" handle cable located on the instrument panel. Our flight was over the Snake River in the magnificent Hell's Canyon. The sun gave a glare from the East, so I didn't even try taking photographs, and I was somewhat intimidated to fly very low into the canyon but that didn't stop it from being a fun flight. The plane flew well and I could easily have spent many hours flying it.

As the company name implies, McCall Mountain/Canyon Flying Seminars, LLC has several seminars a year teaching pilots how to fly safely in mountains and canyons. From what I understand, it is one of the premier flight training programs in the country dedicated to this purpose, and with its strong emphasis on safety, it is also very highly rated. Several issues of the Pilot Getaways magazine have made similar references about this company. Owner Lori MacNichol wrote me in an e-mail, "Aviation safety is what I promote and represent". Although there are many thousands of pilots who learned to fly in mountains and canyons without the benefit of such professional instruction, for those pilots who are inexperienced, taking such a course just may help keep them alive. Sometime, I would like to take the beginning and advance courses that this company offers. I'm quite sure I would learn a lot of very useful information.

After saying goodbye to Marti and Paige, I left for Coeur d'Alene, which is located about five hours driving time North of McCall. It is one of those beautiful places that once again made me ask myself why did I live in Texas.

But besides enjoying the scenery of the drive, I had another reason to go there: To fly a 1946 Piper J-3 Cub on floats with Mike Kincaid, owner of the Mountain Lakes Seaplane company. Before I left Texas he suggested that perhaps I could finish my seaplane rating with him. Since the Stinson could not be flown to Wyoming as originally planned, I thought, "Why not use the money I had planned to use on that trip and see if I could obtain the rating." While I waited for the cub to come back to the dock, I chatted with one of Mike's students, a Hollywood stuntman. The other man who was flying the plane is a pilot of a business jet that goes worldwide. In one of Mike's e-mails to me after I came home, he told me that he was teaching floatplane flying to a former U-2 pilot.

So Mike and I finally took off, with me sitting in the front seat and him sitting in the back seat of the Cub. The original 65-horse engine had been replaced with a 100-Hp engine, but with two people on board and the weight of the floats, it still seems a bit underpowered. We practiced the standard things taught in float plane training, such as normal, rough water, smooth water take-offs and landings, and step and plow taxis, and I had a blast. My throat was cotton dry, and my techniques were rusty, but the exhilaration of floatplane flying had not diminished. Mike was patient with me, and after several splash-and-dashes on and off the water, my hour of flying time was over too soon. During the time I spent with Mike, he told me of his years of flying in Alaska as a state trooper.

July 9th

Three different times on this day I took off with Mike for an hour or so of fun flying the Cub. The first two flying hours of the day I did OK, but the third time I had serious doubts whether or not I could pass the check ride. Mike had me perform rough water landings and take-offs, and I just didn't have the hang of it, although I had done the maneuver well enough earlier. Mike told me to make gentle and small movements on the stick when coming in for a landing, instead of being heavy-handed with it. He didn't want me to flip the plane over in the water, and in all honesty, neither did I! When we came back to the dock, he told me that he knew I could successfully pass the check ride, but that I needed to relax more, and he wrote an endorsement in my pilot's log book recommending me for the check ride. While I was flying, I didn't have much time to enjoy the beauty of Hayden Lake and the surrounding mountains, but I still had enough time in the cockpit to look it over and see the various hues of blue of the water and sky. From the ground, the yellow J-3 Cub sure is distinguishable when it is flying over the lake and trees.

After dinner, I went back to my hotel room and studied for the verbal exam I knew I would be facing the next day. My thoughts were more concentrated on passing the rating than the beauty of Coeur d'Alene, although the images of landing on the lake kept me awake quite a while before I finally went to sleep.

July 10th

At 9 AM I met Mike at the Coeur d'Alene airport at the Civil Air Patrol hangar. Mr. Richard Pearce, the FAA examiner, had flown his twin-engine airplane in from Moses Lake, Washington. Mike left me his keys to the hangar and went back to the dock. Mr. Pearce chatted with me for a few minutes and then started asking me questions. He was relaxed about it, and often gave me little antidotes to my answers. I felt comfortable around him, even though when we landed after doing the check ride, he told me that I needed to relax more. In 1997, he had flown a 1946 Taylorcraft with a 65-Hp engine and no electronics nor electrical system onboard around the perimeter of the continental 48 states. To start it, he had to use the ancient method of hand propping. After the exam, I bought his book, <u>Taylored Around the USA</u>, and read the entire thing while flying home on a commercial airliner (UGH!) the next day, between the times I spent looking at mountains and the canyon lands of Utah.

About 10 AM, Mr. Pearce announced that it was time to go fly. Very diligently I locked the hangar and put Mike's keys in my pocket, which I found at 10 PM that night in my motel in Boise. I mailed them the next day to Mike, but must admit that I was embarrassed about my mistake.

The wind was blowing from the shoreline by the dock towards the lake. Mr. Pearce told me to do a step taxi and turn 180° and takeoff; he said, "Very nice" right afterwards, so that gave me a little confidence. Often, during the flight he addressed me as "Mr. Pilot". We climbed to 3500 feet, where I had to demonstrate a departure stall and a landing stall, fly at slow speed, and perform a couple of 360° turns to the left and right. Then he told me to land in a particular cove, but I missed the one he told me and headed for one that was next to it. After I realized my mistake, he told me to fly over a boat and perform a rough water landing in the boat's wake. Upon landing, Mr. Pearce remarked, "That was more of an actual rough water landing then a simulated one." After the next takeoff, he told me to head back to the dock and then had me do one more rough water landing. I kept remembering what Mike told me about handling the stick very carefully. As we taxied near the dock, Mr. Pearce told me that if I docked successfully, I passed. The last time when I was in Alaska, going for my unofficial check ride, was when I hit the dock. I had butterflies and my stomach churned, and a boat with fishermen was moored just off the entrance to the dock, but I carefully taxied around them, shut the engine off, and drifted into the dock at the correct angle. Mike was there to grab the rope on the starboard wing.

What a great day! After two years of trying, I finally received my "Airplane Single Engine Sea" (ASES) rating in a 1946 Piper J-3 Cub at Mountain Lakes Seaplane in Coeur d'Alene, Idaho, on July 10, 2004. Photo by Mike Kincaid

After two years of trying and 38 hours of flying eleven different seaplanes with thirteen instructors, and in four states, I had finally obtained my Airplane Single Engine Sea rating. Mr. Pearce gave me my new temporary license, Mike and the other two students shook my hand, and I left a very happy camper. I immediately called Karoline, who was on the road heading back to Texas. She did not know that I was even going for the rating at this particular time. I had not told her or anyone else. Then I called Hawks Abbott, Bob Simle, Carl Nepute, and Jim Gardner to tell them the good news.

Soon after the check ride, I left Coeur d'Alene and drove the five-hour distance to McCall, going through Moscow (not the big one and not the one in Texas). Near Lewiston and then again outside of White Bird (if I remember correctly), I drove down some very steep hills with multiple curves that lasted about six miles each. I would have liked to spend more time looking at the geology. Some miles North of McCall, I passed a sign that I should have taken a photo: "45th Parallel - Halfway between the North Pole and the Equator".

"For, lo, He that formeth the mountains, and createth the wind, and declareth unto man what is His thought, that maketh the morning darkness, and treadeth upon the high places of the earth, The LORD, The God of hosts, is His name." Amos 4:13

Seattle and Alaska Flying 2005

March 3rd

It doesn't cost much more to have a stop in Seattle when flying Continental Airlines between Houston and Anchorage, since they stop there anyway for fuel. And I had a reason to stop: Seattle Seaplanes.

This was the fifth time I have flown with Jim Chrysler. The first three times were in his Stinson; the last two in the Cessna 172 with a 180-hp engine and a constant speed prop. In the short hour that we flew together, I took-off and landed at Lake Union, Lake Washington, and at a third lake east of Lake Washington. In all cases, we did glassy water take-offs and landings and Jim had me land and do step turns. We didn't have to contend with much boat traffic; our flight path took us between Mt. Baker to the north and Mt. Rainer to the south. Mt. Baker glistened in the sunlight, its snowcap a brilliant white against the cloudless blue sky. We didn't fly by the Space Needle this trip; on previous flights we could see people waving at us. For not flying seaplanes for several months, I think I did reasonably well. Had I not been heading "North to Alaska" to see the Iditarod race, I could have easily spent every day of the weekend flying with Jim.

My friend Jim Chrysler, owner of Seattle Seaplanes

March 4th

The lady running Talkeetna Aero Services recognized a tourist wanting a flight around Denali, but at the same time she didn't act like she felt the need to scalp me of all the money I had with me. A DeHavilland DCH-2 Beaver with both wheels and skis sat on the ramp outside her office. She said that a group of four people were going to fly in it around Denali, and said I could go for $150, which is the bottom line pricing for just touring the South side of the Mountain, but she wouldn't charge me any more for going all the way around. Four people walked in as I told lady I would fly, and shortly afterwards, Don Lee, the pilot, showed up. As we walked towards the plane, I asked him if I could sit in the co-pilot's seat and he said I could. WOW!

Earlier, I wrote about flying in a Taylorcraft floatplane near Talkeetna. Don owns Alaska Floats & Skis, the same company that owned the Taylorcraft. I recognized the name on his jacket, so when I told him I had flown in his airplane with one of his instructors, I started off on the right foot with him. As we flew around the mountain, he gave me some verbal instructions about flying along mountain ridges. And flying around the mountain is what we did – all the way around. At one point he said we were twenty-five miles away; it looked like only a mile away. Clear visibility, low turbulence. We flew over the ridges at eleven thousand feet; the top of Denali towered over us another nine thousand.

DeHavilland DCH-2 Beaver, located at Talkeetna Aero Services, that Don Lee flew around Denali with me in co-pilot seat

Our flight path took us up the Ruth Glacier, around the mountain, over Shelton's Amphitheater, over Shelton's cabin, the only private cabin on the mountain. Don Shelton is probably the best known pilot that flew around Denali. He is famous for delivering climbers to-and-from their starting points, rescuing stranded climbers, making numerous glacier landings, and being a good guy on top of it all. Don Shelton has been dead for many years, but his legend lives on. Don Lee seems to have inherited the Denali flying skills of Don Shelton. The photos I took of the trip can never do justice to what I saw flying around the mountain, but instead of filling the page with a lot of superlatives, I'm just going to include a few photos anyway. After we landed I told Don that I was planning on bringing the Stinson up in July, and if I land in Talkeetna, I will let him fly it. Then when I said I might come back next year around Iditarod time and take some glacier landing lessons from him in ski-equipped planes, he grinned and said,

"Put some skis on your Stinson and fly along the Iditarod Trail all the way to Nome"! I must admit I like that idea!

Denali, as viewed from co-pilot seat of DeHavilland Beaver

Another great view of Denali, from the Beaver's co -pilot seat

March 7th

Don flew this same plane with another group of tourists along the same route to Denali. While flying, the plane's wings started extreme and dangerous fluttering. Don's years of experience kicked in, and he successfully landed at Talkeetna and saved everyone on board. On the AOPA website, there is a link where Don talks about this event, called "May Day on Mt. McKinley". He is a terrific pilot.

Floatplane Trip to the Arctic Circle, August 2005

Franklin Lake, north of the Arctic Circle

After performing the emergency landing in my Stinson in May when the crankshaft broke, my plans to fly it to Alaska this summer quickly evaporated. With my available funds for the Alaska trip quickly diminished because of engine repairs, but with vacation time still on the books, I looked around to see where else I might go. Even before I obtained my SES rating in 2004, I had been watching the web site of Adventure Seaplanes (www.adventureseaplanes.com) located at Surfside Seaplane Base at Lino Lakes, Minnesota (about a thirty minute drive from the Minneapolis/St. Paul Airport). Their Arctic Explorer Tour intrigued me. From their web page, I quote:

- Maximum 4 Seaplanes
- (Churchill, Baker Lake, Arctic Circle)
- 35-45 Hours flight time
- Fly your plane or we may supply one for you
- See Beluga Whales, Polar Bears, Moose, Caribou, Musk Ox, Wolves
- Unbelievable fishing for Grayling, Arctic Char, Lake Trout, Walleye & Northern Pike
- This is a TRIP of a LIFETIME

"Wow, flying a float plane from Minnesota to the Arctic Circle should be a blast!" I thought. Not only is Adventure Seaplanes one of the few companies in the United States that rents seaplanes to qualified pilots, even more unusual, pilots are also allowed to fly the planes into Canada. Thinking that I could handle the Cessna 172 or the Piper PA-11, I called up owner Brian Schanche. Yes, there were still openings for the August trip. Even though I had over forty hours flying seaplanes in three years, I had only flown five hours since I obtained my SES rating last year. About 20 of my hours were obtained in Cubs or Super Cubs, and only 5 hours were gained in a C-172. By the time the details of the trip were finalized, Brian astutely accessed my lack of proficiency in flying seaplanes and decided that I would fly with him in his Cessna 185, switching off with a German by the name of Wolfgang Fischer. Our trip was scheduled to leave on Saturday, August 13th.

But the week leading up to the 13th gave me the highest of the highs and the lowest of the lows. After completing a very successful mission, the crew of the space shuttle STS-114 mission was scheduled to land on Monday, August 8th. This was the first mission since the ill-fated Columbia mission two-and-a-half years earlier, and there was no way that I was going to miss watching the landing on the NASA channel, scheduled around 3:30 AM. But the landing attempts that day were waved off due to potential weather problems at the Cape, so the mission was extended one day, so on Tuesday I sat holding my granddaughter Camyrn as we watched Discovery land at Edwards AFB, the first space shuttle mission in her life. Shortly afterwards I drove to work, feeling absolutely ecstatic all the way. That same morning my good friend Mike Gentry left a phone message for me at work; I figured that since his job is to provide the media with astronaut and space mission photographs, he had called to tell me about some terrific photograph regarding the shuttle landing. Wrong. Mike's message told me to call him; when I did, in tears, he told me that Butch Head, our mutual and very good friend and even better person, had been killed as a result of a car wreck the day before. Butch and I had met during the trip to Russia in 1992 to watch the launch of Soyuz TM-15. His father had been a close friend of Gus Grissom, one of the original Mercury Seven astronauts. He should have worked for NASA as an official space historian, because nobody knew the facts of space program better than Butch; he could easily recall the names of every

American and Russian space crewmember and on what mission they had flown. Oh, my heart was heavy that day. Within one hour I went from being on top of the emotional roller coaster to the very bottom.

On Wednesday afternoon, the STS-114 crew returned to Houston's Ellington Field. I stood near the front of the roped off area, listening to the crew's excited speeches and watching their gestures as they shared their adventure with the crowd, refueling my own dream of going into space. One of these days those dreamlike sparks are going to ignite into the combustion of the main engines.

Before I boarded the plane to Minneapolis on Thursday, I assisted in the removal of the Ku-Band antenna that we have in our lab; the antenna that is just like the ones that fly on the space shuttles. Twenty-six years of my life have been devoted to the space shuttle's and space station's Ku-Band systems.

Later that evening, Brian Schanche's girlfriend Lori picked me up at the Minneapolis – St. Paul airport. We went to a restaurant, where we met up with Brian and a French couple who often came to the States to fly around the country in either wheeled planes or floatplanes. On Friday, we packed the planes and I met the other men who were going on the trip, all anxious for the Saturday morning departure. I got to know Eric Weaver and Kirk Spangler when we ate dinner together on Friday evening, along with Wes Moore, a flight instructor that works for Brian. Interesting enough, Wes received his seaplane training from Mike Kincaid, the owner of Mountain Lakes Seaplane from whom I received my last hours of training when I obtained my seaplane rating last year. Eric has a Winnebago that he kept parked at Surfside. On this night I slept on a couch in the RV. Eric gave a white blanket to use; the next morning I asked him if I could take it with me on the trip to use along with my not-so-great-in-the-warm-department sleeping bag. Wrong choice on my part! I put it in Brian's plane where it haunted me like a ghost for the rest of the trip.

August 13th

Everyone going on the trip met at the Surfside Seaplane Base about 6:30 AM. Nine guys, four fully loaded seaplanes, waiting on one more. Craig Johnson was there with his Cessna 206 (N932DB) fit with amphibians (floats with wheels, so the plane can either land on the water or on runways); Bruce Johnson (Craig's brother) and Bruce Hendry were his passengers. Mike Andrews flew another Cessna 185 (N2397E) with Gary Wilson as his passenger. Eric owns a Cessna 180 (N2990C) that Wolfgang Fischer started off the trip flying right seat. Initially, Brian was going to have three seats in his plane; Wolfgang and I would either fly left seat or sit in the back, while Brian would always fly right seat. Prior to the trip, however, Brian took the back seat out of his 185 and decided that Wolfgang and I would switch off between his and Eric's planes. Brian and I flew in his Cessna 185 (N185AS). Wolfgang had arrived in Minneapolis just a few hours earlier from Germany and Brian knew he would be exhausted, which is why I started the trip flying with Brian.

All seaplanes at Surfside are lifted in and out of the water using a modified 4X4 that has had the back removed and the wheelbase replaced with extension tubes that are about twenty feet long. The tubes are rolled under the struts of a plane between the floats, and then a hydraulic mechanism with spreader bars is used to secure the plane, and operates much like a forklift. (I should have taken a photo but didn't.) As a result, the floats themselves are clean, and don't show much of a water line like most seaplanes that are always docked with the floats still in the water.

By 7 AM, all five floatplanes were in the water, and most were gassed up and ready to fly. Oh, yeah, I hadn't mentioned the fifth plane, a Cessna 150 (N23191), flown by Kirk. He is a pilot for Southwest Airlines and is based out of Orlando. Eric and he are good friends; Kirk keeps his plane at Surfside and had vacation time that he had planned on spending with his son, but his son had just graduated from college and had started a new job about three days earlier. So Kirk was just hanging around and talked about accompanying us to the Canadian border. He had had a problem with his electrical system the night before, and had let it charge overnight, but hadn't fueled the plane yet. Pilots of floatplanes often sit on one wing to gas up, and then slide across the windshield to the other wing. On this particular morning, Kirk accidentally scored the top of his plane's windshield, and then used a piece of that magical duct tape about two-feet long to cover the scratch mark.

Single file, we all slowly taxied down to the south end of the lake. Two or three other planes departed before Brian and me. Since the plane was heavy, Brian gave it some nose-down trim prior to takeoff; we accelerated onto the step, and as the north end of the lake came closer, Brian expertly popped it off the water by quickly pulling the manual flap handle to 40° and shortly afterwards he gave me the controls. I think we climbed to 2000 feet and headed north, over the well-kept farms and some of the 10,000 lakes that Minnesota boast on their car license plates. About an hour after takeoff we flew over the farm where Brian's parents live. I could see them waving at us. Shortly afterwards, Craig announced that he had a low voltage light and could not clear it, so we diverted over to Ely Seaplane Base. With Brian coaching me, I did my first landing in a C-185. In fact this is the first time I have ever flown a 185. We spent about two hours on the ground while mechanics worked on the 206. Gary borrowed a vehicle from the airport and brought us all back some hamburgers. After some part swapping of alternators and voltage regulators we left, with the planes refueled and our stomachs full. Set the flaps for twenty degrees, check that the area is clear, lift the water rudders up, give it full throttle, bring the nose back, push nose forward a little, climb onto the step, rotate, once airborne adjust the prop and throttle to 25 square, go to ten degrees of flaps, and once the climb rate is established, bring the flaps all the way up. For me, it is not automatic yet, and I simply need to fly a bunch more in seaplanes and high performance airplanes to improve my seaplane flying skills.

Maybe it was 1 PM or maybe it was 3 PM – it doesn't matter, but we landed at Crane Lake and taxied to Sand Point to clear Canadian Customs. Sand Point is located on the northern side of Crane Lake that is shared by both the United States and Canada. Brian paid the $25 for a gun permit because he had a 12-guage shotgun on board, a bear gun and/or a survival gun that is also required by Canadian law. After clearing customs, we walked a short distance to a souvenir shop where I bought a sweatshirt with several floatplanes on front, and Brian bought some ice cream for us.

Kirk decided to go with us to Red Lake, Ontario. Once all of us had cleared Canadian Customs, it was time to leave. As I flew over the thousands of lakes I wondered about the toughness of the men and women whom had settled this country, or at least parts of it. Perhaps we could fly for a hundred miles or so and not see and signs of man's presence. But the scenery is beautiful, so once we settled into a level altitude and a straight course, I could relax and enjoy it. We kept in contact with each other by radio. Prior to landing at Red Lake, Mike announced that he was experiencing a low voltage light in his plane, which is kind of unusual for the same problem to occur in two different airplanes on the same day. There is something to be said for traveling in groups. Coming in for the landing, I upset Brian when I pulled power just prior to touch down on a rough water landing. Rightfully so. Most of my experience is in wheeled airplanes, and pulling power is something you do just prior to landing. He took over the controls and averted a potential disaster. I was angry at myself for the rest of the evening.

Sitting next to the fueling docks were a couple of yellow Norseman aircraft owned by Green Air. These planes look a lot like the DeHavilland DCH 2 Beaver, but they have 600 horsepower engines, as opposed to the 450 HP in a Beaver. I talked to one of the pilots and he said he likes the Norseman better than the Beavers. These planes were built in the '30s. I don't know if they were built at Red Lake, but Red Lake calls itself the Norseman Capital of the world. After fueling the planes, Brian went looking for a place to stay, since he hadn't planned on staying here this night. He found some rooms at the Red Lake Inn that only cost $22 a night. Not fancy, but clean. We all then went at dinner at the Red Lake Lodge.

Norseman at Red Lake

Eighteen-year old Kayla was our waitress that night. Gary asked how old she is. She did a good job of serving ten guys steaks and fish and drinks. At dinner, Bruce Hendry suggested that we all give a brief introduction to ourselves. He is a retired stockbroker and lives in

Minnesota. Craig has a contracting business, and built wastewater treatment plants; his brother Bruce is a lawyer specializing in international law. I think Craig lives in Wisconsin, but his brother lives in Minnesota. Both Gary and Mike live in Minnesota, and work in separate commercial heating and cooling businesses, and have known each other for several years. Mike lived in Alaska for nine years, but wasn't a pilot then. Gary travels the world in his business, and physically, he is a very big guy. Wolfgang is now the principal of a German high school. He used to teach math and physics. Eric Weaver is from Florida; a year earlier the restaurant and hotel that his family owned was wiped out in a hurricane. For nine years he had put in 100 – 120 hour weeks, so now was in semi-retirement. As I previously mentioned, Kirk Spangler is a pilot for Southwest Airlines. Brian has over 6500 hours flying, loves the outdoors and is an expert hunter and fisherman and pilot. He did a good job of making the trip happen.

August 14th

Our day started with breakfast at the Red Lake Restaurant. Gary, Bruce Hendry, and I shared the same booth. Bruce or Gary started a mini-tradition of flipping coins to decide who was buying. I think Gary lost the toss. We flipped coins three days in a row, and Bruce didn't loose. I did, but don't remember if I bought one or two times. Gary asked the young waitress her name. Kaila. Does she know the other Kayla? Oh, sure. How old are you? Fifteen. Seems like I had heard this conversation before.

Mike, Gary, and Brian disappeared to see if the airplane mechanic located across the lake could find the source of the low voltage light. Before he left, Brian told me to walk down the road a ways and see the Norseman on display. As I walked down the street, I noticed several hand-painted banners hanging on the streetlights. They depicted life in Ontario, with several scenes showing wildlife and seaplanes. One that caught my attention was titled, "The Flying Bandit". I wondered what stories were behind that banner. Thirty minutes later I walked back to the motel, having exercised my shutter finger many times photographing the Norseman and the banners. Eric and Kirk sat around a table on the motel's outside deck; I went across the street to the Red Lake Restaurant to buy the three of us some coffee, and ended up buying a couple of books about flying that were on display near the cash register. Just couldn't help myself.

Later in the morning we migrated to the dining room at the Red Lake Lodge. Seems like some guy named Mr. Red Lake owns the town, the inn, the lodge, the restaurant, and the museum. It rained while we drank coffee. Wolfgang told me that he had learned to fly in Peru during the four years he worked there teaching math and physics at a high school. He has over a thousand hours as a pilot and received his commercial and instrument ratings in the United States. In addition to having his seaplane rating, he also pilots his own plane in Germany. He spoke of flying in South Africa, which is one of my own dreams. During the trip he wrote extensively in his journal, so he could tell his wife about it. She is gradually going blind, and he wanted to share with her in great detail our adventures. Because of his fluency in Spanish, and the fact he is such an easygoing person, I would like to fly with him to South America in my Stinson sometime. And it wouldn't bother me to fly with him around Germany and Austria in his airplane.

Around noon, Brian came back and said that Mike and Gary were going to fly over to Winnipeg to fix the low voltage problem. After we ate lunch, he said he was going to take a nap. That left Sunday afternoon to do some exploring around the town. So I did. My camera decided that it needed more batteries – of course I had all kinds of time before I left to make sure that I had fresh ones, but failed to do so. Not many places were open, but those that were didn't have the right batteries. After wandering around town for about an hour, the Kodak film store opened. The owner had the two-hard-to-find batteries that I needed, and something else: a bookstore. On a shelf behind the counter, laying like a panther ready to pounce on me, there was a book that caught my attention: The Flying Bandit. Having just seen the banner with the same title a few hours earlier, my curiosity needed an answer. The owner explained to me how this guy robbed banks in the Sixties and used his airplane to fly away.

In fact, the guy owned a Stinson! Now that doesn't mean that every Stinson owner is a bank robber! Let me be clear on that point! Then he graduated to robbing a gold shipment in Winnipeg that had originated in Red Lake. Eventually, he was caught. After he served his time, eventually he ended up being president of the Red Lake Chamber of Commerce. Unfortunately, I don't remember the robber's name either because I no longer have the book. The bookstore man told me I needed to visit the museum; after I left the store I heard a horn honk. He gave me a ride to the museum. Walking into this new building, the first things I saw were more banners. The lady there explained to me that a local high school teacher had started the project a year before. Along the wall were photographs of the banners on display on the main street, as well as a little biographical information on the artist. It turns out that Kaila, our waitress this morning, had painted one.

When I left the museum, I walked back to that restaurant, but it was closed. I hoped to tell her how much I admired her banner. By this time it was nearly four o'clock. I read about half of The Flying Bandit in the lobby of the Red Lake Inn while waiting for the planes of our group to show up. During the afternoon, as I wandered around town, I missed seeing the planes take off, but noticed they were gone when I came back from the museum. By now, the weather had cleared. Around 6 PM everyone started showing up. They had tried to contact me, but couldn't find me since I was in the rambling mode. Off to the West of Red Lake is a place called Fletchers, and that's where Brian, Wolfgang, Eric, Kirk, Craig, and the two Bruce's had gone. Although I hated to have missed more flying, I had enjoyed the afternoon being by myself. While we were eating dinner, if I remember correctly, Mike and Gary flew in from Winnipeg, with their low voltage problem resolved. Once again, we ate dinner in the Red Lake Lodge, and then we went our separate ways for the night. Brian knew of another place about twenty miles away called Vermillion Lodge (I think) where he would have liked for us to stay, but we sort of mutually agreed that Red Lake was probably a better choice in terms of logistics and airplane maintenance.

August 15th

Today was the first day that I flew with Eric (What a fun guy to fly with!), so Wolfgang flew with Brian. Although I flew left seat in Brian's plane, when I flew with Eric I always sat in the right seat. We taxied to the north end of the lake and took off towards the west, then headed in a northerly direction towards God's Lake (they all are). Kirk always left first since he had the slowest airplane. Throughout the trip we always kept in radio contact with each other and tried to maintain visual contact. Shortly after take off, Brian led us over Vermillion

Lodge, and from the air I could easily see why he wanted to stay there. We climbed to about 2800 feet and continued on to God's Lake. Eric often gave me the controls, so we would switch off flying. When he needed to use his video or digital cameras to film one of the other planes he would tell me the direction to move so he could line up his shots. By the end of the trip I was more adept at handling the Cessna 180 while Eric did his excellent photography.

Eric also has the best toys and is good at using them: On the left yoke he had the new Garmin 396 GPS receiver mounted, which was connected to a satellite radio/music receiver from which he could download some weather and cloud information, and an i-Pod filled with his own music, wired to the plane's intercom. He used his laptop for route data and flight planning. He kept a DC-DC converter plugged into the plane's cigarette lighter socket to charge the digital camera and the laptop. At 35, he has that youthful exuberance and self-confidence and the skill level and familiarity with his airplane that makes him a good pilot. My Introduction to his abilities occurred enroute to God's Lake, when he decided to take the controls and fly low along some lake. Low, as in ten feet above the water, diving between the trees and pulling out at full throttle, commanding the airplane to go exactly where he wanted, while he played a song from his i-Pod about a wild cowboy roping and a'riding, naturally at a high volume. With Eric at the controls, I never felt any apprehension after the first couple of times, but I also know that he flew at a much higher skill level than I will probably ever have. We arrived at God's Lake behind the others – we could hear them on the radio but couldn't spot them, and even sometimes when we were flying on the deck we were out of sight radio range. Then we had us an air show. Kirk took off in his Super-150, flew over us fairly low, and then performed one-float landings while Eric held the hammer down on the video camera. Brian and Wolfgang took off and circled us a couple of times, then Craig and Mike took off in their planes.

For lunch, we stopped near Gillam. A lady driving a pickup with a huge fuel tank in back came out to where we docked and gassed up the planes, and then the ten of us clamored into and onto the truck for a ride into town to eat. We didn't secure Eric's plane well enough and found it had drifted away about one hundred yards. He walked into the water to grab it, and then he taxied it to the dock. Prior to takeoff, he took off his shoes and turned on the plane's heater to help dry them out. It was somewhat uncomfortable, but we had such an exciting ride that afternoon that I paid little attention to the cabin warmth as we flew down the Nelson River to York Factory and to Churchill.

Kirk's "Super-150" over the Nelson River. Photo courtesy of Eric Weaver

Hey look! Somebody named a river after me. Well, maybe I could be related to whomever the Nelson River is named after; perhaps he and I share the same grandfather thirteen generations back, as I do with Edwin Hubble, the astronomer that discovered telescopes. Or was that Galileo? At any rate, Eric and I had fun flying low over the river. We both wanted to go under one of the bridges, but had no desire to deal with the Canadian Federales wearing red coats, Smokey the Bear hats, black shining boots, and running with a German shepherd named Rin Tin Tin, so we didn't. What a crazy name for a dog! Sounds like something somebody would dream up in the Fifties. But today wasn't in the Fifties, and we weren't flying fifty feet. Eric told me to hold the plane steady while he shot videos of Kirk. As the river curved, so did I, keeping the altimeter on the mark, thrilled but nervous at flying about ten feet above the water, climbing only when necessary, and weaving a flight path with Kirk that may have looked like a strand of DNA. We passed a herd or a school or a group or a covey or a gaggle or a bob or a colony or a crash or a harem or a pod or a rookery or whatever you call a bunch of seals. There were some great geological formations that would have been fun to closely examine, especially if we had a geologist with us. I think Brian and Craig flew behind us; every now and then we saw Mike. Most of my memories of flying over the Nelson River consist of me concentrating on flying the C-180 while keeping track of Kirk in his Super-150.

Somewhere near where the Nelson River entered into Hudson Bay, Brian took the lead and headed south a few miles, to the mouth of the Hayes River. From a vantage point of about five hundred feet or so, York Factory of the old Hudson Bay Company looked as white and as impressive as the Taj Mahal, standing out in contrast to the gray ocean water, gray clouds, and dark foliage. This place was very active during the fur trading days. The trappers brought their furs here, and from here, they were shipped to England. At one time there stood many buildings, but now only the three-story square building remains.

From the air it looks very interesting, and hopefully, sometime in my life I can tour it. Dr. George Erickson, a retired dentist from Minnesota, wrote a good description of the place in his book, True North. He flew around Canada in a Piper J-3 on floats a few years back and wrote good details of his adventures in the book. It turns out that our flights to the Arctic Circle followed very similar routes that he described in the first part of his book

Even as we circled York Factory, the rain splattered over our windshield. A few miles to the north, the rain diminished, but the grayness of the clouds had not, and the ceiling had dropped to about two hundred feet. Horizontal visibility was OK. Brian, Mike, and Craig flew ahead of Eric and Kirk, north towards Churchill. They reported seeing polar bears. It took a little while, but then we saw them, and I had my first real lesson in precision and formation flying. On our Eastern side we had the Hudson Bay; on the West we had marshy flat lands; to the North we had beaches, and to the South - well that was behind us so it didn't matter. Except for the polar bear mounted at the old Anchorage airport terminal building, I don't remember ever seeing one. We probably saw about one hundred of these magnificent animals. Kirk circled some bears; we began to circle behind him. Eric and Kirk have many hours flying in sync with each other; they are like two dolphins. Always, they communicate, constantly giving position reports. They watch out for each other, because their lives depend on it. They know each other's flying skills, and they respect each other. And

I had the good fortune to fly with them! Trim the nose a little high. Keep the RPMs up. Maintain a constant altitude and speed. Maintain a constant bank angle. Watch out for the other guy. Eric had me fly while he captured the bears on videotape and silicon chips. My film shots of the bears didn't come out nearly as well as did Eric's and Kirk's. As the C-180 and the Super-150 waltzed through the air, my flying proficiency improved, at least for these invigorating moments. Kirk claims that he had his window open, and one time he could hear one of the bears loudly growl at him over the noise of the engine. I have no reason to doubt him.

Eric and Matt flying in Eric's plane. Photo courtesy of Eric Weaver and/or Kirk Spangler

Polar Bears south of Churchill. Photo courtesy of Eric Weaver and/or Kirk Spangler

Near the town of Churchill there is an old shipwreck of the freighter *Ithaca* that lies in the bay. Once again, Eric gave me the controls of the plane while he photographed it. We flew over the airport and the people in the tower directed us to the seaplane base, where shortly after securing the planes for the night we were met by a young girl driving a bus to take us into town. But instead of stopping, she drove us through town, to a park, where we saw some beluga whales. We drove past several empty tundra buses that looked like the skeleton remains of bombed out buses, because they had no sides. With their huge tundra tires about five feet high, I thought of Ivan the Terrible, the bus in Antarctica that meets the incoming planes, only Ivan has walls and a top. In November, tourists fill the tundra buses to watch the polar bears come into Churchill, and perhaps wander through the garbage dump. I am glad we saw them in the wild. Perhaps they are not as big in our photos as they are in those of the people riding the buses, but I don't care.

The bus driver took us to the Seaport Hotel, and then went behind the counter to assign us our rooms. Wolfgang and I shared a room that night. We all met in the dining room for a good dinner of ribs. After dinner, I used the computer in the lobby to check my email, where I read Bob McCullough's account of Butch Head's funeral. I would have been there had I not gone on this trip. He had died a week ago on this day, and I felt sad reading about his funeral. Goodbye, good friend.

August 16th

One of the things I like best about travelling is meeting interesting people. Bill Layman was in the lobby of the Seaport Hotel chatting with Craig prior to breakfast. He had just returned from a month long canoe trip with Lynda Holland on the Hanbury and Thelon Rivers. He is a topnotch canoeist and outdoors person. I think he even went over some maps with Brian. I think he was waiting to catch the train to Winnipeg. Although he was on his way home, Bill was ready to turn around and go fly with us. He easily strapped on his "light" backpack, which weighed about 50 pounds, and looked like a keg of beer. It's a waterproof container. Typically, the "keg" might weigh 85 pounds. Perhaps I listened to Bill for fifteen minutes at the most; I would very much enjoy hearing his stories for hours.

"*Bill Layman and Lynda Holland live in La Ronge, Saskatchewan in Canada's north. Bill's mining exploration company and Lynda's work as an educator put them in close contact with the Athapaskan Dene who lives along the edge of the tree-line. Now both largely retired, a fascination with these people's ancestral lands has seen Bill and Lynda venturing by canoe each summer for the last decade into the so-called "Land of Little Sticks." Recently these trips have taken them further afield onto the barrens and the land of the Inuit.*

Bill writes for KANAWA, the paddling magazine of the Canadian Recreational Canoeing Association and for a number of Web sites about their canoe trips. For the last two summers he has been doing a daily internet journal, live from the river and complete with pictures, using a Globalstar satellite phone linked to a handheld Hewlett Packard PDA. Diaries of their Dubawnt River (40 days 750 miles) and Thlewiaza River (55 day 1000 mile) trips, as well as other articles about the Coppermine, Kazan, Thelon, and other northern rivers can be seen at www.out-there.com."[1]

Bill also emailed me that this website has his trips from last year and this year posted: http://www.townoflaronge.ca/features/blayman/.

Eric and Kirk and I went into a hardware store. Kirk needed some clothes, since by now he had decided to go all the way to Chantrey Inlet with us. One of the contributing factors was that while in Red Lake he had tried his ATM card and money started spitting out as if he had been playing the slots and won in Las Vegas. I bought a better raincoat. I had one in my backpack, but that was in Brian's plane. Then we all went back to the planes, where we had to fuel up using a hand pump screwed into a 55-gallon barrel. Brian had prearranged a fuel drop. While fueling the planes, a guy came out to fuel either a DeHavilland Beaver or a Norseman – I can't tell the difference. He had access to the electric pump, so his task was easier. Brian gave him a

---

[1] http://www.equipped.org/bill_layman.htm
Copyright © 1994 – 2003; First Published: January 21, 2003
Douglas S. Ritter & Equipped To Survive Foundation, Inc.

hand while a half a dozen Danish fishermen waited to fly in this magnificent airplane.

While eating breakfast together, Craig told me about some of his work as a contractor building waste treatment facilities. When I asked him how he started doing that work, he told me that when he graduated from high school he needed a job and went to work as a laborer for a construction company and eventually worked his way up the ladder high enough to start his own company. He may not be doing much of the type of labor that he did as a young man, but he certainly gained the experience to know what it takes to do a job right. He goes around the world on exotic hunting trips. One of them had taken him to Mongolia; when we were all introducing ourselves a few nights earlier, Bruce Hendry said he had never met anyone whom had gone to Mongolia, but here at the table sat two of us.

Rain squalls passed over us in the morning; while we waited, Brian suggested that we walk to the museum at the Churchill train station. It's not a big one, but I found it interesting. Swampy Cree life and fur trapping exhibits and polar bears are on display.

When we took off around noon, I felt my stomach that looks full on the outside begging for something to fill the gap on the inside. Fortunately, Eric shared some ham sandwiches that he had bought at the restaurant, quieting that persistent beggar. Over the western shore of Hudson Bay we did fly, taking great delight seeing many white beluga whales. Actually, these animals are not part of the whale species, but that of dolphins or porpoises. It didn't matter to me. I still enjoyed flying over them, as did the rest of the gang. But once again, Eric and I and Kirk lagged behind, as we choreographed our own ballet in the sky, "Dances with Whales" – perhaps somebody ought to make a movie with that name. Onward we flew, hugging the coastline, sometimes over the gray cold water and sometimes over the rocks and sand and tundra's edge; what distant oceans had the whales travelled, where's their destination, questions that even the ancient mariners asked, and look at that abandoned hut – single hut, not *kanata* which means a collection of huts from which the name Canada is derived[2]; hey, a caribou just passed under our right float, wondering about the biggest mosquito he had ever encountered; as he wondered we

---

[2] Round the Globe in Old and New Paths, M'Collester, Sullivan Holman. Boston: Universalist Publishing House. 1890. Pg. 11.

wandered North, no, not to Alaska but to Rankin Inlet, "Eric, please hand me my camera", "I can't because I put it in the back", OK, just look at that beautiful water now, from three thousand feet little islands of clouds and the azure color of the water look like we are flying over the Caribbean Ocean, an unexpected pleasure of blues, cobalt, sapphires, once more evidence of the exquisiteness and splendor of the handiwork of God.

By the time we arrived at Rankin Inlet, the other three planes had already landed and had their fuel tanks filled. Eric circled around the planes and talked with the other pilots on the radio. "Why is he landing downwind?" I asked myself, but kept quiet because I thought he wanted to do it for some reason, and he is more experienced than I am. Good splash down anyway. He told me I should have said something. We all make mistakes. No harm was done except that it would have been his turn to buy (everyone else who drank) a beer that night if we were heading for a place that sold it. While he sat on the plane filling the tanks and I turned the pump handle mounted in the 55-gallon barrel, a man that Brian had met a couple years ago drove up. He told Brian that he owned a fish camp located about eighty miles to the West, and that we were welcome to stay there for free. Actually, he wanted to sell the place, and hoped by us staying there that Brian would buy it. Whatever the reason, the timing was just right and I was glad that he came along when he did.

After Kirk landed and fueled the Super-150, we all headed to the Arctic Skies Outposts. Once again, the Super-150 and the 180 performed their aero waltz. Upon arrival, we flew low over the water near the camp to check for rocks and floating logs, hazards that can poke holes in the floats. Before we left Churchill Brian had all of us put on our breathable chest waders; I was glad that I had it on, because when I stepped off the float near the shore I fell in chest high water. The fleece shirt I had bought at the Seaport Hotel is the only thing that became wet, and that quickly dried.

Sometimes, besides water, you just fall into things. For being out in a remote area of the tundra, we couldn't have found better accommodations. It had a floatplane and/or boat dock, several cabins, and a huge main room complete with food supplies and cooking gear. Gary found a generator inside one of the cabins that he started and plugged in an extension cord that ran to the big room. There was propane in the tanks, and even a barrel of avgas that the guy offered to let us use. We found boats and motors and for some, the fishing started that night. Declaring in advance that this was "Trout Taco Tuesday", Brian caught our supper, as did Craig, his brother Bruce, and Bruce Hendry. (At least that's how I remember it.) Hungry mosquitoes swarmed around us, but I still managed to take some decent photos of the sunset. Eric put his chef skills to use as he cooked the fish, making bar-b-que nuggets for an appetizer. Even for a minimum fish-eating guy like myself, I must admit that the nuggets tasted good and the two fish tacos I ate tasted even better. In all my years of eating tacos, I had never once before eaten a fish taco, let alone two. Given a choice of beef or fish tacos, I would choose beef, but given the choice of eating a fish taco or going to bed hungry…well, these were good enough I have no complaints. Eric is an excellent cook.

Eric Weaver's C-180 and the C-185 that Mike Andrews flew (back)

Brian took a couple photos of me standing in front of the main Arctic Skies Outposts building, wearing my Seattle Seaplanes long sleeve shirt. I started off the trip wearing my Mountain Lakes Seaplane baseball cap, and had no problem wearing the shirt I had bought from Jim Chrysler, owner of Seattle Seaplanes. Flying with Jim Chrysler and Mike Kincaid gave me the foundation to go fly with Brian to the Arctic Circle. Now, I'm wearing my Adventure Seaplanes hat that Brian gave me, and had I been able to fly with Alan Crawford in his C-172 on floats here in Texas on Veteran's Day weekend, I would have gone flying with him wearing my current hat. I respect most of my flight instructors equally, and don't mind wearing something with their company's name on it.

Craig took a nasty fall off the porch of the main cabin; the next day he showed us a bruise about three-inches wide; by the end of the trip it was the size of a saucer and quite red. If it hurt at bad as it looked, I feel sorry for the guy.

Just before we all went to our cabins, somebody noticed the full moon rising over the water. My photography doesn't do justice to the actual event, but it does remind me of the beauty of the moonrise. Content, I went to my cabin, lit a mosquito repellant coil, and quickly went to sleep.

August 17th

Calm waters, hot coffee, warm oatmeal, and good company. For two or three hours I dinked around the camp, not doing much that I remember. Bruce Hendry asked me if I wanted to go fishing with him in one of the boats. We weren't gone a long time but Bruce certainly knows how to drive a boat. He told me stories of his younger years when he had owned his own C-172 and had flown it to Alaska a couple of times. His flight hours totaled about 1000, about twice what I had. Neither one of us had any luck fishing, but that was OK, too. Shortly after going back to the dock Wolfgang came in, quite happy that he had caught his first fish. In his life!

For lunch, Mike gave us some sandwiches he had made. Brian announced that it was time to go fly fishing, or go to the fish flying. Not in those exact words, but his meaning was clear. Mike and Gary opted to stay behind and fish out of a boat; Bruce chose to hike around the area, and Wolfgang wanted to write in his journal. Craig and his brother Bruce, Eric and Kirk, and Brian and I wanted to keep the airplanes happy and fulfill their destiny and dreams of flight, so that's exactly what we did. Flight time from the Arctic Skies Outposts to the river where we landed perhaps lasted thirty minutes; the next few hours or so bought us extra time in our lives, for as the saying goes something like this: "God doesn't take off from the days of your life the number of hours spent fishing (and flying)".

Bruce Johnson with a Grayling

Brian and Kirk with a flying Grayling

Fishing is what we came for and fishing is what we did. On my very first cast I hooked a grayling about 15" long; within twenty minutes I landed eight fish. The biggest one that I caught was an Arctic char, about two feet long, and near the back of its neck there was a yellow mark shaped like a heart. At one point, Brian told me to step back to give Kirk a chance, so I walked down stream about ten feet and landed another one. But Kirk was no slouch either, using his small telescopic rod. He managed to catch several fish, as did most of us. Eric may or may not have landed fish – I don't remember, but one time he caught one and the fish broke his line and escaped, and I instantly felt a tug on my line. When I reeled the fish in, we saw that in addition to my lure, Eric's lure was hanging out of his mouth. We caught many more fish than we took back for supper, because of the catch and release policy, but also because there was no sense in killing the fish if we weren't going to eat them. After the fish I caught warned the others not to bite at these shimmering shiny things, they understood so my luck changed. Eric decided to take a nap and I wandered up towards the other guys to see how they were doing. Brian, Craig, Bruce, and Kirk had caught several. While Brian filleted the fish, Kirk fished nearby. He caught one and had released it on a rock. He asked me to take a photo with his camera. The fish started flopping around so Kirk grabbed it and threw it away from the water, and I managed to photograph the fish in midair.

Three or four hours later we hiked back to the planes and loaded up. It was amazing to see all the rivers and lakes in the area, each a brilliant blue (as opposed to a dumb blue?), reflecting the color of the clear blue sky. Although pretty flat, the landscape beneath our wings told stories of millions of years of rivers eating granite for breakfast and their endless quest to flow to the sea, and their nostalgic efforts to return home by evaporation into the clouds and then heading homeward bound in raindrops seeking their way back into more rivers.

(Ecc 1:7) *"All the rivers run into the sea; yet the sea is not full; unto the place from whence the rivers come, thither they return again."*

Once again, we all enjoyed Eric's cooking of the day's catch. Wolfgang made sure that he ate some of his fish. I think Mike and Gary had also caught more fish. Bruce Hendry told of his observations of the eco system in the tundra and he also saw an arctic fox. He said it was like a miniature forest that only stood eight inches tall. Most everyone else but me drank a beer or two; naturally, the conversations of ten men out in the boondocks covered the gamut of topics, such as flying, fishing, hunting, sports, cars, and wonder of all wonders, women, who really are the wonders of all wonders.

August 18th

And I must admit, when I woke up this morning, the idea of meeting a dozen of those wonders never occurred to me. By the time you the reader finish reading about today's activities, you will have a better idea of what I am writing about.

Coffee. Breakfast. Clean dining room. Load planes. Take off. Take off to where? Kazan Falls, that's where. Wider than Niagara Falls. Not quite as well known, and for that great reason, not very many touristas, either. Look at the musk ox, perhaps thirty of them. Fly past Thirty Mile Lake, communicate, fly in loose formation over the falls, and do it again, and again. See that colorful tent – who belongs to it? So we land a mile away (seems like a strange word when flying a plane on floats) – OK, so we splash, secure the boats, grab fishing gear, and hike. Hike past an old refrigerator – where did that come from? Hike over the tundra and cross small streams until we reach the river. Wow, that water moves fast. Wolfgang stops near a rocky overlook. Wouldn't be fun falling into that. Catch up with Eric and Kirk, who are having fun taking photos of each other, framing their faces with an old picture frame that Kirk found. Brian and Bruce and Craig Johnson fish, maybe Bruce Hendry does too. Somewhere along the way there's Mike. Meet up with Gary. Walk to the falls sign. Hear the roar of the falls in the distance. Take photos. Place a caribou antler on our heads and take more photos. Who are those people Kirk and Eric talking to? Seven – count 'em – seven young ladies. High school girls on a 45-day canoe trip, heading to Baker Lake. So, that's who belongs to the colorful tents we saw!

Gary with six of the girls from the
Manito-wish YMCA, 2005 Canuck Expo.

All of the seven girls are members of the Manito-wish YMCA out of Boulder Junction, Wis. They started canoeing when they were ten years old. Now, they were nearing the end of their month-and-a-half long journey. When we met them, they were about to portage around the Kazan Falls. Big Brother Gary asked them their names and soon had his photograph taken with six of them standing around him. Laura, the seventh girl had taken off walking with Eric. At 24, she was the elderly lady of the group, and was serving in a leadership role. A day or two earlier this group had camped at Thirty Mile Lake and Laura had left her camera on a rock near the river. Eric offered her a ride in his plane to retrieve it, which she eagerly accepted. After Gary and the girls had their photographs taken, three of the girls expertly turned over a canoe and stood under it. The two girls on the ends helped the one in the middle balance it, and then they stepped out and the one in the middle started walking with her sixty-five pound load. Twice more the scene repeated itself, because these girls had three canoes to portage. While Eric flew Laura to pick up the camera, Gary helped portage the packs of the girls – not once but twice. Brian said that Gary has a hundred pound heart in his two hundred and eighty pound body. It didn't take long before we could see Eric's plane flying around the falls.

Gary Wilson at the Kazan River Falls sign

The sign reads:

"The Kazan River Valley is the home of the Caribou Inuit, the first people to live year-round on the treeless barrens. Here they have depended for generations on the vast caribou herds that migrate seasonally across the river. The Kazan was unknown to Europeans until 1770, when it was crossed by Samuel Hearne, and unmapped until 1894, when it was surveyed by renowned Canadian scientist J.B. Tyrrell. Today, this wild river, cascading through the rugged Precambrian Shield, offers experienced canoeists spectacular whitewater and view of abundant wildlife, as well as insights into the way of life. For these outstanding features, the Kazan River has been proclaimed a Canadian Heritage River."

On my way back to the planes, I walked by a caribou carcass and naturally had to photograph it. By the time I arrived an hour later, Eric was chatting with Laura, who was ecstatic that she had flown over the Kazan Falls on her first float plane ride and happy to have her camera back. Since it was a yellow waterproof camera, she easily spotted it from the plane on a rock near the river. While talking to the other six girls near the falls, we learned that another group of girls were canoeing to the Chantrey Inlet and should be near the end of their 90-day expedition. Laura asked to look for them, and on the off chance we might find them, she wrote a note to them and gave it to Eric. She said her sister was travelling in this group. Tired Gary came trudging back, we said our goodbyes, and boarded the planes again. Laura gave Eric a big hug.

Within minutes we were airborne once more to Baker Lake. Even without any charts, we could have found it without difficulty, because the Kazan River flows into it. The town of Baker Lake has a tower-controlled airport where Craig landed his C-206 for fuel; the rest of us landed on the lake and taxied to the sandy beach. Brian told the man in the tower that five Cessna floatplanes were inbound; the slow-talking air traffic controller took forever issuing landing instructions. On final approach, as Brian waited for the controller to finish his long-drawn out words, he told me to keep the airplane ten feet above the water and fly towards the shoreline so we wouldn't have to taxi far, but I didn't hold it as steady as I should have. We did a slight bounce on the water; irritated, Brian took over the controls. Once again, dumb me.

We were still securing the planes when this native guy drives up and very casually asks if we have fishing licenses. Since he offered to sell them on the spot, and the paper we filled out had little boxes for individual letters, we sort of had the impression that he is the local game warden. Guess what! We sort of felt obligated to buy this piece of paper from him. I think I threw my Nunavut fishing license out one day by mistake, even though it was expired. When five floatplanes with U. S. registry fly in, talk on the radio, and a bunch of guys jump out, it didn't place a heavy burden on the game warden's deductive reasoning skills to determine that some of these guys might be thinking about fishing in his territory. So we bought licenses. Soon afterwards a fuel truck arrived. Brian and Wolfgang and I walked to the trading post, which I expected to be very small. Nope – it was a super market with

Kentucky Fried Chicken and Pizza Hut. Brian gave me $20 to buy a pizza. Then he left and walked back to the planes. I added another $20 or so and bought some chicken and maybe another pizza. That stuff didn't last long.

One of my regrets is that I didn't go into the museum at Baker Lake. There is a sign or plaque that tells about Charles and Anne Lindbergh stopping at the town on their way to the Orient in 1931.

Despite the fact that my floatplane flying skills need to be improved, I really enjoyed flying with Brian in his C-185. He is such a good pilot, and has such a vast knowledge of the countryside. We flew together for hundreds of miles over the Canadian Shield, and I relished every minute. Besides having a good visual on the screen of the Garmin 296 GPS receiver, he kept his aeronautical charts handy, making notations as we flew, and pointing out different landmarks and rivers to me. Obviously, I am glad we did not encounter any emergency and/or survival conditions, but had we done so, I am fully confident that our chances of survival would have been greatly enhanced by having him along. When we crossed over the Arctic Circle (Latitude N 66°33'), he reached over and shook my hand.

From Baker Lake we flew almost due north, crossing over and then flying along the Back River (*Thlew-ee-choh*[3], or "Great Fish River") enroute. I think it was on this section of flying that I saw ancient rock rings. The Back River flows into Franklin Lake, which was our destination; within a kilometer of the inlet into the lake stood the Chantrey Inlet Lodge, a rugged assortment of abandoned buildings that became our campsite for the next two nights. It was great staying here, although I thought the Arctic Skies Outposts was in a little better shape. On the bottom of the Chantrey Inlet Lodge sign, the words, "Northwest Territories Canada" had been painted. By those words alone, I knew that the lodge had been built before this area of the Northwest Territories called the District of Keewatin (or Keewatin Territory) had a name change to Nunavut around 1999.

By the time Brian and I arrived at Franklin Lake, Craig and Mike were already securing their planes. Eric, Wolfgang, and Kirk were nowhere to be seen, but having flown with them I figured that they were just doing more extensive sightseeing. Brian and I taxied the C-185 to about 100 feet from the shoreline where the Chantrey Inlet

---

[3] Email from George Erickson

Lodge lives. As soon as I stepped off the float I saw a fish that looked to be two feet in length. About ten feet from shore my old tennis shoes that I wore over the boots of the waders bogged down in the mud. In order to make it to shore, I had to leave the shoes behind. I never saw them again. My prize pair of $11 shoes! But the plane still needed to be unloaded, so I gingerly walked back to the plane and brought more essential junk back to the shore. Soon everyone had their gear in, so we made our portages from the lake to the cabins. I checked my GPS receiver and saw that we were at N $66°$ 42.700' and W $095°$ 47.613'. Almost due north of Houston, only 2616 miles away! My home in Bacliff, which is southeast of Houston, is located at N $29°29.732'$, W $094°59.385'$.

Then it was fishing time. Although the others walked on the right side of the lake (as viewed from the camp), I chose to go to the left side. I didn't have any luck fishing but enjoyed my own little exploration among the rocks. When the three stragglers showed up, I wandered back to the camp. I noticed that they were unloading their gear, but so had we, so I thought nothing of it. Then Eric and Kirk took off again. "What was going on?" I wondered. It wasn't long before Kirk and Eric landed; five young women emerged from their planes. This was the group of canoeists that the first group we saw earlier in the day told us about.

"I've got canoes" Eric Weaver, the seaplane pilot of Cessna 185, tail number N2990C, gleefully radioed to Kirk Spangler, the pilot of "Super 150 Chick Magnet, N23191. After circling a couple of times around the two canoes filled with five astonished women, the two seaplane pilots landed just north of the Arctic Circle on the Back River, near the entrance to Franklin Lake, which flows into Chantrey Inlet south of the Arctic Ocean. Huddling together like the herds of musk oxen they had seen on their 1200-mile canoeing odyssey, the bewildered young women probably discussed having their 12-guage shotgun ready to use if necessary. Eric landed first, and grinned as he read the names of Beth Halley, Karen Stanley, Emily Stirr, Nina Emery, and Meg Casey off a sheet of notebook paper. Beth grabbed the note from his hand and finished reading their special delivery airmail from Nina's sister Laura, whom Eric had flown around the Kazan Falls earlier in the day. Amid the hoops and hollers, Kirk landed and paddled his Cessna 150 over to the group. Except for scheduled food drops approximately every three weeks, the five courageous women of the Borealis Paddling Expedition (BPE) had not seen any other people during their nearly ninety day journey across the Canadian wilderness and tundra. (www.borealispaddlingexpedition.com)

Eric's co-pilot, Wolfgang Fischer from Germany, was sworn to secrecy not to say anything about seeing these women when the three pilots left them behind and flew over to the Chantrey Inlet fishing outpost, about seven miles away. Wolfgang came in the lodge and told me that he needed to sweep out his cabin – he was actually cleaning out a bunkhouse for these girls; a few minutes later I asked him where Kirk and Eric were going and he gave an evasive answer. About a half-hour later I was chatting with Bruce Hendry when the planes landed and shortly thereafter the five women walked into the lodge. Sitting in a circle and not being shy about sampling liquid refreshments, these highly educated women told us about their accomplishments and dreams. Their adventures included watching a bear rip to shreds one of their tents. Bruce talked a little about one of his adventures when he was a young man, hitchhiking to Central and South America and riding down the Amazon River. A short time later I walked out of the lodge in time to see Kirk and Bruce Johnson walking up with four fish. After landing, Kirk walked over to Brian Schanche and told him that we need fish. Brian handed Kirk his fishing rod and Kirk landed a three-foot lake trout on his fourth cast.

That night, Brian and former chef Eric received high compliments from everyone about the tastiness of the fish. As a full moon rose over Franklin Lake, I talked to Meg and Emily, telling them how much I admired them for going on their expedition. Hearing the laughter of all these young women sure sounded better than hearing the stories of the nine other men I had been traveling with over the past week."

(Lev 11:9) ***"These shall ye eat of all that are in the waters: whatsoever hath fins and scales in the waters, in the seas, and in the rivers, them shall ye eat."***
(Psa 8:8) ***"The fowl of the air, and the fish of the sea, and whatsoever passeth through the paths of the seas."***

August 19th

After we all ate breakfast together, Eric and Kirk flew the five girls back to their canoes; the rest of us fished. Using a "Five of Diamonds" lure, I caught eight fish, each around two feet long. The two Bruce guys don't look too sad in the next photo.

Bruce Hendry and Bruce Johnson with Lake Trout at Franklin Lake

We followed the shoreline to where the Back River enters Franklin Lake. Gary decided to go for a swim/bath, and most of the other guys followed, but I had no desire to go swimming with a bunch of naked guys, so I turned my back on them and fished some more. Wolfgang caught another fish, a lake trout that was maybe 30 inches long. He was quite happy!

Brian holding Wolfgang's Lake Trout at Franklin Lake

Craig Johnson. Photos on this page are courtesy of him

Brian's 41" Laker

Mike Johnson

Gary Wilson and one of his Lakers

Bruce Hendry

Look at me with 3-foot long Lake Trout on Franklin Lake!

We all made our own way back to the lodge; as I was coming in I couldn't help but hear another plane come in. Two guys landed a two million dollar Cessna Caravan on floats; the owner is seventy years old and had made a lot of money and had worked hard for many years building up a crane rental company. Now, he was off enjoying life and spending his money. He owned helicopters and a jet and said that he was planning on flying the jet to Los Angeles on Tuesday. The two men came into the lodge shortly after I did and had lunch. For those people that had gone to the plane, he gave them t-shirts printed with his company's logo. Somebody – probably Brian – handed the old man a fishing rod and he caught five fish in eight casts. He said that this was the best time he had had on his whole trip. An hour or so later they took off for Gjøa Haven on King William Island, which borders Chantrey Inlet on the northwest.

These guys reported avgas was available at Gjøa Haven. Later that afternoon Kirk and Eric took off in Eric's C-180 to buy some. They have their own stories to tell about their experiences with the Inuit people living there, especially the children. Remembering what Bruce Hendry had said about the tundra having its own miniature eco system, I used up an entire 36-exposure roll of film (the kind of technology used before digital cameras! Ha! Ha!) photographing some of the plants and small flowers and berries on the shore of Franklin Lake.

A boat had been found with a little gas in its tank; the motor started after about ten pulls and avgas kept it going the rest of the day. Eric later remarked that he had been so busy at Franklin Lake that he never even put a line in the water. Not so for the rest of us. As far as I know, the other nine of us did well. Craig and Bruce Johnson are good fishermen; they were always catching good-sized fish. Brian caught the largest one, a forty-one inch lake trout. Mike didn't do too bad himself.

Late in the afternoon Gary and I went out near the rapids where the Back River enters the lake; before we had fished much we heard our names shouted, and there on the rocks stood Beth, Karen, Nina, Emily, and Meg. They went back for their canoes and were chatting with us about ten minutes later. Gary and I fished for about an hour, and I landed my biggest fish ever, a three-foot long lake trout.

Gary started out-fishing me, and then we went over to where the girls had set up their tents for the night. Gary went back out fishing in the boat and caught a bunch more big fish, while Karen and Beth paddled me in one of their canoes around the calm lake as the water reflected the purples and pinks of a setting sun. I sat in the "duffer" seat in the middle, slightly embarrassed about my lack of canoeing experience, while I watched Beth's and Karen's strides on the paddles that were natural as breathing. **(Eze 27:26)** ***"Thy rowers have brought thee into great waters."***

Borealis Paddling Expedition entering Franklin Lake on the Back River

While we circled the lake, Emily, Meg, and Nina cooked the guys a coffee cake over a small burner. Earlier in the day I gave them decals from the space shuttle missions of STS-107 and STS-114, pointing out the names of the women on those missions. One of these girls stuck a set of these decals on their wooden backpack cabinet used to hold their pots and pans. Somehow during the conversation they said that in preparation for the trip they had gone to Bill Layman's house to study his detailed charts of the area. All these little circles.

Two of the ladies from the Borealis Paddling Expedition at the Chantrey Inlet Lodge.
Courtesy of the girls.

All 15 of us at the Chantrey Inlet Lodge sign.
Photo courtesy of Borealis Paddling Expedition

August 20th

Our day started off eating the delicious coffee cake that had been cooked the night before. Then, it was time for some photographs. After loading the planes and receiving hugs from the girls, we all departed Franklin Lake. Three of the planes headed south; I flew with Eric in close formation with Kirk, who flew north in his "Super 150 Chick Magnet" and performed a glassy water landing on Chantrey Inlet. We then turned south and headed to Franklin Lake, looking for canoes. Several minutes later we spotted them and did a couple of fly-bys; Kirk landed near them on one float. All five women stood in the canoes waving at us. I think Eric waggled the wings on the C-180, our way of waving goodbye. By the time we arrived in Minnesota on Monday, the following write up appeared on the web page of the Borealis Paddling Expedition (these women had a satellite phone which they used to leave messages that were later placed on their web pages):

"Bums and Fishes, Part 3: They Came from the Sky
Emily
08/21/2005, Back River, Nunavut; GPS Coordinates: 67 deg. 6 min. north; 95 deg. 17 min. west

Preface: The events I am about to describe are true. The title is a reference to a song sung at Manito-wish and should in no way be associated with the ten wonderful people we met in the past week. If anything, we ourselves are the bums, but the trout we ate was incredible.

The fact that in the vast expanses of the tundra, news had just reached us from a group that included our friends, sisters and campers was astonishing. We had just received airmail from the Kazant to the Back, delivered by our new friends, Eric and Wolfgang, pilots from No joke; there we were. Our two canoes rafted together facing the Cessna 185 boat plane that had just landed a few hundred feet away on the glassy waters of Franklin Lake. Only moments before, the plane had come over the ridge behind us, almost without a noise and had circled a few times before landing. We sat in astonishment wondering who it was, if the pilot was just curious, or if they were bringing news from the outside world. Unsure, brimming with excitement and slight apprehension, we drew together as the plane taxied forward and decided to paddle up to it and meet whatever was in store for us. I don't think any of us would have ever guessed at the incredible series of coincidences that came together to shape the next few days. "I'm looking for five women," the pilot said, as he stepped out onto his float.

His smile growing as he read each of our names and handed us a note, laughing at our disbelief. Beth read the note out loud immediately, not even stopping to ask questions until she reached the end, which was signed "with love, from the 2005 Canuck Expo." Laughter and questions filled the air until it was established that the two men in the plane were part of a group of ten men in five planes that were flying over the tundra on an adventure trip (see www.adventureseaplanes.com They had run into a group of girls from Manito-wish at Kazant Falls, and had been instructed to keep an eye out for us on the Back River since they were heading up our way. The fact that in the vast expanses of the tundra, news had just reached us from a group that included our friends, sisters and campers was astonishing. We had just received airmail from the Kazant to the Back, delivered by our new friends, Eric and Wolfgang, pilots from Florida and Germany, who had just dropped out of the sky.

While all the explanations and introductions were taking place, another plane, which we would soon come to know as a Super 150, came up the river from the east, buzzing crazily close to Eric's plane and our boats before landing. A man in waders got out, sat on his float and paddled his plane over to us and so it was that we met Kirk, another pilot from Florida on the northern edge of Canada. The Adventure Seaplane group was staying about seven miles down the river at an old fishing camp and we were promptly invited to join them for dinner. It may seem that we have been receiving dinner invitations left and right, but such is not the case. We have not seen any other canoeists for 86 days and the only people we have seen we had anticipated meeting at all of our re-supplies. To have ten of the most generous and welcoming people drop out of the sky right next to us, bearing notes from our friends, was incredible. Meeting anyone up here in the northern reaches of the Canadian tundra is special in and of itself, and you immediately share the unique connection of the land you are traveling through for a call at home for any period of time.

Meeting the group of seaplane adventurers was an unexpected gift. Not only did we have the opportunity to catch a glimpse of the tundra from the air, after being escorted by our pilot friends to dinner, but we had the opportunity to see our enthusiasm and love for the land reflected ten-fold through different means. I have never heard of a float plane adventure trip before, but as we soared above the Back River, *zooming over the astounding hydraulics and the rapids out of Franklin Lake, I was convinced that there could be no better way to experience the Arctic than by seaplane, except by canoe, of course. The planes landed and we caught our breath, and found ourselves wading through murky waters, to scattered outside buildings reminiscent of Tuckto Lodge. The buildings that had once made up Chantrey Inlet Lodge were now the temporary lodging for a group of pilots, chefs, fathers, husbands, adventurers, fishermen, professors, lawyers, inspectors and guides who shared their space, stories, intrigue and encouragement with five young women from Wisconsin and Connecticut. Over an amazing dinner consisting of fish tacos, Oreos and popcorn, we talked to Bruce, Matt, Brian, Bruce, Craig, Gary and Mike, who like Eric, Wolfgang and Kirk, shared a love of flying and a love of adventure. We were delighted to swap tales of our current trip and past travels and we were excited to make connections of colleges and hometowns. It truly is a small world, even above the Arctic Circle.*

The following day after being transported back up the river to our regular life, we began the much slower journey back to the lodge. While we had attempted to scout the rapids from the plane, a rare opportunity to say the least, it still took us the rest of the day to make our way down the river through incredible whitewater and over calm stretches of flat water before coming once more to the white buildings of the old Chantrey Inlet Lodge. We set up our camp and while Nina was fly-fishing with Bruce, Karen and Beth took Matt for a paddle, and Meg and I chatted with Mike, Wolfgang, Craig, Bruce and Brian as we baked them a coffee cake for the next morning. That evening, as we enjoyed another amazing meal of fish, the moon glowed huge and orange above the horizon at the cabin next door and again we watched the stars and the northern lights play in the sky. When it came time to leave the next morning, we packed up our boats, paddled over to where the pilots were loading up, getting ready to head south again. We said the final round of good-byes, hugging Gary from our boats as he stood waist deep in the water, Brian's words "Run for life" echoing in our ears. I think it is fair to say that anyone you meet while traveling above the Arctic Circle will definitely remain a friend for life, whether you meet again in the future, or simply carry the energy of the memory with you to share with others along the way. It is difficult to express how genuinely touched the five of us were by this chance meeting on the

Back River. It could not have come at a better time. Being able to share our stories with such interested and appreciative listeners put an incredibly positive twist on the bittersweet ending of our journey.

The night before we met our friends, I stood outside watching the sunset, willing it to last as long as possible and for the day not to end. The thought of being so close to the end of our trip was overwhelming and it hurt to count the small number of days left. Our time on the Back River has been beautiful. A huge river, carving its course out of smooth bedrock on one shore and rolling green hills, dotted with caribou and musk oxen on the other. The best thing about our meeting with the Seaplane Adventurers was not only their incredible generosity, but the opportunity to share with them the ability to dream big and always be thinking of new beginnings. As we left that morning, we had not paddled far before the roar of engines filled the air and the planes took off one-by-one, tipping their wings and buzzing over us as they climbed into the air. Leaving us alone in the tundra again, looking at each other in disbelief for confirmation that all this had really happened. We tried to sing to lift our spirits, holding on to a bit of hope that even though we had watched each plane disappear over the horizon, that one might come back. Sure enough, the humming sound reached our ears before we could spot the two tiny dots that we knew were Eric and Kirk, coming to say a final farewell that we knew would be good. Eric's 185 came in first with Kirk's Super 80 close behind. As the planes approached, they split, circling around each side of us, while we stood in our boats, waving and belting out the song from Top Gun, "You've Lost That Loving Feeling" at the top of our lungs. Eric flew over Kirk, one plane 100 feet above the other, while Kirk did a full circle above us, skimming along the surface of the water on one float. One final pass from each plane, Kirk's arm waving out the window, and they were gone. We kept singing as the planes were lost in the endless blue sky.

A heartfelt thank you to our seaplane friends, we truly enjoyed meeting each of you."[4]

(NOTE: This is but one of the many journal entries on the BPE web site. Great reading, highly recommended.)

---

[4] http://www.x-journal.com/journal/borealis/?xjMsgID=5603

"...we stood in our boats, waving and belting out the song from Top Gun, "You've Lost That Loving Feeling" at the top of our lungs." BPE

For my part, you are quite welcome, and we all enjoyed meeting each of you as well. After leaving these adventurous canoeists, we headed south to Baker Lake. Trying to describe in words the number of lakes we crossed, or their multitude of colors and shapes is a difficult thing for me. Just as I was fascinated by the colors, I also thoroughly enjoyed seeing the reflections of clouds on the surface of the lakes. One day I told Karoline that we must have seen a million lakes, but she found that hard to believe. Brian mentions 100,000 lakes on his web site. Whatever the count, it's a bunch.

Our welcoming committee at Baker Lake consisted of a dozen or so kids and a million or so mosquitoes. We donned our head nets before we even opened the doors of the plane. Craig bought us chicken at the trading post and afterwards, the kids wanted to do what they could to help fuel and secure the planes. Our pied piper, Gary, led them away towards the museum so they could all have their photographs taken, which sort of relieved the anxiety of the plane owners because the kids kept walking on the floats. One boy about nine helped me hold a rope to keep one of the planes from drifting out to sea, not knowing that the plane was still tied up. George Erickson captured the essence of these modern day Inuit kids with this paragraph in <u>True North</u>, while he was at Chantrey Inlet:

"A small child ran down to the river, holding high over his head the primary symbol of change for the Arctic, if not the world—a bundle of twigs tied into the shape of an airplane. Though his grandmother might tell him that geese fly off to the Old Woman Who Never Dies every fall and return with the promise of spring, this child-of-the-airplane will also learn the facts of migrating birds. Airplane

held aloft, he flopped onto a nearby caribou hide and flew his bundle high, his body cushioned in caribou hair, his mind far off in the sky."[5]

Shortly after takeoff, Kirk spotted three canoes. The first group of girls from the Manito-wish YMCA, 2005 Canuck Expo that we encountered two days earlier was crossing Baker Lake a few miles south of the town with the same name, their final destination. Eric tied his plane nose-to-nose with Kirk's plane. He was non-committal when asked if we had seen the group of five canoeists; but when he asked one of them to place a decal of the Borealis Paddling Expedition on his airplane, the cheers erupted.

Borealis Paddling Expedition decal. Photo courtesy of Eric Weaver

Chomping down the Oreos™ at Baker Lake with the girls from the Manito-wish YMCA, the 2005 Canuck Expo.

They marveled about the quickness of the "Polar Airmail Express". They declined the offer of Snickers™ due to a peanut allergy, but quickly devoured the two packs of Oreo™ cookies that Eric had bought at the store in Baker Lake. It was kind of funny when the girls saw the cookies. They all looked back at Laura, questioning if

---

[5] <u>True North</u> by George Erickson. The Lyons Press. Guildford, CT. (2002) Pg. 101.

it was OK, but she craved them as much as they did. One of the girls said that she had been talking about eating Oreos™ all morning. Not long afterwards, we said goodbye to the happy Oreos™ Chompers!

Southwest of Baker Lake are the Dubawnt River and Dubawnt Lake. Bill Layman and the girls of the BPE had both told us that we needed to see the Dubawnt Falls. So that's where we all headed next. Although we were told that these falls are more spectacular than the Kazan Falls, I personally liked the Kazan Falls better. However, I am still glad we flew over them. And then we flew over Dubawnt Lake! Sixty miles of lake – glad that our planes had floats. We flew over a fishing camp, and I think this is Tuktu (the native word for "caribou)" Lodge's Outpost Fishing Camp that Emily mentioned in her journal entry. On one of the earlier BPE journal entries, Nina wrote,

"A Day in the Life on the Shores of Tulemaliguak
Nina
07/08/2005, GPS Coordinates: 63°, 22" North, 101°, 7" West

Dubawnt Lake, Tulemaliguak, in Inukituk, is the sixth largest lake in Canada. Straight across it is 60 miles from where the Dubawnt River flows in at the southwest corner and Outlet Bay where it again heads north."[6]

As I mentioned before, I encourage everyone who reads my story to read the all the journal entries of the BPE on their web site. It's a great adventure story.

As we flew towards Kasba Lake, our stopping point for the night, we could see the glint of the sun being reflected from the many lakes. Once again, I almost blew it, as I reduced power on Eric's plane just prior to a rough water landing. Once again, the owner of the plane kept us from having a bad day. Having done that twice on one trip, the experience is seared into my mind; hopefully, I will never ever make that mistake again. I don't think I will. Sorry Eric and Brian. Thanks be to God and to Jack Clodfelter, the Guardian Angel He gave me.

Kasba Lake Lodge has its own gravel runway, where Craig landed with another low voltage light, and a dock for floatplanes and boats. We were lucky that we could stay there, because the place had

---

[6] http://www.x-journal.com/journal/borealis/?xjMsgID=4690

officially closed the day before. Although I had never heard of it before this trip, the lodge is known for being the place to go for trophy fishing of Lake Trout, Arctic Grayling, and Northern Pike. Brian had called ahead and made arrangements. One of the guides still there cooked us two batches of fish, but Eric is a much better chef. The caretaker for the winter had been divorced about six years ago; he planned on home-schooling his fourteen-year old daughter who was staying with him. His goal was to teach her about caribou hunting, but she seemed squeamish. It ought to be an interesting winter for the two of them, because they hadn't spent much time with each other since the divorce. We were each charged $84 Canadian for the rooms and dinner and breakfast, which considering the location was a good price. It's too bad that I can't remember any of the colorful phrases that the guide uttered the next morning. Without being dirty, his words came from the heart of a poet. It wouldn't bother me terribly much to land either a seaplane or a wheel plane at Kasba Lake Lodge and spend a couple days fishing there, and have him for a fishing guide.

August 21st

Craig was able to start his plane and brought it over to the dock; shortly afterwards we all took off. On this day I flew with Brian. Brian chuckled that it was Craig's time to buy the beer tonight, since he took off with his water rudders down. Brian had to do the same type of take off that he did at Surfside, popping the flaps to 40° in order to go airborne. The water was even rougher than it had been the night before. As we journeyed south, more and more our odyssey took us over massive forests, replacing the tundra that we had flown over the last several days.

For lunch and fuel, we stopped at the town of Thompson located on the Burntwood River. Brian complimented me on my good glassy water landing. Ah, hamburgers! It was noon, we were hungry, and my meat-conditioned body was in withdrawal after eating fish for the past several days. But then I negated my good landing. After Brian refueled his plane, he moved it to another dock, and tied the left float to it. He climbed in and moved to the right seat and started the engine. I was supposed to untie the float and jump on board, but I hesitated a second too long and the plane passed me. Brian circled back after me and told somebody on the radio that he almost left me behind. He may not wish to fly with me again, but that doesn't change my opinion of wanting to fly with him some more.

My takeoff was decent, we turned south, and after a while Brian took off his headset and took a short nap. Along the way we passed two different heart-shaped lakes. Eric woke us all up when he blasted some German beer-polka music over the radio. He laughed as he told of Wolfgang dancing in the cockpit! Mike and Craig led in their planes; Kirk and Eric landed near some other fishing lodge. We climbed to 6500-feet for smoother air. Not only was it smoother, we also had a good tailwind: Our ground speed according to the GPS receiver was 158 mph - typically we were around 110 or so.

The next place we landed was Kenora, the hometown of Lori, Brian's girlfriend. Like Red Lake, this is another town where I really could enjoy living. While we fueled we talked to a pilot that flew DeHavilland Twin Otters exclusively. He learned to fly in one, and had flown one for tourists around Thailand before the great Tsunami of 2004. It probably won't surprise anyone when I say that I had steak for dinner instead of fish! Brian and I took off before Craig; he had a hard time making his 206 go onto the step, so he went back to the dock and Brian and I landed. After Bruce Johnson jumped out, Craig was able to fly off the water. Bruce rode with us on the next segment, which was to the twenty-two acre island and lake home that Craig owns on the Lake of the Woods. What a fantastic place! Brian buzzed both Mike's and Craig's planes that had already landed. Then we landed, and waited for Eric and Kirk to show up.

The house is built like a ski lodge. If I had to live away from the Rocky Mountains, I could force myself to live there. We all chilled for the night. Using his laptop computer, Eric showed us some of the many digital photos he had taken on the trip. (He had also done this at Chantrey when the girls were around). Craig made good on his beer debt for leaving the water rudders down.

After Bruce Johnson, Kirk, and I washed the breakfast dishes, Craig took us for a short boat ride. The planes were made ready; our German friend Wolfgang helped Mike fold up the American flag. Craig's plane wouldn't start, but either Brian or Mike used their battery to start it. Eric and I took off in his 180 and flew along with Kirk to Crane Lake. This was the first time I had ever entered the United States in a small aircraft. Eric kept in constant contact with air traffic controllers in Canada and in the U.S. We landed at Crane Lake near the U. S. Customs office. Eric showed him registration for the plane and the gun permit he had for the shotgun and the agent examined my passport and asked me if I had bought anything in Canada. I told him about the few things I had bought and he quickly dismissed us. Then it was ice cream time. Perhaps we were there for an hour.

Once airborne, Eric headed down some river, playing his roping and a'riding music. We all flew over the farm of Brian's family and Gary asked if we could fly over his farm, which wasn't too far away. A couple hours after leaving Crane Lake we were back at Surfside. I kind of wished we were back on the Back River. Once we started unloading the planes, Bruce Hendry gave us all a very poignant DVD of his cancer survival, and Brian came up to me with the white blanket I had borrowed from Eric. During the journey, it had often irritated him because it was always in the way. He said he was giving me "The Blankey Award".

Next time I fly with him I won't bring it along. Bruce Hendry hopes to fly around Baffin Island, and Brian has talked about doing a trip there, as well as some of Canada's other lakes, such as the Great Slave Lake and Great Bear Lake. Hopefully, someday it will happen, and I will be along for the ride, and will also be a better seaplane pilot. But I sure learned a lot on this trip, had a great time, and thoroughly enjoyed the company of everyone on the trip.

The Widgeon in Florida, 2006

When I went to Florida to see the launch of the New Horizons spacecraft heading for Pluto in January 2006, I was hoping to see Eric Weaver and Kirk Spangler. Kirk wasn't around, but I managed to talk to Eric a couple of times, although I didn't see him. Last summer we talked about flying around in his Cessna 180, but it was having either a paint job or its annual inspection. But that didn't keep this seaplane pilot away from the water. Not this kid. The Seaplane Pilot's Association web page (http://www.seaplanes.org) lists state-by-state names of the seaplane-training instructors. Just as a spider spins her web to catch flies, the Internet spins a web to catch flyers like myself. It not only spins the web, but baits it as well. And the bait that caught me is the Grumman Widgeon (G-44) that Chester Lawson owns at Spruce Creek. Check it out: http://members.aol.com/h2oflight/

Hear those mighty engines roar! Not hear that mighty engine roar. Hear those mighty engines roar! Plural. Multi-engine. Lock the tail wheel. Hold the yoke with your left hand, reach up with your right hand and advance the throttles and adjust the pitch of the props for the climb position. Keep it steady down the runway. Push the nose forward. Accelerate and rotate. Lift off. We have lift off. And the pilot sitting in the left seat is as excited as the astronauts who lift off in the space shuttle fifty miles to the south, our sort of direction, but not quite. Climb to 1000 feet to the nearby lake. Fly lower and look over the lake for obstacles. Go through the checklist. Splash down. Not once, but six times. Before you can splash again you have to take off. Hold the yoke back, give it full throttle, push the nose forward, now we're on the step, then we're airborne. Could talk about things like 25 square, power and rpm settings, but we're flying, setting up to do another splash-and-dash, step taxi, rough water demonstration, a glassy water approach, stay on the step and take off, or pull back on the yoke after touching down, reduce power, and feel the water sloshing against the hull. Poetry. Poetry in motion. Poetry in the air. Poetry on the water. Flying for fun. Be safe, but have fun. Have fun, but be safe. Don't worry about chasing the Multi-engine Seaplane rating today. Maybe someday. Now just enjoy the hour. Already an hour! Guess we have to switch seats and head back to Spruce Creek so Chester can do the landing on the runway near his house.

Chester Lawson's Grumman Widgeon – great airplane to fly

That was last January. When I flew with Chester again in May, we landed on four different lakes. The flight in the Widgeon was every bit as exhilarating as the first time, so I won't go into more details. Before I flew again with Chester, I flew with Rich Hensch, owner of Florida Seaplanes, www.floridaseaplanes.com. Rich also flies this Widgeon, but uses his own Maule 7-235 to teach the SES rating. That plane just pops off the water. Of the sixteen different seaplanes that I have flown, the Widgeon, the DCH-2 Beaver, and the Maule 7-235 are in the top three. Look for logs on the rivers; watch out for crocs, step taxi on the river, wow, look at the size of that croc!

Canadian Trip, Fall 2006

For the past several years, Karoline and I have taken a trip together, just the two of us, usually in the Western part of the United States. We have seen the balloons of Albuquerque, the Grand Canyon – generally on the Northern side, the canyons of Utah, Crater Lake, the launch of SpaceShipOne in California, Mt. Rainer, Las Vegas, and of course, the mighty Tetons. We have learned that the Fall is a good time to travel, because the students are back in school, the weather is cooler, the prices are somewhat lower, and it's a good time of year to see the changing colors on the trees. This year we decided to go to British Columbia. So, on September 27th, we flew to Seattle. The next day we were in Coeur d'Alene, Idaho, so I could fly with Mike Kincaid in his

J-3 Cub on floats, and somehow I reckon everybody will know that the Alaskan bush pilot wannabe that hides within me snuck out and thoroughly enjoyed spashin'-and-dashin' one more day, and did his best to convince me to buy a floatplane. He hasn't won yet, but if he ever does, tell Karoline I will be home for Christmas!

We drove part of the time and took the train roundtrip between Prince George and Prince Rupert. Each way takes 12 hours, but it is beautiful ride, with scenes of glaciers, mountains, rivers, and Fall colors and colorful water falls. Prince Rupert is a nice harbor town, but we arrived too late in the season to go on a whale-watching cruise, and there was no one at the seaplane base that gave floatplane training, although they do have a nice seaplane base. After we went back to Seattle, I just had to go fly with Jim Chrysler again!

Prince Rupert, British Columbia Seaplane Base

Havasu Seaplanes Adventures

March 4, 2007

Matt and Dave Bartholome and the Havasu Seaplane Adventures C-172

London Bridge. I didn't even see it, although I saw the sign for it, while on my way to the Havasu City Airport. But enroute from Casa Grande, I did see a lot of tumbleweeds, blowing dust, and saguaro cacti (I guess that's the plural of cactusus!) However you spell it, I saw a bunch of them. Had I not had an appointment with Havasu Seaplane Adventures, I would have used up what film I had left and filled up the memory card on my pocket digital camera photographing those emblems of the old West, even though in the past I have photographed them. But I did have an appointment, and it was one I didn't want to miss. As it was, I was twenty minutes late. Soon I was trying to taxi a 1978 Cessna 172 on amphibs. Amphibious seaplanes have floats designed to land on both land and water, as opposed to straight floats, which are only built for water takeoffs and landings. You try not to ride the brakes, but to turn the plane while taxiing on land you must use differential braking. Do the mag check and set $20°$ of flaps. Line up on the runway, and give it full throttle. Rotate at 55 knots. After a positive rate of climb is established, bring the flaps to full up. Retract the landing gear. CHECK for the blue light (associate this with water), and CHECK that the red flags on the floats indicate that that the wheels are up. The one thing that a pilot must REMEMBER EACH and EVERY time before landing on water is to double or triple CHECK that the wheels are UP. If not, the plane will nose over in the water, and sink. That wouldn't be a good day for anybody. Instructor Dave Bartholome drilled this into me.

Don't forget the checklist, and don't forget to have fun. Beautiful day, enjoy the scenery. Watch out for the boats. Land on the water and take off again. Grin. Do it again, and again. Fly past the town of Parker and land on the Colorado River. Grin again. Head on back, but do a few more landings on the lake before heading back to the airport. Run through the checklist again and lower the landing gear. Think Blue light for water, and Green light for grass or ground. CHECK that the red indicators on the floats are in the land position. Landing on the water is easier than landing back on the runway, because of the technique and knowing when to flare. But I can learn it, and hopefully I will have more chances to practice and fly with Havasu Seaplanes Adventures.

Take a side trip to Sedona, on the way to Prescott, to fly across the Grand Canyon!

Flying Across the Grand Canyon (in a plane without floats)

March 6, 2007

Before I left Texas for Arizona I searched the Internet to find a flight school where I could rent a plane and fly across the Grand Canyon. Although I knew I could be checked out in a plane and go by myself, I opted to fly with an instructor because I figured he or she would be more familiar with the area and the special restrictions the FAA has imposed upon pilots who want to fly across "The Ditch". No longer are you permitted without special permission to fly beneath the rim of the canyon. Well, what do you know? SKY School out of Prescott has Norm Kalat for their chief instructor. When I saw his name, I knew that I wanted him to be my instructor, because he was my main instructor in Alaska in 2002 when I was first trying to obtain my seaplane rating – you know, the time when I ran the owner's Super Cub into the dock and he didn't give me my rating! Norm is a good instructor and a good guy.

Some days the conditions are right to go fly and have fun! Norm and I took off in a Cessna 172 with a 180 Hp engine. We climbed to 11,500 feet, he programmed some waypoints into the GPS receiver, and an hour or so later we crossed the rim of the Canyon northbound in the Dragon corridor, flew as far as Marble Canyon, descended to 10,500 feet, and headed south across the Zuni Point corridor. Naturally, we had to take a photograph or two along as we flew across the canyon. Our total flight time was 2.5 hours; our words and photos don't do justice to God's handiwork, we both enjoyed the flight, and I want to go back and fly across the Grand Canyon again. It wouldn't hurt my feelings if I did it in the Stinson, nor would it bother me to fly with Norm again. I did pick up some pointers flying with him, but I also realize that I could have flown the route easily enough by myself, and have the confidence built up now that it wouldn't bother me to fly across the canyon solo. Of course, having somebody else who is also a pilot fly with you has its benefit – you can let him or her take the controls while you practice your skill as an aerial photographer!

Look! I'm finally flying across the Grand Canyon!

Flying Floats in Montana, Idaho, Minnesota, & Alaska 2007

June 15th

Look at that lake! Do you see what I see? Canyon Ferry Lake, located between Townsend and Helena, Montana, which sure looks like a good place to fly a floatplane on and off the water. But floatplanes cost more than our land cost us, so I doubt that I will be buying one anytime soon, if ever. Our daughter Cheri, her husband John, and our granddaughters Camyrn and Cheri moved to White Sulphur Springs, Montana, and we helped them move. Townsend is about 45 miles away from White Sulphur Springs, and we ended up buying a one-acre plot of land that overlooks the lake for our retirement home. Maybe, when I'm sitting on my back porch I will see a floatplane touch down and take off again. Maybe I will be able to become acquainted with the owner, and have an opportunity to fly a plane off that lake someday. Until then, I guess I will just have to rent, but in most cases, renting a floatplane requires going up with an instructor all the time, due to the high cost of insurance. That's OK, because I always learn something and I don't fly floats enough to stay current, anyway.

Where do I go in Montana to fly a floatplane? A good place to start is with Montana Seaplanes, located near Marion, on the Little Bitterroot Lake, which is West of Glacier National Park. Roger and Michelle Weltz have just started this summer instructing in their Super Cub 150. They are friends of Dave Bartholome. Roger flew the heavy iron for several years and now wants to share his love of floatplanes with those of us who want to fly them. Karoline and I stayed in Helena the night we bought the land, and then we drove the next day to Little Bitterroot Lake, passing by Flathead Lake, a bunch of mountains, several deer, and spectacular scenery along the way. One sentence does not equate to the several hours spent driving in this beautiful part of the state. Nor does a few sentences equate to the fun I had flying with Roger, flying on and off the Little Bitterroot, McGregor Lake, and the middle chain of the Thompson Lakes. He says there are a good fifty lakes nearby to fly to; on the way back he pointed out a peak in Glacier National Park. Hopefully, within the next two or three years, my fingers will hammer and bang out another flying story on the computer machine telling people that I landed the Stinson at the airstrip near the

South end of the Little Bitterroot so I could fly in the Super Cub with Roger. Oh, did I say anything about how much fun I had flying the Super Cub? Guess I need to!

Roger Weltz and his Super Cub, on the northern end of the Little Bitterroot Lake, Montana.

Mike Kincaid and his J-3 Cub, Coeur d'Alene, Idaho

If I remember correctly, this is a 1958 Super Cub, and that 150 HP engine sure wants to go onto the step and take that plane into the air quickly. Maybe, after about one hundred hours of flying floats, I'm beginning to acquire a little skill. Maybe Mr. Piper had guys like me in mind when he designed his planes to be so responsive and fun. Whatever the reasons, the day I flew with Roger everything seemed to come together, the plane felt comfortable with me and I felt comfortable with it. It was an all-American day: The Cub, painted with red and white stripes, flew off the blue water into the blue sky and back on the blue water. Do the old CARS check (Carb heat off, Area clear, water Rudder up, Stick Back), ease into full throttle, GRIN, (No acronym here, just GRIN as far as you can, stretch those smiling muscles), and STEP it up! "And we have Lift Off, Lift Off of the Space Ship Super Cub!" GRIN some more. Set up for a glassy water landing. Smooth splashdown---almost like I have done this before. Keep it on the step. Remember to close the Carb heat, give it full throttle---whoops, not so fast, lift a float, and we're airborne once again, so GRIN, head for another lake, repeat the procedure, go on until the money meter goes to a notch higher than I can afford, and then reluctantly head for the beach, and think for the rest of the day about my exciting flight in another seaplane.

Now, when I go to Montana to visit my kids, I have a place to go to fly floats. When I retire, I have a place to fly floats. If somebody in Montana is going to separate my much less than a measly half-a-million green dollars from me so I can fly red and white striped airplanes that take off and land on blue waters, Montana Seaplanes is the place for me! Roger and Michelle are on my good people list!

(Unfortunately, Roger and Michelle had to close this business due to the high cost of fuel the year fuel prices soared like the space shuttle being launched. Karoline and I still moved to Montana in 2009, and they are still on the good people list!)

June 16th

Maybe you can't go home again, but you sure can go back to places where you had a lot of fun and sometimes be lucky enough to have some more fun, such as flying with Mike Kincaid in Coeur d'Alene again in that yellow J-3 Cub. Instead of doing the usual splash and dashes on Hayden Lake, we flew around to some others. In once case he had me do a low pass and turn at the same time, coming out of a small canyon onto a lake, like we were doing some real mountain flying. Then I followed the river for a ways, clearly seeing the wall of a mountain approaching, but I could also see that the river turned right, so just as I was ready to bank right, Mike asked me if I saw that mountain. I flew like I knew what I was doing, picking up on the responsiveness of the Cub, and flew over the river, touching down on another of Idaho's scenic lakes. Enroute to the first lake we flew over an area where a mama moose and her two calves live, but we didn't spot them. Anybody who knows me must also know how disappointed I was after spotting a small herd of elk instead. All too soon my time and money were spent; not only did I spend money flying a fun float plane again, but I also ordered a copy of Mike's book, <u>Alaska Justice</u>. A few days after I arrived home the book came in the mail, along with two hats. It's a fictional novel, based upon actual events that occurred during the twenty years Mike work as a pilot and Alaska State Trooper. A book with a Cessna 185 flying over a glacier on its front cover and written by a pilot might have a flying story or two inside, and Mike did his best not to disappoint me by leaving those stories out.

June 19th

Today Karoline and I drove into Minnesota and found our way to the motel near Rice Lake, which is part of the Lino Lake chain NE of Minneapolis. Why? Perhaps the word lake might give a clue! Matt, you already have had two floatplane flights on this trip. But you see, I have this addiction. My name is Matthew A. Nelson, and I have this problem. I am addicted to flying seaplanes as often as I can, and my problem is that I don't have enough funds to buy my own floatplane, so I have to make do by renting one as often as possible. Brian Schanche, owner of Adventure Seaplanes, bases his Cessna-185, a Cessna-172, and a Piper PA-12 at Surfside Seaplane Base on Rice Lake during the summer. Two years ago I flew with Adventure Seaplanes on the trip to the Arctic Ocean. Now, I would like to fly with him again to Northwest Canada in August, but won't be able to do it this year. So what, I can still fly with him in the PA-12 tonight. Better make that tomorrow morning. Gusting winds here today, too. Let's eat. Karoline and I rode with Brian and Lori to meet Gary Wilson and his friend Karen and Mike Andrews and his wife Jackie. So eat we did. Big-hearted Gary bought dinner for everyone. Gary and Mike also flew to the Arctic on the same trip I did. Good dinner, good company. Good flight the next day!

Adventure Seaplanes PA-12. Would you believe that's me with the grin you can almost see?

Oh No, Not Alaska, again!

October 6, 2007

Made it back to Alaska. Delta Airlines had a roundtrip fare of $352 from Houston to Anchorage. Great to be back home! You kind of expect that the temperature in Anchorage is cooler than in Houston, and you know what? My powers of deduction are just as good or bad as they ever were. In Anchorage, it wasn't quite as warm as 75° F. like it was in Houston when I left. But the 40s weren't bad either. Dave and Jean Bieganski had prior commitments, but that didn't stop me from going back to the Cattle Company in Alaska and eating a Texas-sized steak called New York. After waking up around 4 AM, not sleeping much on the planes, and being old and tired or tired and old, my raggedy body decided for me that it was time to go back to my room at Ace Hangars and dream of flying any one of a bunch of colorful taildraggers at Merrill Field instead of wandering around wishin'-and-a-hopin'-and-a-covetin' the seaplanes at Lake Hood. I know coveting is a sin, but that's what I did when I first arrived in Anchorage and drove around Lake Hood.

October 7th

Since it was such a severe clear and visibility unlimited (CAVU) day and Denali could be seen from Anchorage, I decided to drive towards Fairbanks and stop in Talkeetna to see if I could fly with Don Lee up to Denali. We had plans for me to fly with him a couple days from now, but with it being such a beautiful day I thought I would chance it today because I had no idea what the weather would be like on Tuesday.

While I drove on the spur to Talkeetna, Don called me on my cell phone. Next thing I know I'm at Lake Christensen waiting for Don to fly some people out in his PA-20S to pick up some moose antlers. An hour or so later I'm giving full throttle to the Pacer, we're up on the step, and then airborne towards Denali. Now, flying no higher than 8000 feet, it's fairly obvious that we aren't going to fly over the top of the mountain, but we were high enough to fly up the Ruth Glacier, around Shelton amphitheater, and look at the area where famed aviator

Don Shelton built a cabin. Once Don Lee was stranded in that cabin for five days with four strangers before the mountain cleared. He has seen enough of that cabin that he has no burning desire to go back.

Don Lee's Pacer 20S

Mt. Foraker, no slouch itself at 17,400 feet, looks every bit as impressive as the 20,300-foot high Denali. Clear day, beautiful, light winds, big WOW! factor. One spark plug was a little fouled, and the oil temp climbed to edge of green arc, while we were flying over the Ruth on the return segment, but Don did a good job of leaning so the slight roughness of the engine didn't last long. Don pointed out what the clouds were doing, "they tell a story" – top of Denali had blowing snow, some clouds near the base went straight up, calm; I felt very comfortable flying with Don. He pointed out the far side of the canyon walls most dangerous – we could see the walls that appeared very close, we could fly a lot closer, but you have to give yourself room to turn around, so other sides could be more dangerous because you might not have as much room as you think, or they could hide oncoming traffic, etc.

Flying in the Pacer, we didn't have quite the power as we did in the DCH-2 Beaver in 2005, and we didn't go as far or as fast, but this time I was the pilot, so in that regard I enjoyed it as much, if not more fun. I asked Don what happened to the Beaver three days after I flew with him in 2005 and he gave a vivid description of trying to control it. Once again, I highly respect him and his piloting skills. I think he told me that the investigation found out one aileron was 17 ounces out of balance with the other one. He gave me the reason why, but now I don't remember what he said.

Before Don and I left for Denali, I had to wait for Esther and Anna to come back in the Pacer; Esther was Anna's seaplane instructor, but Anna has a lot more flight time - she flies Aero-jets for a telecommunications company, one day she might be in Barrow, Alaska, and the next day she might be going to Washington, D.C. She is from Gillette, Wyoming, graduated from the University of North Dakota (where I received my Master's Degree in Space Studies), she had Warren Jensen for instructor, and I did, too. She substitutes as a fourth-grade teacher. Anna has more flight time at age 26 than I will ever have. I am almost ten years older than the combined ages of Anna and Esther. How do you spell "O-L-D G-O-A-T"?

Esther is also about 26, she obtained her SES rating last year from Don, then during the Winter went to Arizona and picked up her CFI, and then she started working for Don this summer as an instructor. She told me that she has the best job in the world, loves living in Alaska and flying the floats. She is from Louisville, Kentucky.

Excited but nervous because of the threat of bears, both Esther and Anna wanted to go out and retrieve the moose antlers. Had I not been going flying with Don, I would have liked to have gone myself. Don had spotted a moose dying while he and Anna were flying on Saturday. Shortly after I arrived at Lake Christensen, he took off with his son Andy to see if they could spot the moose again. When they did spot it, they could tell a bear had buried it. So retrieving the antlers became their objective for the day.

Andy works up on the "Slope" for part of the year, lives in Anchorage the rest, and often works as a white-water rafting guide. His 25th birthday was only a few days away. Good kid.

His friend Dustin also lives in Anchorage, and he is an instructor at a water-survival school. At the school, they have a helo-dunker and an airplane dunker, kind of like what I went through while in the Navy reserves. I asked him how he wound up there, and he said that he also had worked on the slope, had a lot of outdoors training, worked as an EMT, and somebody recognized his talents and asked him to go work at the water survival school. He also used to live in Gillette, but I had the impression that he wasn't raised there like Anna was.

Don Lee's Pacer PA-20S with the fresh moose antlers

Answering the call from Don to go with them for the moose antlers, Jason quickly responded, and showed up with all kinds of bear artillery. He really was loaded for bear. The moose had died about a half mile from where Don landed the plane on Larson Lake (probably no connection with my son-in-law John Larson), so everyone had to be on a high lookout for bears. The bear had done a lot of damage to the moose. I think Dustin is the one that carried the antlers out. I guess the moose stunk quite a bit. Jason is from Rhodes, Michigan, which is located near some of the same territory that my Hubbell and Gremel relatives are from. He is a PE teacher and coach, a terrific hunter and outdoorsman. I think he is about 35. When he received the call from Don, he was installing rock around the fireplace in the cabin that he is building. Sometime earlier, he had shot another moose, so for dinner that night he cooked up several moose burgers. I didn't have any problem eating those!

I don't know much about Lynnette, Don's better half, but she welcomed us all into their home while we ate, and seems very nice, She said each day is about as crazy as the next, so while it isn't an everyday occurrence for Don to fly people out in the middle of bear country to retrieve some moose antlers, it was just another event at Alaska Floats and Skis!

There is a good chance I won't see all of these people again, even though I hope to fly with Don many more times. But their company was enjoyable, the moose burgers were good, the scenery was fantastic, and the flying was on the good side, too. Good day.

Don built a four-bedroom lodge during the winter three or four years ago, so that his students could have a place to stay. I could easily live in it as my own home. He told me to pick out a room, and the one I chose had a good view to the stars. During the night I watched Orion march in a clockwise direction, at one time trying to camouflage himself between tall pine trees, but Orion is so used to having his bright stars shine brilliantly - instead of shining dully, I guess – that he couldn't stay camouflaged for very long or very well.

October 8th

Columbus Day, or at least the day listed on calendars this year. I decided to celebrate this day by seeing the Alaska he discovered! Say What? So I headed to Fairbanks, but stopped in the town of Talkeetna for some coffee. The morning sun woke up the Mountain, gently, softly changing its hues from a grayish-bluish color to a violet and pinkish tint, letting the Mountain emerge from its slumber gradually, instead of blaring it wide awake with the full white radiance reserved for later in the morning.

Prior to leaving Texas, I emailed Chuck Thomas, saying that I would be in Fairbanks today. Chuck has written <u>Wings Over Wilderness</u>, a biography about his good friend Paul Shanahan, an older Alaskan bush pilot whom he respects very deeply. A few months earlier I saw the advertisement for this book in the "Alaska" magazine, and bought it.

Paul had more things happen to him in the first few chapters of the book than I hope I ever have as a pilot. I thought I would quote Chuck from the chapter called "The Professionals":

"He had just landed on a gravel bar on one of the many small rivers draining the Alaska Range and was right on time for an appointment with a flying customer...His rider was not there... Instead of relaxing in the airplane Paul decided to stretch his legs with a walk down the gravel bar. He climbed down from the tall Stinson SR-6 and set off downstream, footloose, happy, humming a tune, unarmed...

The first sign that the pilot might be in the wrong place at the wrong time came as he heard the very clear signs of something, or possibly some things, heavy and in a hurry pounding through the thick willows at the edge of the gravel bar. ..

With no other viable options, the man who would one day be called Qayuuttaq stood rooted to the gravel beneath him as a cow moose burst into a clearing running flat out, apparently making for the river. She was about eighty yards from him an on her current heading, would be much closer by the time she reached the shoreline. Scant seconds after the cow emerged from the brush a large grizzly hove into view, head low, hackles up, and pedal to the metal in hot pursuit of lunch. Paul immediately dropped to the ground, hiding as best as possible behind a river-worn cottonwood log. He flattened himself on the gravel, hoping not to become a part of this everyday natural drama. He peered over the log just in time to see the bear overtake the moose, ending the chase with a cat-like swipe of a pile driver paw...

After what seemed like more than enough time, even for a big bear, the grizzly finished eating and began to cover the carcass with gravel and debris he raked from the gravel bar with his powerful paws. Swinging his head to and fro, nose working constantly, he surveyed his surroundings before he began to amble towards the treeline, putting valuable distance between him and the interloper behind the log. It took will power to wait long minutes after the bear's wide rump disappeared into the spruce before Paul stiffly got to his feet and, hugging the edge of the river, swiftly and quietly made his way several hundred yards back to the airplane where he found his passenger just emerging from the trailhead. In retrospect, he feels the whole incident took far less time than it seemed while he was going through it. He had simply witnessed a food-chain situation that takes place countless times every day in the big, wild country off the pavement."

From <u>Wings Over Wilderness</u>, by Charles M. Thomas, Jr. Chapter 30, "The Professionals". Sixty-Below Press, Fairbanks, Alaska. 2004. Pages 157-159

When Chuck invited me to dinner, he didn't mention how great a cook that his wife Pat is! Roast pork, crab cakes (which I didn't try but should have), fresh salad, good green beans, potatoes, bread, and homemade apple pie! I had a wonderful evening with them, and Chuck and I even managed to talk about an airplane or two! He has a PA-18 Super Cub that he puts on floats during the summer. Pat grew up in the same town in Pennsylvania where Mr. Piper produced his famous airplanes for many years before the company moved their operations to

Florida. Their youngest son Coby works as a commercial fisherman, and their oldest son Ian is an Alaskan State Park Ranger. Ian had told Chuck and Pat that recently a bear had killed a moose. He helped field dress the moose (I wonder how the moose felt about having a dress on), and then he had to keep people away from the bear that showed up at the moose's gut pile. A lady with two young children was adamant about taking them close to the bear just to take photographs, but finally relented when threatened with a possible arrest for endangerment to children. Some people don't have an idea how stupid they can be, or how dangerous a bear can be. Chuck can attest to the second part – he showed me photos of a Citabria he once owned that he flew to the Brooks Range many years ago on a sheep hunting trip. While he hunted, the whole fuselage of his plane was ripped out by bears. Both sides, from the tail to the wing were peeled like a banana. His friend's Super Cub had the left flap destroyed also. The friend took off the flap, flew back for some canvass and duct tape, came back the next morning, and the two guys used the tape and canvass to make a temporary fuselage. Nervous, but determined, Chuck successfully flew the Citabria home the next day. Just another day in the Alaskan bush! What's even more weird about it, the Super Cub had had a similar bear encounter the previous year. Chuck wrote an article about the incidents that was published in <u>ALASKA</u> magazine in 1982, and another article for the now defunct <u>Alaska Flying</u> magazine. Chuck talked about how humble of a man that Paul Shanahan is, and how strong he and his wife Mabel are as she fights a courageous battle with cancer. Thank you Pat and Chuck for the dinner and your thoroughly enjoyable company, in the very nice log cabin that you built. (A few months later Mabel lost her battle, which I was sorry to hear.)

Chuck Thomas's PA-18 Super Cub with Denali in background. Photo courtesy of Chuck

More Floatplanes in Florida, 2008

February 16th

Judi, Hawks Abbott's wife, asked me if I could come up with a place for Hawks and me to go to celebrate his 55th birthday. On his 50th, we went to Jackson, Wyoming, flew a Cessna 172 near the Tetons, and watched a lone wolf wondering across the Elk Refuge, before we saw a migrating herd of about 3000 elk steaks-in-motion. This year, we made plans to be in Florida to see STS-123 launch and fly floatplanes over the upcoming three-day weekend. But shuttle delays happen. The launch of STS-122 occurred on the 7th of February, and STS-123 was delayed until March. Hawks and I kept our plans to fly floatplanes over the President's Day weekend.

My plane arrived in Orlando on the 15th about three hours before Hawks came in. We finally arrived at 3 AM on the morning of the 16th at the Oak Harbor Lodging and RV Campground, which is located on the shores of Lake Lowery outside of Haines City. We rented a very nice two-bedroom duplex for three days at a reasonable cost. By the time we left, we seriously considered going in half and buying a small cabin to rent out, especially for pilots interested in picking up their floatplane ratings. Once again, it was time to fly with Brian Schanche, owner of Adventure Seaplanes, whom I flew with to the Arctic Ocean in 2005, and in Minnesota last year. Brian established a winter-time operations at Oak Harbor. He would have had the yellow PA-12 that I flew last Summer in Minnesota down there, but a 20,000 hour airline pilot who knew better stalled it out over some trees. Brian told me that he made a mistake that a student pilot would probably not have made.

By 8 AM I was on the dock in front of the duplex where a yellow Piper J-3 on floats was tied down, but I didn't see any Cessnas. Brian gave me a call on my cell phone and gave me directions to his place. Two beautiful Cessnas – a 172 and a 180 - with sunlight glistening off them were impatiently waiting for me to yell, "Clear Prop!" And I was anxious to do the same thing. Richard, my instructor pilot, has taught flying for 40 years; he worked for 17 years as a commercial water-skier at one of the local amusement centers. We flew for 1.1 hours in the 172, splashing-and-dashing on-and-off about 8 - 10 lakes. Naturally, that hurt my feelings. Adventure Seaplanes is one of the few places in the country where you can fly floatplanes solo, due to high insurance costs. I haven't done it yet, but one of these days I hope to be signed off to go out on my own. Until then, I will continue using an instructor. However, I do think my skill level is improving – it ought to be by now – and I am hoping one of these days to be fishing in the lakes of Minnesota or Florida from one of Brian's planes.

Gregg Anderson owns the Oak Harbor Seaplane Base. OK, so it's really called the Oak Harbor Lodging and RV Campground! Well, when I'm flying a seaplane, as far as I'm concerned I'm in an RV, so it's easy for me to swap names. He has quite a collection of arrowheads and pottery remains that he has found along the shores of the lake. Later in our stay, Hawks managed to find some more pottery pieces made by the Indians who used to live in the area. Gregg owns the Piper J-3 I first saw.

After I finished flying – well, after I stopped for the day – I walked back to the duplex, knocked on Hawks' door, and told him he could waste the day sleeping or go fly a floatplane. He managed to drag his carcass out of bed, swigged down some coffee, and wondered on down to Brian's area. He flew with Matt in the 172 for 1.7 hours. I wish I could say it was with Matt, as in Matthew A. Nelson, Esq., STS-144, but there are at least two Matts in the world! World, are you ready? When Hawks came back after flying 13 takeoffs and splashes, it was a good thing that he wasn't playing poker, because the grin on his face was larger than that of a Halloween pumpkin.

Hawks went for a fly-about in this Cessna 172

While Hawks was preparing to go fly, two floatplanes came over flying low and I thought they were going to stop. They didn't, and I was disappointed. I recognized those planes were Eric Weaver's Cessna 180 and Kirk Spangler's Cessna 150.

February 17th

Today is Hawks' birthday. Happy Birthday, CAPT Hawksorius Oozic! It is also the birthday of Keith, my son-in-law, and my friends Bob McCullough and Kathy Noble. Happy Birthday to you all of you! Somebody else I know has the same birthday, but I don't remember who it is, so happy birthday anyway.

Matt at the controls of the C-180

Hawks and Brian

Despite his Senior Curmudgeon status, Hawks pushed his carcass out of his bed earlier than yesterday (I say that, because that must have been that loud thud I heard coming out of his room while I was in the kitchen making coffee), either because I had plans to fly the Cessna 180 and had invited him to tag along, or because he knew that if he didn't wake up, I would go fly anyway and then let him know what a wonderful time I had while he was trying to catch up on his much needed make-him-look-better-sleep. Notice that I did not say the oft-repeated phrase "Beauty sleep". Except for what I am writing now, the words "Hawks" and "beauty" just don't go well in the same sentence.

Although the guilt feelings crept in when I chose to go flying instead of going to church, they were not powerful enough to stop me from eagerly taking the pilot seat and giving Brian the chance to exercise his privilege as a CFI while riding shotgun in the right front seat next to me. Boy, did we ever go flying! And in doing so, I once again admired the beauty of God's creation. We flew like the fowl of the air in our manmade flying machine, sweeping down upon the water and flaring at the right moment to make a perfect landing... OK, maybe not perfect landings, but we had fun anyway making our splashes-and-dashes. For a while I flew, and then I exchanged seats with Hawks, who had been sitting in the back. Shortly after he did his first splash down I saw a gator creature that must have been at least ten feet long. *"And God said, Let the waters bring forth abundantly the moving creature that hath life, and fowl that may fly above the earth in the open firmament of heaven."* Genesis 1:20. *"The heavens declare the glory of God; and the firmament sheweth his handiwork."* Psalm 19:1.

One of these days I might even convince myself to fly another seaplane or two. It wouldn't bother me if I flew this yellow cub that belongs to Gregg, or the white/blue Cub Crafters that belongs to one of Gregg's tenants!

Gregg Anderson's Piper at Oak Harbor

Closing Thoughts, March 2011

Of all the flying I have done, I like flying floats the best. As I mentioned earlier, we moved to Montana in May 2009. Three weeks later I flew with Mike Kincaid again in Coeur d'Alene. He and I have flown several hours in that yellow J-3 Cub, but won't be doing it again, since he sold it. He now owns a Savannah Light Sport Aircraft (LSA), and has put amphibs on it. Looks like another floatplane for me to fly!

Brian Schanche has moved his winter operations to Cherry Pocket Fish Camp at Lake Pierce, Florida. Eric Weaver now is part owner of Jones Brothers Air and Seaplane Adventures at Lake Taveres, near Leesburg, Florida, and teaches the Multi-Engine Seaplane Rating (MSES) in a Republic Seabee Twin funny-looking plane. (www.mesratings.com). There is a photo of it in the back of this book.

Finally, after looking at Canyon Ferry Lake here in Montana, I had a chance to fly onto it. Steve Palinkos, a local pilot in Townsend, has a Cessna 185 on amphibs, and one day in November 2010 we did four splash and dashes. For not flying a floatplane for nearly a year-and-a-half, I didn't do too badly. Steve was with me every step of the way (and that's what you do when you take off – get on the step!), but I did the actual landings, and even managed to put the plane back on the hard surface at Townsend airport. Great day! Although I had a camera with me, I didn't use it – darn – and Steve doesn't have any photos of the 185, so I am not inserting any in this story. He and I are talking about flying to the Little Bitterroot Lake to see Roger and Michelle Weltz, and to Lake Hayden to see Mike. If they are nice to us, they might even have a chance to go for a ride!

I thank God for all the seaplanes I have flown, and I'm certainly looking for many more opportunities to do it again. I would like to thank all the people and companies that I have flown seaplanes with in the last 9 years. I have received topnotch instruction in seven states and in Canada, all at beautiful places. I have had a very good time, thanks to all of you. God Bless.

(Isa 41:18) *I will open rivers in high places, and fountains in the midst of the valleys: I will make the wilderness a pool of water, and the dry land springs of water.*

Sounds like an invitation to me for places to fly floatplanes!

A Vagabond's Story of Hopping a Freight Plane, the Antonov An-22

The An-2, with the old paint job (top) and the new one (bottom). Photos made by and are courtesy of Ken Gray, a professional photographer (www.helicopterphotos.com)

Flying the Antonov An-2 in Alaska, 2003

Introduction

Altogether, over the years, I have made a dozen trips to Alaska. I wasn't born in Alaska, and I certainly do not have the navigation skills of a salmon returning to the same stream where she had been hatched. Airplanes, mountains, glaciers, caribou, moose, grizzly bears, bald eagles, salmon, whales, not too many people, Denali. Primordial stirrings, ties, or whatever. I have to answer my own call of the wild. I have to return to Alaska as often as possible.

In Alaska, one can see planes of every description. I was on a fishing trip to this state in 1999 with my friends, Hawks Abbott, Brian Collier, and Bob Simle. While walking around and looking at all the aircraft at the Lake Hood airport in Anchorage, Hawks exclaimed, "Look at that An-2 Colt!" The An-2 is a Russian designed bi-plane aircraft that served the communist countries for many years. Until that day, I had never even heard of it. On the tail of this plane there was the flag of The Explorers Club, of which I am a member. When I saw this monstrous bi-plane I knew then that I wanted to fly one someday.

An-2 Colt in Anchorage, which later ended under the ice at the North Pole

A year after we went to Alaska, this same An-2, owned by Ron Sheardown, was flown to the North Pole by Ron, Dick Rutan of Voyager II fame, along three or four other people. The plane fell through the ice, and is now on the bottom of the ocean near the North

Pole. No one was hurt, and all managed to be rescued. (Reference: http://www.explorers.org/newsfiles/archivefiles/biplane/index.html.)

Seven months later I had gone to Mongolia to bring in the new Millennium with Kazakh Eagle Hunters. When my plane from Beijing landed at Ulann Baatar, the capitol city of Mongolia, I saw several derelict-looking An-2s just lined up on the tarmac. Immediately, I started trying to figure out how I could finagle a ride on one of these planes, but it didn't happen on this trip, because I came down with pneumonia just before I left the country on the Trans-Siberian train, and was so sick that I had no desire to fly. If I have no desire to fly, you know I must have been sick.

When I left home to go to Alaska in June 2003, I had no idea that I would be back in August to fly to Russia in N87AN, a U. S. registered An-2. Nor did I know that I would more trips in this plane.

June 28th

Four hours after takeoff from Seattle, I saw a bull moose at the end of the runway in Anchorage, as we landed near midnight.

June 29th

It would almost be criminal not to go to an air show when you are in the same town at the same time when one is going on, so since I didn't want to go to jail, I went to the air show at Elmendorf AFB. While waiting for the USAF Thunderbirds to perform, I wandered around looking at the airplanes in today's Air Force. One of the first planes I saw was the AWACS, the Boeing-built jet with the thirty-foot rotating radome on top. In Seattle, I had walked through the Boeing 707 that became famous as Air Force One when President Kennedy was shot. Touring the AWACS plane gave me nostalgic feelings from the time I served as aircrew on the EA-3B in 1968. Given a choice today, I would much rather be assigned to the AWACS than I would Air Force One, because there are many electronic consoles on the AWACS and there is too much spit and polish on Air Force One.

I walked past the over-priced hamburger and soft-drink booths. I walked past a gray C-130, a gray F-15, a gray B-1B, a gray C-5A yawning, a black-and-orange Goose, and Whoa! Sitting on the tarmac is a white and orange An-2 Colt with "Lithuanian Airlines" painted on its side. Maybe, this is the starting point of the story. But it's time to watch the Thunderbirds fly. Now, everyone's leaving. I walk upstream past the crowds to the Antonov. I meet one of the owners, Douglas Fulton. Reluctantly, he lets me go scope out the cockpit. I ask if it is possible for me to fly it. He tells me yes and what it costs to fly that plane for one hour. I know if I am frugal for the rest of the week that I should be able to afford it. But he lives in Valdez. No problem. There is no way that I am going to go home without flying the An-2. And then Douglas goes fishing:

"We are taking this to Russia next month." The hook is set and the line zings. "Do you have any room for one more person?" "We are looking for three more people to fill the plane." Zing! "What's it going to cost?" "About $750 per person." (Ended up a little more, but that's OK.) Douglas and his partner Neal can't make any money off the plane, but are allowed to share operating costs with others. I certainly wanted to share costs. Wow! Right then and there I phoned Hawks to see if he was interested, but couldn't reach him. In 1988, Alaska Airlines flew a Boeing 737 from Nome to Provideniya, Siberia on a friendship flight. Since then, tourist ships dock at that port city. Partly through the efforts of the Alaska Airmen's Association, a VFR route had recently been legally opened between those two cities. Initially, the plan was to fly over and back from Nome the same day, but then the talks gyrated towards spending one night in Provideniya.

I have been around military aircraft for years. I have even flown in a few. If I were offered a chance to fly in an F-15 or and F-16, or even an SR-71, I suppose I might even say "Yeah, I guess I'll go for a flight, if no one else wants to". You know, it's a dirty job, but someone has to do it. Turning down a ride in an SR-71 would be like me saying to NASA, "If you want me to fly on STS-123, I guess I'll go, but I was really hoping for a ride on STS-144". I approached the chance to fly in the An-2 with the same half a nanosecond delay – after all, I didn't want to appear over eager! That night, sleep played its elusive game, as if I were a child on Christmas Eve, and not because I had visions of sugarplums dancing in my head.

The next few days I roamed around Alaska, and made plans to fly to Valdez with Marc Paine, a pilot whom I had flown with in 2002.

He has a Decathlon that he uses to teach aerobatic maneuvers and recovery from unusual altitudes. We discussed flying to Valdez in it so I could fly the Antonov.

July 3rd

Antonov An-2 at Valdez Airport

Marc met me in the afternoon at Merrill Field in Anchorage. By 3 PM, the weather had cleared good enough to fly his Decathlon to Valdez. I sat in front of the tandem plane and did some good old stick and rudder flying. We flew on the northeastern side of the Turnagain Arm, crossed over the mountains near Whittier, and then flew over a bunch of islands in Prince William Sound as we headed to Valdez. A rainbow off our port wing enhanced the beauty of this wonderland. Occasionally, we could see the cruise ships. Numerous icebergs the size of houses had calved off glaciers on our left. From the air, they didn't look very big. Marc pointed out the Columbia Glacier and a place where the cruise ships stop. If the passengers on the ships take a helicopter ride over the glaciers, they see what we saw; if not, they only see one wall of this massive glacier that's about 400-feet high. Over the years, I have seen many glaciers, especially in Antarctica, but they never cease to amaze me. It's exhilarating to fly over them, but I always give a sigh of relief when their plane-eating crevasses are behind me.

As we approached Valdez Airport, there was no doubt which plane was the Antonov. Actually, there were very few planes in sight, but just like at the air show in Anchorage a few days earlier, I had no problem picking it out. A bi-wing airplane with a 60-foot wingspan and a huge 4-bladed prop is easy to spot!

We landed and taxied to the Antonov on the West end of the airport. Douglas told me to give him a call when we landed, and he would come over from his dry wall construction business. While we waited for him, Marc and I just marveled at this gigantic feat of aeronautical engineering. Before we pre-flighted the plane, Douglas took us into his hangar, where he has a Stinson 108 waiting for me to fly sometime, and an upstairs lounge area that he built as a winter project. During the pre-flight, I called Hawks Abbott on my cell phone to tell him that I was about ready to fly the An-2, but he didn't answer, so I just had to leave an "eat your heart out" message.

As veteran pilots of radial-engine planes know, oil in the bottom cylinders has a tendency to pool, so the prop is turned a few turns to redistribute the oil. Otherwise, a cylinder might crack during startup. At least that is my understanding. "Propping" a 4-bladed prop with each blade as long as I am tall would be a good way to work out, if done for an hour a day. It takes a lot of muscle effort to turn the prop on the Antonov.

I climbed into the co-pilot's seat and read off each item of an extensive checklist as Douglas performed the actual functions. I don't fully understand how the brakes work, but the air-operated system has to be up to the proper pressure. After Douglas stepped his way through the checklist, it was time for him to start the engine. At the right precise moment, Douglas did his magic and there was that rough cough, puffs of smoke, a satisfying roar, and then a smoothing of the engine as all nine cylinders started firing. Douglas taxied the plane to the East end of the runway, pushed the throttle in, and then all of sudden we lifted off.

Twenty-four windows in the cockpit provide almost unlimited visibility. We slowly climbed out between 80 and 100 knots, and once we were above 3000-feet, Douglas gave me the controls. Marc stood in the cabin, just behind the cockpit. We flew West, and banked North, over the Columbia Glacier. When Marc and I flew into Valdez, we could see the glacier a few miles away. Now, we were flying right over it, flying over the moraines, the rivers of ice and rocks that curve like a super highway, and over the crevasses. Turquoise pools of water glistened in the sunlight.

Flying this plane, as one might guess, gave this pilot one of those smiles that takes forever to evaporate. It mattered not that that the yoke felt heavy. So what – the plane responded to the control inputs, perhaps a little sluggishly, but I didn't care as we soared over the glacier. Douglas occasionally talked to the ground using the black solid-looking Russian built radio. Near my left knee an ADF indicator the size of a Frisbee was mounted on the panel. It didn't operate, but I was impressed with it anyway. For about ten minutes I traded places with Marc, to give him a chance to fly this wonderful flying machine. All too soon we had to go back to Valdez. I flew it until we entered the pattern to land. Douglas took over, and made the landing flare way too high, I thought. Then we touched down very smoothly. I had forgotten that one sits much higher off the ground when in the cockpit of this airplane than in any airplane I have ever flown before. Even if I had not flown the An-2 on this trip to Alaska, I still would have signed up to fly it to Russia.

July 4th

Independence Day! Temperatures in the 70s. Clear blue sky, but no clear destination. So I drove around Lake Hood to see the floatplanes and by Merrill Field for another look at the taildraggers, and just sort of kept on going down the highway towards Palmer and Glennallen. I even thought about turning South at Glennallen and going to Valdez again just to take another look at the Antonov. Halfway between Anchorage and Glennallen is the Malanuska Glacier. There is a restaurant and lodge overlooking the glacier where I had stayed on a previous trip to Alaska. Why not have a hamburger? So I did. While waiting, I overheard one lady telling her friend that the original owners had bought the property with the idea of putting in restaurant for people travelling down the highway, but they first saw it on a drizzly, rainy day, and did not see the glacier. People travelled that highway for twenty years before the owners made it back again. They were astonished to see this beautiful looking glacier right on their property. I did not know it then, but looking at the Anchorage Sectional, it is obvious that the Malanuska Glacier is a Northern finger of the same ice fields as the Columbia Glacier.

A few miles down the road at a construction site, somebody in a powered hang glider flew over the snow-capped mountains. East of Glennallen, 14,000 and 16,000-feet peaks of the Wrangell-St. Elias gave me something to ooh-and-ah about as I drove into town. As I headed North on the Richardson Highway, the road ran parallel to the Trans Alaskan Pipeline. I gassed up the van at Paxson, and made a choice to turn west on the gravel road called the Denali Highway, instead of driving North to Delta Junction and Fairbanks. I could have eaten at the restaurant located a few miles West of Paxson, and I had enough money to do so, but wanted to camp somewhere along the way. But I stopped there anyway, to beg for something to boil water in to cook my backpacker stew. I had scrounged some firewood earlier and I had me a plan. But I didn't have any silverware to eat the stew, and I didn't realize that fact until another mile down the road. I drove back to the restaurant, and begged some more. Disgustedly, the same lady whom had given me the number 10 can to boil water gave me a plastic spoon. So I bought a coke out a machine for a buck and drove about twenty-five more miles until I saw a stream on the South side of the road, and white mountains of the Alaska Range to the North telling me to stop and camp. Ah, the life of a hobo! Well, not really, but cooking stew on a open fire with no one around but the mosquitoes and I can make them disappear by standing in the wood smoke, and drinking hot coffee and admiring beautiful mountains and listening to the popping and crackling of the logs as my Fourth of July fireworks, and watching the sunset near midnight, and thinking of my family and my good friends and the airplanes I have flown and the places I have travelled and my dream of flying in the space shuttle, and then later on, look at all those stars - well, color me content.

July 5th

There comes a time, no matter how warm the sleeping bag is, or how low the temperature has dropped during the night, you simply have to face a very urgent reality. Once up, I guess I might as well drive to Anchorage, especially since the big airplane will take off whether I am on it or not. Someplace that had a Super Cub on floats also had cabins and a small café that served hot coffee and breakfast. In Cantwell, the Denali Highway dead-ends into the Parks Highway. Turn

North, and you go to Fairbanks; turn South if you want to go to Anchorage. Little did I realize that I would be seeing Cantwell again a few weeks later.

Stop and take photos of Denali. Drive through America on the Parks Highway: Colorado, Honolulu, Montana, Houston to go to Houston. I took a shower at a general store, gas station and restaurant in Trapper Creek (the same store from where I had called Norman Vaughan a few years earlier), and later, ate lunch in Talkeetna, even though it's off the main highway. Not necessary in order of the other towns listed, I pass through the towns of Igloo, Hurricane, and Caswell. Is there any connection to my friends Dawn and Bill Caswell? Keep on going through Wasilla and Eagle River and drive past Merrill Field again and break the Tenth Commandment by coveting many of those airplanes.

A man named Andy gave me a ride to Anchorage Airport after I returned the van. I told him about the upcoming flight to Russia in the An-2. He told me that he flew the first An-2 from Russia to Alaska about ten years or twelve years ago, and that he offered to let Ron Sheardown borrow his An-2 skis for his ill-fated North Pole expedition, but Ron declined. We all make mistakes that we regret. I would not hesitate to fly with him to the North Pole in another An-2, given half a chance.

So now, another trip to Alaska has ended, but not without the anticipation of another adventure flying an An-2.

August 7th

Finally, the day came for me to head "North to Alaska" and on to Provideniya. Numerous telephone calls and creative financing and a rushed visa application were now things of the past. My Continental Airlines One Pass account now read 47,250 miles less than I wanted, but I didn't have to pay for another plane ticket to Anchorage. Beggars can't be choosers – it would have been faster to go non-stop from Houston to Anchorage, but having a free ticket made it OK to change planes in Detroit. It took almost as long to fly the Detroit – Anchorage route as the return flight from Anchorage to Houston.

Sitting next to me on the Anchorage flight was Bill Kenaston, a 747-pilot who works for Polar Air Cargo. I told him of my planned excursion to Russia in the An-2. When two or more pilots start talking to each other, you can be sure that somehow, the subjects of flying and flying stories and airplanes may accidentally creep into the conversation. We both kept this tradition alive! Bill came to Lake Hood airport the next morning to watch us depart.

Flying into Anchorage is like going home for me. This journey made my tenth trip to Alaska, and the last seven have occurred since 1995. I am as familiar with this city as I am with Christchurch, New Zealand. After checking in at my motel, I contacted Douglas, and he told me to come to the party on the Lake Hood strip. One of his friends agreed to pick me up, but our paths didn't cross until I reached the big An-2, after walking around Lake Hood. Walking for 45 minutes around a bunch of colorful floatplanes and tail-draggers isn't a bad way to spend an evening.

Douglas introduced me to the other adventurous travelers of our group: His wife Jeanne Passin, their friend Mary Lou Rarra, Neal Oppen, who is the other owner of the AN-2, and Sonja Sabel, a bush pilot out of Fairbanks who works for Warbelow's Air Ventures, Inc. Many of their friends had gathered for a giant send-off. I guess this was only proper, since the An-2 is a giant of a single-engine airplane. While in many of the conversations the name Provideniya was mentioned, the item that generated more attention than even perhaps the gargantuan An-2 and its destination was the margarita / mixed drink mixer attached to a gasoline-powered weed-eater engine. Ice, bags of fresh fruit, and rum were all poured into the blender, and then, watch out! I don't drink anything alcoholic any more, but I enjoyed watching the others as they participated. At 10:30 PM, a friend of Douglas's gave me a ride back to the motel. My ragged old body was still on Houston time, and it felt like it was 1:30 AM.

August 8th

The driver for the motel took me to the An-2 at 8:30 AM. I was the first one there. A few minutes later, Bill arrived in a taxicab. Eventually, the others arrived. By 10 AM, Neal had the plane loaded, we had a group photo, and then it was time to leave. The lady at Lake Hood tower gave us taxi instructions; we took off from the gravel strip, and shortly after take-off, she radioed, "Beautiful airplane!" I know, because I sat in the cabin behind Douglas and Neal, and had my headphones plugged into the spare headphone jacks located just behind the cockpit. Right after takeoff, Douglas discarded his sandals and operated the rudder pedals with his bare feet.

L-R: Mary Lou, Douglas, Jeanne, Neal, Sonja, Matt

Sonja, Jeanne, and Mary Lou sat in the back of the plane. We weren't airborne more than five minutes before they opened the outside door, which was a little unnerving at first. As we flew along towards Nikolai, Denali could be seen off the right side of the plane. If I remember correctly, we climbed to 8500 feet to clear Rainy Pass, and after that, all of our flights were at a lower altitude. This day was a clear day and we had very little turbulence. Neal stepped out of the co-pilot seat and invited me to take it. No problem! Sonja stood behind Douglas and me, and after I rode shotgun for a while, I exchanged places with her. In this Americanized version of the An-2, the pilot's altimeter displays thousands of feet and air speed is read in knots, but the co-pilot's altimeter is in meters and the air speed indicator is in kilometers. It was no trouble for me to make the transition, but you definitely have to be conscious of the difference. This is the first plane I had ever flown with electric trim controls for ailerons, the rudder, and the elevator. Douglas said that there is an onboard electric pump to refuel from 55-gallon (or the metric equivalent) barrels on the ground, since it is easier to place fuel barrels into remote landing strips than it is a fuel tanker. There is an elaborate checklist that must be meticulously followed to start the engine, including turning the magnetos on at the precise moment when the prop has been cranked four times, or the battery will die. Once the magnetos fire, that wonderful cough and deep roar of the radial engine resonates as white puffs of smoke belches out and reminds me of the bygone days when steam locomotives gave that sweet and mournful sounding whistle that no diesel locomotive can ever hope to imitate.

George, and Roger Jenkins

Two-and-a-half hours after take-off, we landed at Nikolai. It seemed like every person living in this town of about 100 people turned out to watch our landing. Even before we landed I saw some people riding on 4-wheelers near the end of the runway. A Russian-designed biplane with a copy of an American Curtis-Wright 1000 HP radial engine that can be heard for miles may have had something to do with our warm reception. The first person that I talked to was George, whom had driven his 4-wheeler up to the plane. His first words to me were, "Are you a tourist?" I stammered out, "Yeah, I guess I am". Then he smiled. He has his own Piper J-3 Cub, and is retired from the Alaskan Department of Transportation. While I chatted with him, City-Councilman Roger Jenkins handed out pens with the words, "City of Nikolai, Alaska On Iditarod Dogsled Trail" written on the barrel. Roger and George stood by the plane so I could take their photograph.

We six flying vagabonds had our photos taken by several of the villagers, and the next thing I knew I was riding on the back of a 4-wheeler with Sonja, going down a dusty trail to someplace. It reminded me of being in China when I blindly trusted non-English speaking taxi drivers taking me down roads whose signs I could not read to destinations that I did not know. I needed not to have worried, for we were dropped at John and Marty Runkle's place. There are some 24-hour periods in one's life that to describe fully, would fill the pages of a book, but not to describe at all would do a great injustice to those people who are right with God and the world.

The Runkles

We were welcomed by John and Marty, and their children, Sharon – age 21, Andrew – age 19, and PJ – age 9. Sharon gave me a cup of coffee; we all sat down and chatted, then John and PJ gave us a tour of the place, after telling us that he had been on the Internet trying to buy a church bell from Russia that morning. John came to Alaska 23 years ago on a construction project for the school. He and Marty had cleared the land, chopping down the trees so not to disturb the undergrowth, built a log cabin and then expanded it over the years, built a smaller cabin for Andrew, a smoke house, a sauna, and John was in the process of constructing a shed for his saw mill, where he debarked the trees and cut them up into lumber. Oh, yeah, although they have indoor plumbing, he also built the outhouse where one can sit with the door open and view a small lake that is often visited by moose and bears. All this was done when he wasn't driving heavy machinery to extend the runway, or remodeling the only church in town, or working on the schoolhouse and serving on the school board, or hunting, fishing, and trapping, or running his own guiding business out of four camps and a lodge that he had built in the mountains. He wore a Tee Shirt that had many different tools on the front, with the saying, "So many tools, so little time!"

I didn't have much conversation with Marty, who is a Native-born Athabaskan Indian, and just as nice as she can be. But boy can she and Sharon cook! Sharon was back in Nikolai after going to school in Seattle. Andrew had just been accepted to go to work at Prudhoe Bay up on the North Slope. Apparently, it is quite competitive to work there, and he passed some practical tests well enough in Anchorage to earn the right to go to a three-week training course. He is an excellent hunter and fisherman in his own right – the steaks we ate for dinner were from the 40-pound King Salmon, which he had caught. He told me that he wants to learn to fly, and I can certainly understand that idea. If I ever had to survive in Alaska, little PJ could certainly be the person helping me stay alive. This kid knows the bush, the plants, what to eat and what not to eat, and said that beaver tastes better than porcupine! Later, when we toured the town riding on the back of the town truck – a Chevy flatbed pickup – PJ scampered about, pointing out berries to us while giving a rundown on the local plants and trails. These kids grew up driving 4-wheelers. On the spur of the moment, several would hop on one and take off to see their friends. I observed no fighting among this close-knit family. They were really a pleasure to be around.

Sometimes our positions altered, but we started touring the town with Sonja, PJ, and myself riding on the back of the truck, with Neal inside the cab, while Douglas, Jeannie, and Mary Lou followed on a 4-wheeler. First we went to a nearby lake, then back to the plane where we ate lunch. Afterwards, John took us through the town along the Kuskokwim River, stopping at an abandoned cabin, then at the school. John showed us a dog sled he had built, and took us through the three classrooms. The upper level class had a computer for each student. Along the main hallway were photos of the "Elders", a glass case that contained various artifacts about Alaskan village life, including an animal skull that PJ had found. Hanging on one of the walls were snowshoes homemade by one of the elders, an art form that is dying. Marty's youngest sister is three years older than Sharon. She had gone to this school and then had gone on to college, graduating with a 4.0 average and then worked for a US Senator, as I recall. We were told that this is typical among the Interior villages. We stopped next at the Russian Orthodox Church, which is the only church in town. A small ornate cemetery nearby had colorful fences around many of the graves. After we walked around the cemetery for a few minutes, John invited us inside. John told us that he had been working on the floor, so the fact that there were no pews didn't surprise me, but then he mentioned that there aren't any, since the doctrine of the church wants the people to be somewhat uncomfortable during worship. Many icons and paintings adorned the walls. John said that the people do not worship them, but they are simple reminders of the events in the life of Jesus. Candlesticks made from the wax of honeybees are used during the services; these had their own rich aroma, as well as some bottles of incense that we could buy. While the church building is small, I was still impressed with the inside. I had to laugh at PJ when he said he liked it when the priest came to town, because he could have wine and bread. From the church we walked a small distance to visit Grandpa Bobby Esia, Sr. He is one of the elders of the church and the village. In church, his position is the Reader. It was evident that John respected the old man very much. He said that Grandpa Bob always rode around on his own 4-wheeler, carrying a camera and rifle everywhere he went. When he encountered someone who said that he was trespassing, he acted like he couldn't hear them, then took a photo of that person, and rode off, whether it be on that person's land or not. We all gathered around his kitchen table, and he sat on a well-worn chair in the corner, please to have company. Much of the wall to his left was covered with Russian Orthodox icons.

Inside the Russian Orthodox Church

John told us that Bobby was hard of hearing, but loved to tell his many stories. With only a little encouragement, once settled in his chair, he slowly began one of them. Several hours later, I tried to write as much as I could remember of what he said, but obviously, listening to him was a more rewarding experience than I can convey second-hand. Here is the story he told us, as best as I recall:

Grandpa Bobby Esia, Sr.

"I am an old man, not to much interesting, not much to tell. I'm almost 85 years old. I used to go camping all over, living off the land and carrying my gear in a burlap bag. Not like the people today with all of their coolers. For 11 years I have lived by myself, since my wife died. We were married for 47 years. I believe in God and I believe in Jesus. When I was 17, I was mushing a team of dogs. We were going through long grasses near the river. The river was iced over. When I was crossing the river the ice gave way and the sled and the dogs fell into the river. It was icy cold. I managed to get the dogs up on the ice, but the sled and I were in the water and I couldn't get out. I cut the dogs reins. I was in the water 1½ hour to 2 hours. I believe in God and I believe in Jesus (as he clutched the cross that he wore around his neck). *When we were young we always carried a picture of Jesus with us. I pulled out my picture of Jesus and prayed. Right after that some people came along. They tied some rope (quarter-inch rope it was) to some long poles. I cut the dogs loose and tied the rope to myself. The people pulled me out of the water. It was very cold, and I was in the water for 1½ hour to 2 hours."* Wow! In the water for 1½ to 2 hours!

I don't do justice to his story. We were in his house about 15-20 minutes, maybe a half hour. We took photos of him, and he asked up to sign his guest book. But the one thing that I took home with me is the insight that there are millions of old people in this world that have their own stories to tell. Later that evening, I remarked to Sonja how I would like to return to Alaska and listen to these people tell their stories. She asked me if I had read the book, <u>Shadows on the Koyukuk</u> by Sidney

Huntington (as told to Jim Readen). When I said no, Andrew brought me one of his four copies to take with me. (I finally finished reading it in October, glad to have had the chance.) Although I don't know if Sidney and Bobby knew each other, there is a good chance that they did. They certainly had similar life styles of trapping, hunting, fishing, and mushing.

When we left the old man's place, I rode with John in the truck to the lake where several kids were swimming. Along the way, he told me that he and Douglas had been very good friends for over twenty years. I have a few long time and very good friends, so I can understand the mutual respect. I hadn't figured on swimming in Alaska, especially in a cold lake, and I hadn't taken any swimming trunks with me. So I watched the others of our group enter the frigid water and have water splashed onto them by the kids. I remember swimming in lakes in Wyoming as a kid while adults wearing sweaters stood around and watched. PJ put his dog in a canoe and paddled out around the other kids; soon, some of the kids were playing in the canoe. I admire the people who went swimming, but I did note that the kids were still having fun in the water while all the adults came out one-by-one.

Back at the log cabin, John started the bar-b-que for the salmon steaks. Even though fish is not generally a favorite meal of mine, I must admit we all ate a very good dinner. Afterwards, I didn't have any trouble at all eating Marty's homemade chocolate cake and frosting. After dinner, some people went into the sauna, another result of John's handiwork.

Around 11 PM, we all went back to the plane. I walked behind PJ, Sonja, and Neal, going at my own pace and catching up with them at the plane. Roger Jenkins had told them that there was room available at the town's guesthouse, but nobody wanted to stay there after seeing what a mess the construction workers had made. Jeannie, Mary Lou, Neal, and Sonja pitched tents, and Douglas slept in the back of the plane, where he has built a bed. Earlier, John offered to let me sleep in the cabin where his son Andrew usually stayed, and there were two beds, so I thought I would have the extra bed. As it turned out, Andrew slept in the main house on the couch, saying he does it all the time. Andrew's cabin is definitely not the product of someone brought up on MTV. Several furs hung on the walks, including a black bear skin rug. In all of my travels, I think this is one of the best-decorated rooms I have ever stayed in. Thanks, Andrew, for letting me stay there. Thanks to the people of Nikolai for all of your hospitality. Hopefully, in two years, I will be able to fly the Stinson to Alaska and stop there for a visit.

August 9th

After a breakfast of fresh coffee and homemade pancakes made with handpicked blueberries, it was time to pack the plane and continue the odyssey to Nome. Once again, many people of the village rode their 4-wheelers to the plane to say goodbye. I looked around to see if PJ was stowing away. He didn't, but Roger Jenkins had decided to hitchhike with us to Nome, wait for us to go to Russia and back, and then fly to Anchorage in the An-2. He is a man whose sense of adventure just naturally fit with the rest of ours. Roger came to Alaska as a young geologist about 40 years ago from Duluth, Minnesota. Along the way he migrated into city engineering and then into politics, at a high enough level to have served in the Alaska Legislature. He has a unique prospective of being an honest politician – he often laughingly said that he would stay in a town until the people ran him off, then come back a few years later and become a councilman again. I told him of my interest in geology and satellite remote sensing, and he told me he could line me up with people who might be able to offer me a job. I have no doubt that he would be true to his word, and who knows, there may be a time that I give him a call.

Our flight to McGrath departed with a good send-off from the people of Nikolai. Since the flight time was only for a few minutes, Neal stayed in the co-pilot seat, and I stood behind him and Douglas. I quickly understood why Andrew said that the air distance between Nikolai and McGrath is about 40 miles, but the river distance is 120 miles. From the air, the Kuskokwim River looks like a piece of Christmas ribbon candy. About halfway into the flight, Douglas pointed out the area where a Stinson 108 that he piloted had crashed about twenty-five years ago in the winter. The plane started to ice up badly so he chose a place to land; the snow hid the fact that the ground was semi-frosted. After the plane went into a ground loop, it came to a halt upside-down in the trees. Fortunately, none of the four adults and the year-and-a-half old baby on board was injured. Douglas admitted to me that he was much younger and inexperienced than he is now, but I bet he learned some lessons that he will never forget. I learned some lessons that I won't forget. They fed the baby two Granola bars, which was the total food in the plane, and they melted snow in their mouths to give the baby water. Nobody had any matches to start a fire, so they tried to spark the battery against a gasoline soaked rag, but the battery had been damaged in the crash. For two days they hiked for along the river, to find after they were rescued that they had traveled a straight-line distance of only about a quarter-of-a-mile, due to the extensive winding river. Rescue came after people flying in a Cessna saw the wreckage, located Douglas's party, and indicated to them to head back towards the plane. Either the Cessna didn't have room for them, or could not land, but its pilot radioed the Civil Air Patrol to send a plane to pick them up. They were picked up on gravel bar in the Kuskokwim River. In McGrath, they slept on floor of the flight service station operator's house, and flew commercial to Anchorage the next day. Douglas didn't say anything about them eating anything in McGrath, but I reckon they probably did. Even though the landing at McGrath was only the second of our journey (at least for me), it became readily apparent to me that the giant dragonfly *antonovusrex* attracts wistful onlookers as fast as spawning salmon attract fishermen. Dinosaurs and bumblebees aren't supposed to fly but the Peter Pan that lives in children and pilots and those wishing they could fly know that Puff, the Magic Dragon, of the pterodactyl species, does soar.

 In McGrath, while Neal and Douglas fueled the plane, Roger managed to acquire a pick-up truck for all of us to tour the town. Our first stop was to check the weather and file a flight plan at the FAA Flight Service Station, the only building in town that has an elevator - your tax dollars at work. Jeanne drove the truck around McGrath, one or two others sat in front, and the rest sat in back on the side of the box for the five or ten minute drive. One of the shops sold large chocolate chip cookies so I bought enough for us to chomp on as we had the grand tour. Our last stop was to the McQuire's Tavern, since Roger told us that this bar had been mentioned in Sue Henry's book, <u>Murder on the Iditarod Trail</u>. About an hour after landing, we took off for Nome.

 Sonja flew in the co-pilot's seat most of the three-hour flight from McGrath to Nome, and I managed to grab one-and-a-half hours in the pilot's seat. Following Douglas's example, she dumped her sandals, while remarking how cool the pedals felt. Her bright red polished toenails contrasted against the dull gray pedals. During the entire trip Neal and Douglas were very good about giving Sonja and me time at the controls. Quite often, she and I sat in the front, and Douglas and Neal were in the back. Sometimes she would be in the left seat and I would be in the right. I imagine that since Sonja has flown quite a bit in Alaska, and is a very experienced and good pilot, is the reason why we were both allowed to be in the pilot and co-pilot seats at the same time. For this segment, I started flying just prior to crossing the wide Yukon River. As we flew towards Nome, Sonja pointed out some of the different towns and areas she had flown to, such as Unulakleet. She is an interesting person. Furloughed from United Airlines after September 11th, she went to Alaska looking for a flying job, and found one with Warbelow's Air Ventures in Fairbanks. She has all kinds of experience and ratings, including the floatplane rating I eventually hope to have, and type ratings in Boeing 727s and 737s, which I never expect to have. She rolls her own cigarettes, and for fun, mushes a dog team. One day during the trip she told me that some of her friends have hinted at starting a company with her to fly a DC-3. I told her if that happens to let me know, because I would love to fly one, even if from only the right seat for only an hour or two.

Douglas and Neal took over for the landing at Nome. We sat up tents near the plane, and then caught a ride into town with some other people heading for Russia. Several people planned on making the trip, so there was a coordination dinner and meeting at a restaurant that overlooked the Pacific Ocean. Two pilots from Wasilla, Alaska sat across from me. After telling them that I worked at the space center in Houston, one of the pilots told me that his father had worked for Grumman in Long Island, New York during the Apollo days. Grumman built the lunar lander; after the Apollo 13 near-disastrous mission when the astronauts saved themselves by climbing into the lunar lander, the workers that had worked on the lander were presented mission patches that actually flew on-board Apollo 13. Usually, flown patches are reserved for VIPs, but I would guess that in the minds of the Apollo 13 astronauts, no one was more important than those lunar lander workers. The man telling me the story said that he still has that patch.

At the briefing that night assignments were given to the prime pilots of each of the dozen or so aircraft expecting to go to Russia. Each plane had a designated time to take off. I think we were scheduled to go at 10:10 AM the next morning. The An-2 does not have a Type Certification in the United States. In order to do so, each bolt and part would have to have traceability back to the factory, each part would have to meet rigid testing standards, it would cost millions of dollars for a plane that has been flying for over fifty years, and Beechcraft, Cessna, and Piper are being protected by the FAA (in my opinion). As I understand it, for the Antonov to be registered in the U. S., it can only be done as an experimental airplane under very tight restrictions - it can't be utilized to haul cargo or passengers for hire and can only be flown for air shows and special events. The VFR corridor between Nome and Provideniya hasn't been opened long and all flights are heavily scrutinized. The Russians balked at the word, "Experimental", even though it is their design. So at dinner that night, we were told that special permission had to originate in Moscow for the Antonov to fly to Provideniya, and due to the time differences, we would have to wait another 24 hours before we could take off. I guess even the State Department became involved. Had the application been worded slightly different, there probably would not have been a problem. I am an optimist, and having heard the way the Russians typically make people stay in limbo, then grant permission to do something at the last minute, I felt we would be going anyway. I have been wrong before. We did not go.

Perhaps we could have gone on Monday, but by Sunday morning, the weather did not look favorable to wait. As it turned out, some of the people who did make it on Sunday had to stay an extra night in Provideniya due to a huge front that moved from Russia to Alaska.

But I am ahead of the story. After dinner, we all made our way back to the plane. We were sitting around talking when a lady by the name of Susan showed up. She is a dog musher, but is not the Susan Bucher that has won the Iditarod. Several years earlier she had been mushing a team of dogs in Siberia, starting in Provideniya and heading north. After the race, her and her dogs and other teams were to be picked up by the Russians. Usually they used their heavy-lift helicopters, but in this instance two An-2s were sent. Three dog teams were loaded in the plane that Susan flew on. Nobody knows whether it was lack of experience, dumbness, or whatever, but for whatever reason, one of the dog teams was put in the tail section. Apparently, this altered the center of gravity enough to make the plane extremely tail heavy. Upon takeoff, the plane stalled and crashed; one person who was not strapped into his seat was killed. Susan said seeing our An-2 heading on a pleasure flight brought closure. She sure told her story much better than I do.

That night, I spent my first of three sleeping in the plane. I sort of reclined in the seat behind the cockpit, and stretched my legs into it. Not great, but not bad, either.

August 10th

While waiting final word whether or not we would go to Russia, we were visited at the plane by a uniformed U.S. Customs Officer, Anne Marie Millbrooke. She said she was there unofficially, just wanted to see the Antonov up close. She and I chatted a bit, and I told her that I hoped to see her in her official capacity, which would have meant that we had been successful in traveling to-and-from Russia. The reason I know her full name is that I looked it up on the Internet, under the aviation business name of Jeppersen. Not only does she work for the Customs outfit, she teaches at the local college, and according to what I found on the Internet, she has a PhD, writes for the Nome newspaper, perhaps serves on the city council, and is also a pilot. So why was I curious about this woman? It is because she casually mentioned that she had written a book titled <u>Aviation History</u> that Jeppersen carried. I was actually searching for information on the book and the rest of the stuff popped up. Besides the scenic country, this is what I like about flying in Alaska – you never know whom you will meet nor what they have contributed to mankind.

We watched forlornly as other planes departed from Nome to Provideniya. Even though we all knew that it was bureaucratic nonsense that kept the Antonov from returning to Mother Russia (although this particular plane had actually been built in Poland), we all shared some disappointment. But we couldn't languish long – there are plenty of other places that we could fly to in Alaska. The two things that stuck with me about this gaggle of ragtag vagabonds is that nobody complained during the entire odyssey, and all of us seemed to look forward to whatever adventure each day brought and take everything in stride.

About noon or so we departed northeast to Serpentine Hot Springs. Douglas and Neal did a low pass over the gravel runway, circled the ancient volcanic debris field and landed on the 1000-foot strip. Perfect landing. Not quite such a perfect stop! At the end of the runway near the bathhouse there was a place to turn the plane around. Only problem was, it was spongy tundra. We didn't sink much, just deep enough so that we were stuck. Had I been at the controls, we would probably have been stuck even worse. Then, the work began. All of us pitched in to unload the plane and we took almost everything out, including the gasoline-powered blender and the gasoline powered electric generator and food and beer from the freezer, cooking stuff, camping gear, baggage and sleeping bags, and other junk that people can really do without but don't think so. When everything was piled at outside one wondered how it all fit inside.

We pushed on the wings and the spars and we did it again because the first time and the fifth time the six-ton plane did not budge. And we unloaded some more. Had there been more than ten plastic five-gallon red jerry cans, we would have filled them with the planes fuel. Aviation gas weighs six pounds per gallon; you can do the math and come up with the same three hundred pounds of fuel that we drained. Next to the bathhouse is a large bunkhouse. We scrounged lumber from around the bunkhouse. One piece was about three inches thick, a foot wide, and three feet long. And we dug and dug some more and we built up layers of wooden planks beneath the tires. We could have used a come-along, and two exhausted hikers came along just in time (Sonja's words) to help. What I write in two paragraphs took two or three hours to perform. We all gave our muscles a workout while we raised the wings and pushed with all of our might after Douglas started the engine and opened up the throttle to full power, and the plane moved and Douglas skillfully shut it down before it ran out of boards, and we all cheered, Then we lay down some plywood and pushed the plane backwards onto the runway. And we all cheered. When I take the Stinson to Alaska, the back seats will be out and there will be a plywood floor in the back seat and a hydraulic jack and a come-along in the luggage compartment, because I might not be so lucky to have a ready source of lumber to help me out of some soggy tundra.

Roger loaned me a pair of Bermuda shorts and I went into the bathhouse for a little while, and the others did the same. Neal loaded the plane with the skill of NASA packing the shuttle for launch, while Douglas climbed on top of the plane and poured the fuel back into the tanks. The borrowed lumber was returned to the bunkhouse and the tire tracks we left were the only evidence of our journey to the hot springs.

Roughly four or five hours after our stop at the hot springs, we were once again airborne. Douglas set our course for North East to Kotzebue, which is thirty miles north of the Arctic Circle. For this segment of our journey, I logged 0.7 hour of flight time. Sonja sat in the right seat when Douglas landed the plane an hour or two later. The town looks pretty from the air, but I wasn't too impressed after we set down. We parked near the Alaskan Airlines terminal, and a fuel truck drove up. I think this was the most expensive fueling of the entire trip. I forgot how much fuel that we took on, but the $750 that Douglas was charged worked out to $3.75 a gallon. However, included in the cost was a $55 charge to roll the fuel truck. Ouch! While the fueling was going on, Roger talked to some guy who worked with the airport maintenance crews. He offered to take us into town in his car as soon as the Alaskan Airlines jet took off. Some people walked; I rode. We went through the town by a big building that is supposed to be a good museum, but it was closed. Our tour took us by the 22-bed hospital that looked like it could hold 200 people. We went by the pizza place and an old cemetery that also had graves marked with the Russian Orthodox crosses. We drove by the blue hotel overlooking the gray ocean that I had stayed in when I first visited the town in 1995. Before I Wintered-over in Antarctica, I spent a month in Alaska for training. I took a bump from the airlines, and used the free ticket one weekend to go to Kotzebue, only because it is located north of the Arctic Circle. The Alaskan Airlines 737 had stopped in Nome, and would stop again on the return flight. Before I stepped off the plane I thought I would rather go back to Nome, but the airline said I couldn't do it, unless I wanted to pay an extra charge. I didn't. So, I walked to the blue hotel and ate at the pizza place and watched the young men playing pool laugh and drink beer and then I walked past the graves marked with Russian Orthodox crosses back to the blue hotel overlooking the gray ocean.

Snowmobiles abounded. Whalebones could be seen on the beach, if I remember right. I thought, "Why would people want to live here?" And then I thought, "People might say the same thing about Bacliff, Texas". Onboard the flight to Kotzebue a young man sat behind me, handcuffed to a law enforcement officer, who was taking him to prison. I don't know why. Once, during the flight, the young man told the other man about a caribou hunt. I could tell that the kid was scared, and I felt sorry for him. I have often wondered if he has been released, and is caribou hunting again. But he probably can't hunt with a rifle anymore. Back at the blue hotel I almost felt trapped. And I thought of the kid going to prison, and then I realized that I was leaving the next day and it didn't seem so bad. He would not have minded being at the pizza place playing pool and laughing and drinking beer, nor walking past the graves marked with Russian Orthodox crosses back to the blue hotel that overlooked the gray ocean and whalebones, and hopping on a snowmobile.

  Something else happened that night. While watching the gray ocean from the second floor of the blue hotel, I met a man from Dutch Harbor who introduced me to the Holy Spirit. This is the first time I have written about this experience. Maybe this story on the An-2 isn't the right forum to do so, but it is the one I am choosing. I was drinking a cup of hot chocolate when he came in. I don't remember his name. For a while we sat in silence. I even resented having my solitude disturbed. Then he began to talk, and like a man on a mission, he started telling me about how the Holy Spirit is seldom really discussed, but that It is still one side of the Holy Trinity. He said that a person must receptive to receiving It, and that once It is received, it must be passed on to others. I haven't done a very good job of passing It to others. The discussion went on for perhaps an hour. He asked me if I would like to receive the Gift. So we stood up, he had me hold my palms facing up, and he held his hands facing down about an inch above mine. And he prayed, and asked that the Holy Spirit enter me. He told me that it might take a while for me to notice. A few months after going to Antarctica I was alone and started thinking about this. So I held my hands with palms facing upward, and invited the Holy Spirit in. Several minutes later I felt a jolt of energy surge through my entire body from my hands to my feet, almost as if I had been struck by lightening, and I had such a feeling of overwhelming peace.

I thought about these things after leaving Kotzebue. When we took off, Douglas let me sit in the right seat, and shortly afterwards, Sonja took his place in the left seat. Flying east towards Hughes, we flew over the Kobuk and Hog Rivers and lonely looking cabins and clumps of green marshes and swamps (what's the difference?) that probably had mosquitoes as big as moose. I don't know if we flew for forty miles or for one hundred miles over these wetlands, but I would have hated to land here in an emergency. Sonja gave me some excellent free flight instruction during the half-hour that I flew. The aircraft requires constant attention; I often had to readjust my altitude and/or course, especially after making a slight movement in the seat. Probably, that is a result of my lack of skill in this airplane. There is a Garman 295 GPS receiver onboard that I coordinated to our sectional charts. It was cloudy out and we had a good tailwind, but the ride seemed smooth. When Douglas took over for the landing, Sonja gave directions around the hills to Hughes. We crossed over the Koyukuk River and flew parallel to it for a while, and then made a long approach to the airport, which lays parallel to the river. Sonja is used to flying the twin-engine Navajo that flies much faster than the An-2. Our hundred-knot airplane lumbered along; Douglas gave it more throttle so we wouldn't land short – good idea! But, I have no doubt that had our landing been left to Sonja, she would have landed that plane probably about as well as she does the Navajo. Hughes is where Sidney Huntington was born in 1915.

Parked at Hughes

So instead of sleeping in an expensive ramshackle of a dorm in Provideniya, we pitched camp on the airport at Hughes. While we sat up the tents, Roger introduced himself to the few people around welcoming us at 10 PM. One man came up in a 4-wheeler and told us that he owned the laundromat, and that he would open it so we could take showers in the morning. Usually, it was only opened on Sundays, Tuesdays, and Thursdays. He sure wanted a ride in the Antonov. He came back a little later with tokens that cost $2.00 each to activate the showers for eight minutes. Douglas sacked out early in the back of the plane, Mary Lou and Jeanne pitched their own tent and disappeared, and Roger put his tent up away from the plane and disappeared. So, that left Neal, Sonja, and me telling each other stories in the big tent, until the rain came. Neal said that he, Douglas, Jeanne, and Mary Lou had all been friends for many years. The four of them, and some other friends, have discussed growing old together and watching out for each other, with no nursing homes nor assisted living centers. In an old man's creaky voice, he said, "Douglas, let's take the Antonov up one more time again, now that we are 115 years old", or words to that affect. It was either this night or later that Sonja told of flying an Indian woman who delivered a baby during the flight.

  Cap'n Neal (Dawg) is about my age, we both like adventure, and we both once lived in New Zealand, but the similarity stops there. He has lived in Africa, owns at least one deep-sea diving boat in Valdez that universities charter for scientific research and Exxon has charted in conjunction with the Valdez oil spill. He has also participated in studies of octopus, and has been involved with the discovery of new species. From what I understand, there is another boat that he either owns or has access to in the Caribbean. He told me that he could fly the Antonov, but considers it to be more Douglas's toy. I had no doubt from the beginning that he could fly it. He has flown gliders for fifty hours in both New Zealand and in Africa. We have different religious and political opinions but I followed Mark Twain's advice and discussed neither. He treated me well and I would still fly with him again.

  When we finally hit the sack, I claimed the same seats behind the cockpit that I had used the previous night, only Neal had taken bags out so I had more room; he slept in a hammock hung from the ceiling of the plane, and Sonja used a cot that Neil set up in the mid-section of the plane near the door. The freezer was behind my two airline seats, but in front of the area where Sonja slept. The small table had to be removed so her cot could be assembled. Just like in a motor home, only this one has a 1000 horsepower motor with a big fan attached. I hung my jacket up by the cockpit entrance to keep out the bright light from an annoying rotating beacon located near the plane.

August 11th

When I woke up, Douglas had the coffee perking and pancakes bubbling on the hot grill. I used my shower token immediately. Roger was in the laundromat drying clothes wet from the rain that leaked into his tent. Jeanne and Mary Lou had had a cold windy night in their tent. These ladies had just completed a ten-day kayaking or canoe trip down the Yukon prior to joining the An-2 trip. They were used to camping out, and found the plane confining. Here I was proud of just flying across the famous river, and they had been riding its waves. Makes my flight across it seem kind of insufficient!

For twenty years Jeanne and Mary Lou had taught together, and had traveled the world together. Jeanne told me that she was born in Greenwich Village, New York, to parents that had been "Beatniks". You don't hear that word much any more. In the Sixties, she lived in a commune in Arkansas, then migrated to Taos, New Mexico. Somewhere along the way she moved to Valdez. She has two master's degrees, one of which is in Computer Science. According to Mary Lou, Jeanne is a gifted teacher that gave all to her students, but Jeanne told me that sometimes the school year seemed like a prison sentence. As soon as they both worked the required twenty years in Alaska, they retired. It was either this Monday, or the following one, that Jeanne felt her retirement kick in, because school started or would start without her. Her next big adventure is to ride a horse on a 500-mile trip in Argentina this fall. When you are only around people for less than a week, you don't hear a lifetime of the stories that made them whom they are. The ones I did hear were fascinating.

Mary Lou lives in Hawaii, has owned at least one charter boat, and has a grandson that is about a month older than my granddaughter Camyrn. You would never know it to look at her. She has a smile that could go on a magazine cover. (In fact, each of the three women on the trip looks younger than their actual ages.) Joe, a friend of hers in Hawaii, encouraged her to go on this trip. Even though the plane didn't make it to Russia, all of us in the group had a lot of fun together flying around Alaska. Next summer, the plane will not be based in Alaska. Who knows if it will ever fly across the Bering Sea?

While we ate breakfast, one of the twin-engine Navajos belonging to Warbelow's Air Ventures flew in on a mail run. Sonja talked to the pilot. He visited the An-2, and took some photos with his digital camera. There was a good one of me "propping" the plane, but I don't have permission to use it in this book.

Around 11 AM we took off to Fairbanks via Tanana. We flew over the Melozina River. For this particular flight segment, Douglas stayed in the pilot's seat, Sonja sat in the co-pilot's seat, and I stood behind them with my headset plugged in. Because Sonja has such an extensive in-depth knowledge of the area and Douglas's thorough familiarity with his airplane, it was a good combination of talent in the cockpit (although I would have been just as comfortable if Neal had been flying instead of Douglas). I am sure I could have handled the flying, just not as proficiently as the other three pilots. West of Tanana we could see the Yukon River in the distance off our right wing. Sonja apologized later for routing us over some hills directly to the East that soon became shrouded in rain clouds, but I don't fault her. We did some scud running (dodging clouds) for a little while before we made a Westbound turn straight into a rainbow, then we banked to the South and intercepted the Yukon River. We followed the Yukon to where the Tanana River flows into it, and then we followed the Tanana to Fairbanks. Shortly after leaving the Tanana town area, the weather cleared up, and I sat down in the pilot's seat. Sonja asked me if it was OK if she piloted the plane on into Fairbanks, because she was thinking of leaving our group there. An hour later, she banked the plane on final approach to runway 19 Left before Douglas took over. I had flown on four different days with her. There is no doubt in my mind that she is a superb pilot.

There is a camping strip at Fairbanks airport for itinerant airplanes and people that has pavilions with tables and bar-b-que pits and a place to park planes. Douglas taxied the plane the length of the strip and turned it around and went back mid-field. The right wing was about one foot higher than the roof of the pavilion. The only other airplane on the camping strip was a Rockwell Commander that had just flown in from Oshkosh, Wisconsin. After we landed, Sonja met up with her friend Robert, whom she had flown with to Anchorage in his Maule

4, five days earlier. A few days earlier, John Runkle had given some frozen but un-gutted whitefish to Douglas that he placed in the freezer. Sonja and Robert took the fish to Robert's place for cleaning, and later brought them back along with salad fixings.

The rest of the day was rather uneventful. Roger left to rent a car and stay with friends or relatives. Tents once again popped up. A year earlier I had flown with Michael Vivion in his C-170B on floats, so I called to see about flying with him again, but he couldn't fly that day. Oh well, hopefully, we can fly another day together. Sometime during the day Jeanne paid me one of the highest compliments I have ever received: She called me a true Alaskan. We had been sitting around the picnic table chatting, and in the conversation I talked about the number of times I had been to the state, and how much I liked it, and how much of it I had seen. It would not bother me at all to actually move there, when the time is right.

While I walked around, a pickup stopped and the driver asked me if he could take me anywhere. I told him that I would like a coke, so he drove me to a pilot's lounge. It turned out that he is manager of the airport, or at least someone high up on the scale. Later, when I talked to Karoline from the payphone located a few pavilions down from ours, I saw a Fairbanks Airport Police SUV driven by a lady police officer go by, heading for the plane. For the second time in two days a uniformed woman came to the plane. I thought there might be a problem with the plane's wing being over the roof of the pavilion, but found this was not the case. I don't think she stopped then, but a few hours later she did when I was back at the plane. Prior to her arrival, Neal had asked me if I wanted to take a closer look at that round engine. It's impressive! He had been standing on a ladder next to the open cowling of the huge radial engine while Douglas walked around the upper wings and the top of the fuselage. The lady police officer with razor sharp creases on her uniform stepped out of the SUV about the time Neal went back up the ladder. Her first words surprised me; instead of saying something official, she said that she used to work as an A & P. Her name is Catherine Hamilton. I have to admit I have wondered what events took this woman down her career path to working as an airplane mechanic and then on to an airport police officer. Obviously, over the years she has encountered many different airplanes but this one held a special fascination for her. I wandered off again as she talked to Neal and

Douglas. Later, I found out that she had once been in the Bahamas on a boat with a hot tub in the aft section when Neal had been its captain.

Douglas and Mary Lou with blender that is powered by a weed-eater engine

During the evening, other people came to admire the plane. The fish were cooked over the bar-b-que grill, and the gasoline-powered blender mixed up a few more drinks. Douglas asked me if I would like to have a non-alcoholic drink, which tasted good. I should have walked past the trees to see the sunset, but managed to photograph the plane at that time, anyway.

When the sky became darker and people drifted away, I walked into the plane to find Neal working on the cot so I could have a better place to sleep. He told me that he felt guilty about me sleeping in the plane's front seats, but I told him I had done so by my own choice. Douglas came into the plane and went into his bedroom in the tail section, closing the Japanese-style door behind him. So once again, I had the whole cabin area to myself. I have to admit, sleeping on the cot was more comfortable than the airplane seats, but I wouldn't have minded using the seats, anyway.

August 12th

For the Antonov's size and power, burning fifty gallons of gas an hour probably isn't unreasonable. With a fuel capacity of 317 gallons, the plane can fly for about five-and-a-half hours and still have enough fuel left in the tanks to satisfy the 45-minute reserve required by the FAA. As mentioned earlier, Roger seemed to know everyone.

Because of his connections, a fuel truck came to the airpark and the driver pumped 250 gallons into the thirsty An-2 at about 75% of the going rate of $3.05 per gallon.

Once again, the tents were taken down and everything was loaded back in the plane. Sonja came to say goodbye, as did Catherine, along with Alexander, her son who is about ten or eleven. He may not realize for a long time the gift of seeing this airplane that his mother gave to him. If I had to guess, she probably did not sleep well the previous night because the emotions of seeing that plane and wanting to fly to the end of the rainbow pounced upon her soul so strongly that she knew she absolutely had to share them with him. I encouraged her to bring him along and join us on our southbound journey. Catherine did not give into the temptation of hopping on an airplane on the spur-of-the-moment, only because real life responsibilities of jobs and family commitments overrode her heart's desire. As I strapped into the co-pilot's seat for takeoff, I saw her drive away. I thought she was going to leave before we started the engine. But she parked her car near the South end of the airpark, and stood with Alexander, waiting for the turning of the prop, the cough of the engine, the puff of white smoke, and then, the throaty roar as all nine cylinders started firing. She waved when we taxied by, longing to be with us, not minding the prop blast blowing her hair.

Once airborne, we followed the Tanana River towards Nenana, then headed South, flying East of the Parks Highway (which is the road between Fairbanks and Anchorage) and staying well away from the radomes of Clear AFB. Before we passed through the mountains near Healy, I turned over the co-pilot's position to Neal. We started to encounter some down drafts; right after Neal took my place, Douglas gave it full throttle to climb, but the vertical speed indicator showed that we were actually descending. The fact that I am writing this story makes it obvious that we cleared the mountains, but in retrospect, I think I should have started increasing the altitude earlier, since I was the one flying before Neal took over. I hope I learned a lesson that I never have to use: Strong head winds, downdrafts, and lack of sufficient altitude and visibility when flying near mountains can kill you. How do I know that we had strong head winds? Well, when the air speed indicator reads about 100 knots, and the GPS receiver shows a ground speed of 32 knots, even this rocket scientist can do the math.

Douglas and Neal flew low along the Parks Highway and the river that runs parallel to it, which I think is the Nenana River. Through the portholes on both sides of the airplane I could see both, as well as peaks of trees higher than the wings of the plane. As mountains go, the peaks we saw on both sides of the road, when we could see them, are only about 8000 feet high, 6000 feet higher than the river and the road. The NATO name for the An-2 is the An-2 Colt; this colt bucked as if it was saddled for the first time. We bounced and we bounced. Not wanting to prove a cartographer wrong, Windy Pass lived up to its name. And we bounced some more. Let's land at that runway that's off to the right. Is this where they named the Wind Mariah? I'm sitting next to Jeanne, facing aft, near the center of the plane. She has her head down on her hands, leaning on the table. Running through my head is the old adage, "It is better to be on the ground wishing you were up in the air, than to be in the air wishing you were on the ground". I wished that I were on the ground. I thought I might have to use my hat, the South Pole cap with all the pins, for another purpose than to cover up my bald spot, because I couldn't reach anything else without unstrapping my seatbelt, and to do that could mean being splattered on the door. How can Douglas and Neal even see anything? I wish we would land. Let's go back to that runway we saw a few miles back. The plane went into a sudden bank. A few minutes later Douglas landed us at the gravel strip at Summit, located just South of Cantwell. We stop, and the prop stopped. I didn't notice the prop stopping, because I was opening the door for Jeanne. Somehow, through all of this past hour, I managed not to share breakfast, and once outside, the cold wind blowing the rain on my face helped. It was probably a good thing that Catherine and Alexander had stayed in Fairbanks.

 An hour later the sky had cleared somewhat, the rain had ceased, we were ready to go. I stood behind Douglas and Neal; my thoughts weren't on the unforgettable sound of the radial engine making its dragon roar. As if to prove that it could handle more wind and rain than its human cargo, the Antonov easily lifted off the runway. I don't remember the sequence of whether we tried to go further South, and then turned back and flew to Cantwell airport, or if we went to Cantwell first. I guess it really doesn't matter. When we flew to the Cantwell airport, the conditions just weren't right. Some lady on the ground talked to us on the radio and told us about the landing strip, so we either headed further south or back to Summit. Weather definitely deteriorated to very poor visibility and heavy rain near Igloo, so we turned back North. This time the wind pushed us at a ground speed of 156 knots, as indicated on the GPS display. Once again, we landed at Summit, at approximately 4 PM.

The same massive weather front that we would have had to fight had we gone to Russia was now tearing up the State. For the next four hours, we pretty much stayed inside the plane. For a while, I sat in the cockpit reading <u>Shadows on the Koyukuk</u>. I had left my South Pole hat back on the table. Neal looked at it, and asked me if I had an An-2 pin. Douglas had given me one earlier, but it was still on the hat that my sister's dog had chewed up a couple weeks before. I mentioned that to Neal, and he told me to grab another pin, so now I have two. One is a spare. We ate some of the candy bars that had been bought to give to the Russians. We started having discussions about where we would all sleep. I opted to go back to the seats behind the cockpit, and was ready to take one of the pilot's seats. Jeanne said she didn't want to sleep in the plane, but I don't think she relished fighting the cold wind again. While these conversations were going on, some guy drove up in a white flatbed truck. He said people in Cantwell had been talking about the An-2 flying over, and they figured we probably were out at Summit. He said that there was a bunkhouse where we could all stay the night. It didn't take long before we all gathered a few items and crowded into the truck.

At the bunkhouse the same lady whom had talked to us on the radio welcomed us. I don't remember her first name, but she and her husband Ray Atkins own the bunkhouse near the Cantwell airport, where they also run their business, Atkins Guiding & Flying Service. They make their living as outfitters, and are used to having several people staying there at a time. The guy who drove us there took us to a local tavern, where supposedly we could have something to eat, but apparently, the food cooking wasn't done there anymore, or it was too late, or something. Anyway, we had to beg for a ride to the "Lazy J" restaurant, about two miles away. Noisy construction workers chatted with us. I asked to use the phone to call the "Lazy J" to see if they were still open. The bartender with a big handlebar mustache pointed to the phone behind the bar. I didn't know that the others had been talking to someone about giving us a ride to the restaurant, so I announced while I was behind the bar that I would buy beer to anyone whom would take us there. The bartender said I ought to buy a round of drinks. I forgot that this is Alaska, where the prices are high. I agreed, but only had $40.00 that I was willing to spend. I asked him how much a round would cost, and he said, $70.00. Then he told me I had to leave the area behind the bar. Mary Lou said she laughed when she saw me standing behind it. I asked the others if they would chip in the other $30.00, and I was told basically to shut up. Someone else had already agreed to give us a ride, and wouldn't accept any beer. So the six of us clamored into the back of a small Japanese import pickup and were on our way.

At the restaurant I ordered a hamburger that tasted very good. While waiting for the food, Neal and I talked about the dangers of mountain flying. He said the two good friends of his, both of whom were excellent pilots, had been killed as a result of severe downdrafts in turbulent weather. They used to work for Alaska Air Taxi, the company that I had flown with four years ago when Brian Collier, Bob Simle, and Hawks Abbott went salmon fishing together. I knew of the people whom Neal had talked about, because the blonde lady pilot was featured in the videotape, "Bush Pilots of Alaska". We finished our meal near closing time; the owner agreed to give a ride back to the bunkhouse. One more pickup, a lot more fun! Each of us picked out a bunk and unrolled our sleeping bags. I chose an upper bunk; on the wall above my head somebody had left a dirty baseball cap that had the word "Alaska" and a floatplane embroidered on the front. I hope to find a new one sometime just like it that I can buy. But, like my friend Bob Simle told me about an Alaskan Airlines pilot flying 737s into Dutch Harbor saying that wearing a hat or belt buckle with the words "Bush Pilot" inscribed does not make you a bush pilot. You must be able to read and respond to the weather.

Hot coffee and pancakes awaited us in the Atkins's house. I don't think any of us minded paying the $20.00 they charged each of us for the room and board. Ray Atkins is a master guide and air taxi operator, and it is obvious that he and his wife have put in many years of hard work building their business. They showed us albums filled with photographs of successful hunters and fishermen (and women). Inside their house is a large room with heads of several animals they have taken in Alaska and in Africa. I was able to use their computer and delete the 250 pieces of junk e-mail spam that had accumulated in the last week. Another pilot and his wife had been stranded by the weather, having flown in from Palmer the day before in their Cessna 170. He flies the big stuff for Northwest Airlines. This guy showed me the satellite image of the weather front that dwarfed Alaska. I had a better understanding why the An-2 Colt had been a bucking bronco the day before. Neal and Douglas had gone back to the plane to check it over. As I finished deleting e-mail, the aviation radio came to life: "Cantwell traffic, Experimental 87AN turning base for runway ..." I grabbed my camera and ran outside to the airstrip, managing to capture the Antonov coming in for a landing. We all gathered our belongings off the plane.

Douglas and Neal bringing the An-2 into Cantwell

My plane back to Houston left later this same evening, so I had made arrangements to catch the 1:30 PM bus from Cantwell to Anchorage. Before long, Neal, Douglas, Jeanne, Mary Lou, and Roger had decided to ride the same bus. Ray and his wife drove us to the gas station where the bus stopped. These are good people, and I really thank them for their hospitality. The bus driver announced that someone could take the vacant seat in the front, so I grabbed it. Two or three times a week he drove the 350 miles between Fairbanks and Anchorage. He teaches high school in Fairbanks. Neal and Douglas made a good decision not to fly the plane, because we drove through some pretty (or not so pretty) menacing weather. Riding the bus wasn't as much fun as flying the Antonov, but that day it was much safer. We pulled into Anchorage at 6:30 PM. Roger called a friend to take him to a house that he owns in Anchorage, and the rest of us took a cab to the airport. I had about an hour's wait for my flight back to Houston. I arrived home about 9 AM the next morning, slept a couple of hours, and went back to work that afternoon, exhausted but still vividly at the controls of the An-2.

Flying the Antonov in Alaska for five days gave me a microcosm insight to what bush flying is really about. We encountered political boundaries and stormy weather, became stuck in the tundra, saw some magnificent scenery, and met some great people. Even if I go to Alaska and fly for a year or two in the bush, I could never hope to be as good of a pilot as the old time bush pilots. But I can certainly enjoy flying there as much as they do.

EPILOG

Douglas, Jeanne, Neal, and Mary Lou had a car where the An-2 had been parked several days earlier. I think Mary Lou stayed in Anchorage – but Neal, Douglas, and Jeanne drove to Valdez that night, arriving about 2 AM. Douglas went to work the next morning. I found this out a couple of weeks later, when I called Douglas. He said that it took eight days before the weather cleared good enough for him and Neal to be able to fly their Stinson to Cantwell to retrieve the Antonov.

I hope that I have written this chapter on the life of Antonov An-2 N87AN as worthy as she flew. I may not be able to write all of its chapters, but the idea of Douglas and Neal taking me along on all their trips as the An-2 historian – well, I'm not convinced that there won't be another time for me to sit in front of a computer machine and hammer and bang out more episodes.

My thanks go to God for giving me the opportunity to fly the Antonov and the wanderlust disease for which I hope I am never cured, and to Karoline for allowing me to peak over the next hill, and to Douglas and Neal for inviting me along on this trip, and to Jeanne, Mary Lou, Sonja, and Roger for the fun and company during this adventure, and I hope to cross paths again with each of you, and with all the wonderful people whom I met along the way. God Bless.

Jeanne's words of the trip

"I'm sorry, but your permission to fly to Russia has not yet been granted." The words echoed and a wave of disappointment resonated before our eyes. We had filled out 80 pages of paperwork, gotten our Visas from the Russian Embassy, faxed in our passenger manifest and traveled......all the way to Nome.

We had a huge going away party in Anchorage, well wishers stopping by the big plane at Lake Hood, hors d'oeuvres were served, the blender with the lawn mower engine whipped up delicious drink concoctions and everyone wished us a Bon Voyage. Early the next morning we took off for Nikolai, a native village just this side of McGrath---the first nights stop.

At Nikolai we were greeted by the entire village---barefoot kids, teenagers on 4 wheelers, the principal teacher, village elders, and the city manager handling out pens inscribed with "Welcome to the City of Nikolai—enjoy your stay!" We were invited to tour the school---very impressive, visit the Russian Orthodox Church---charming in its rustic beauty, visit the oldest resident of the village and hear his stories of the Old Times, and enjoy a tasty fish fry in our honor.

We camped happily that evening, and early the next morning (after a blueberry pancake breakfast) the City Manager, Roger, approached us and asked if there was, perhaps, an extra seat on the plane. Yes, there was, and he scurried home, grabbed his sleeping bag and tent and vowed to continue the journey with us! Us being: Sonja, a former commercial pilot for United Airlines, now living in Fairbanks and flying for an air charter service, Matt, an adventure seeker from Houston (Texas, that is!), Mary Lou from Maui, Hawaii (and a former resident of Valdez), Neal Oppen and Douglas Fulton who co-own the big bird, and me! We took off, waving a very fond farewell to all of the wonderful villagers who came to say goodbye.

A brief fuel stop in McGrath was next, and the City Manager proved himself invaluable to our trip---he secured us a truck so that we could all bounce around on the dirt roads and take a tour of McGrath.

I must say, they have the nicest espresso stand around that part of the country---and a very famous bar as well.

Then on to Nome! That famous gold city by the Sea! The terminus of the Iditarod Dog Sled Race! We got there just in time to have a dinner rendezvous with all the other pilots and passengers getting staged for the air convoy to Russia. Basically, 8 other planes and a total of around 20 people were signed up, paperwork in order, fuel tanks filled, GPS's waypointed, ready to cross the Bearing Straits and eager to complete and celebrate the first opening of the VFR route for private planes to Russia. And, alas, as irony would have it, our plane, a Russian Built Antonov AN-2, the workhorse of the Russian air fleet, was the only airplane not immediately granted permission to land in Russia, because it is, only in the U.S. mind you, considered "experimental".

That wave of disappointment that crossed our faces quickly dissipated---there was much to do and see in that part of Alaska, and we were ready!

After a celebratory evening in Nome we departed the next morning for the Serpentine Hot Springs---about 100 miles North of Nome. We were forewarned that the runway was short---oh, about 900 feet in length, be we were told that we PROBABLY would be able to land there---just to be really careful! And careful we were, the landing was skillfully executed, and just as we all clapped and shouted hurray, we realized that the pilots had not shared in our joy.....actually they were pretty quiet, because...we were stuck...in the tundra...in the middle of ...nowhere. The pilots had decided to turn the plane around to prepare for take off, and had just barely left the runway and used a wee bit of the tundra to turn on and then, the big plane had sunk, and was still sinking, and not so slowly.

Did I mention that we had 7 wonderful people on board? Well, everyone pitched in and emptied the plane, an amazing amount of luggage, food and survival gear (not to mention the chest freezer, microwave, tables, etc. etc.) We even removed as much fuel as we could to lighten up the 6 ton beast. And we dug, and pushed and rocked and just when we were scratching our heads, 2 hikers appeared out of nowhere! With the increase in person power and the Antonov's mighty engine, we were able to get unstuck and finally enjoy the Hot Springs.

The Springs flow out of the ground in an area of tors---magna plus from an ancient volcano, at a scorching temperature but when mixed with the cool water from the local stream, make for a very pleasant soak. There is a structure built over pool, as well as a rustic kitchen and a bunkhouse. Certainly one of the nicest, and most remote, hot springs in Alaska.

On to Kotzebue and a grand tour of the City. One person we met there told us that the last time he had visited the hot Springs he saw a Cessna 206 flipped over on one end of the runway and a Stinson overturned on the other. Wow---we felt SO lucky!

We continued on and that night we landed in the tiny native village of Hughes---a beautiful village of around 60 folks in a pristine setting on the Koyukuk River, surrounded by forested hills. We received a very warm greeting in Hughes and the Washeteria was opened especially for us! I wonder if they were trying to tell us something!

Then on to Fairbanks where we camped at the Air Camp Park-- what a terrific idea--just like a car camper park, but for Airplanes! A lot of folks stopped by to visit us and take a tour of the plane, help with dinner, and some even came back the next morning to bring us breakfast---ya gotta love that!

Trying to beat out the incoming weather we left early and had Talkeetna in our visions, but the weather beat us to it and we were forced to land at Summit Air Strip—about 10 miles south of Cantwell. Stuck, we thought, we are stuck and grounded, but before we knew it, a pickup truck appeared and offered to take us to a hunting lodge where we could stay in the bunkhouse for next to nothing! We didn't have to be invited twice, off we went to Cantwell where we had delightful dinner, a cozy bunkhouse, and even a home cooked breakfast in the morning!

The weather report was not looking good for the next 36 hours, so we secured the plane, said goodbye to our generous hosts, and hopped on a bus to Anchorage.

And, you may ask—what is the NEXT adventure? Well, beginning Sept. 12 we will be flying the big plane down to California--- Lake Tahoe and many points in between. And yes, we DO have some seats available, so if you have the time, and the inkling for adventure--- come JOIN us! You can contact Jeanne or Douglas at 907 835-5150. Happy trails!

E-Mails

(to-and-from Catherine Hamilton)
hey neal,

the lumbering antonov and its hugely personable crew and entourage left an enormous vacuum after slowly disappearing into the murky afternoon tuesday. for the next two nights as i patrolled our little airport, my glance down air park avenue revealed a large hole – the space somehow stretched and distorted like a pair of leggings recently vacated by their legs.

alexander and i watched the antonov become one with the air without the slightest appearance of effort. as it lifted off in what seemed an impossibly short distance, something stirred in me. it took me the better part of the day to trace the stirrings back to the "supernatural slow-motion takeoff" of donald shimoda's travel air 4000 in richard bach's "illusions". i enjoyed considering a number of other similarities between their story and yours. for example, both stories involve two barnstorming vagabonds who meet...because each is doing what he really wants to do." and they, like you, share their gifts so that people return home, to their lives, with a wonderful feeling inside. i also noticed that there were no bugs smashed on your propeller...

i consider the antonov mission – as i understood it – the jimmy buffett-esque pursuit of enjoying this life and sharing it with all who wish to partake. it dawned on me, in taking stock of the goodness that i felt in the antonov wake (prop wash), that whether you are aware of it or not, your mission is a humanitarian one. or so i think. i would love to hear what your – perceived or realized – goal is in the antonov wanderings. and like the reluctant believer that richard bach is, i am curious: "what's in it for you?" and, "why do you bother with people like me?"

so neal, thanks to you and douglas and jeanne. also to the others on this particular trip who drew me into the antonov adventure. i hope some day to be a part of it.

peace, love, light, cc

From: Matthew A. Nelson
Subject: Antonov photos from one of its vagabonds

Hi Catherine,

Douglas faxed me a copy of the email that you sent Neal about seeing the An-2 in Fairbanks. I am the guy with all the hatpins that tried to get you and your son to come along to Anchorage. I hope you don't mind that I contacted you. I just wanted to share with you some photos of the plane. The landing photos were taken at Cantwell.

I am in the process of writing a story about our trip, but it may take two-three more weeks before I finish it. If you want, I will send you a copy of the story, along with some other travel stories that I have written, including one that's 77 pages long about my life around airplanes. Please send me your address if you are interested. I am lucky that Karoline, my wife of 31 years, allows me to pursue my traveling dreams when I can afford it and can manage the time off work. Two days after leaving Fairbanks I was in the hot Houston, Texas area and back at work and seeing my 5-month old granddaughter who is my pride and joy.

I admire the fact that you brought your son out to see the plane.

Your email to Neal is absolutely fabulous. It is pure poetry. I looked up "Illusions..", and discovered a book that I will have to buy. I hope it's OK with you that Neal forwarded it to Douglas, and that he sent me a copy. I would like to have your permission to include the entire email in my An-2 story. I don't live the vagabond lifestyle, but I had an opportunity to go on that plane, so I took it. No regrets, even though we didn't make it to Russia.

I am taking the liberty to try and answer the question, "Why do you bother with people like me?".. It is because you are one in spirit with the rest of us. You wanted so badly to board that airplane. It is only because of your love for your family, your sense of responsibility, and the reality of having bills to pay that you didn't come with us.

God Bless,
Matt Nelson

From: Catherine Chandler Hamilton
Subject: Antonov friendship circle

Dear Matt,

What a nice surprise to receive your mail with fond reminders of the Antonov visit to Fairbanks. Now, 3 weeks after the fact, our little airpark here still seems forlorn with the collective absence of that grand airplane and its wonderful cast and crew. It is pretty tough to top an act like that. It is really neat that you are writing about this adventure - one chapter of many in the life of N87AN but one of a very few, I'm quite sure, that ever makes it to paper. Perhaps they should take you along on all of their trips as their historian.... I thank you for your compliments on my letter including your desire to include it in your manuscript - I will happily give you permission to include my letter and accept your offer to read your story (and your other writings) when you are finished. I thank you too for answering the question about 'why you bother with people like me', I definitely felt like I was with kindred spirits in the short time that I got to spend with you all. Neal kindly answered the question too with much the same gist as your own response. As you swelter in the Texas heat, we are taking inventory of the signs of fall time - the geese and the cranes flying through in increasingly larger and larger flocks, clumps of leaves turning yellow like lights coming on in the windows of a big building at dusk, children returning to school, the tundra aflame in regal yellows and reds – a lovely contrast to the tenacious greens. Soon, 3 weeks or so, we'll smell the wood smoke from the stoves of cabin dwellers as they melt the cold edges off early mornings and late, cool nights. Thanks again for writing and sharing - greetings to Karoline and a fortunate granddaughter.

peace, love, light, cc

Flying the An-2 in Guatemala and El Salvador, 2005

PRELUDE *(copied again from the previous page)*

From: Catherine Chandler Hamilton (September 2003)
Subject: Antonov friendship circle

Dear Matt,

It is really neat that you are writing about this adventure (Flying the An-2 in Alaska) - *one chapter of many in the life of N87AN but one of a very few, I'm quite sure, that ever makes it to paper. Perhaps they should take you along on all of their trips as their historian....*

As much as I would like to be the historian for this airplane, at this time I can only add one more chapter in the life of N87AN, but hopefully, will add many more in the future.

About a year-and-a-half had passed since I had last seen Neal Douglas, and Jeanne after our little adventure of flying the An-2 around in Alaska. In September 2003, they flew their plane to California. Later, they took the Antonov to Central America, flying and camping around Mexico, Belize, Costa Rica, Panama, Guatemala, and El Salvador. Perhaps they went to other countries, but I don't know for sure. I was invited to join them on that trip, but didn't. They left the plane at the Guatemala City airport in March 2004 and went back to Valdez, Alaska for the Summer. We kept in touch, and by Thanksgiving time, I had bought an airline ticket to Guatemala, with an "open-jaw" return from El Salvador. In the past few years there has been an air show in El Salvador during the last weekend of January, so our intentions were to fly the Antonov to the air show, and then after the show I would leave El Salvador to come back to Houston. Things pretty much worked out that way, except there was no air show in El Salvador.

January 26th

A few minutes after takeoff from Houston's George Bush Intercontinental Airport, the Continental Airlines Boeing 737 crossed over Galveston Island and then the deep blue waters of the Gulf of Mexico came into view. Occasionally, I saw a freighter. As we approached the Yucatan Peninsula, the color of the water became more of a greenish-blue. As we flew over Mexico, I could see the many small farms and villages, where people are just trying to make a living. Gradually, the farms disappeared into the green foliage of a jungle. Off to the West I could see several volcanoes. Some had the classic conic shape, while others now look tired after millions of years of surrendering to the forces of nature and gravity and erosion. In their younger years, they too had proudly once roared like dragons, with their breath of rotten eggs and their mouths spitting molten fire. Now they are like old drunken men, collapsed, sunken, wrapped with blankets of trees and rocks to keep warm as they bask in the sun, because they long ago spewed their fiery innards from deep within the earth, as I did once spewed my fiery innards from deep within after a bottle of rum. They called me the Volcan Mateo!

Had I been sitting on the left side of the 737 during the landing, I would have seen the An-2 when we taxied to the terminal building. Momentary glancing at my passport, the immigration official smiled and waved me through; likewise, the customs official just collected my form and welcomed me to Guatemala. Douglas told me to meet him on the second floor of the terminal building; as I headed up the stairs he was walking down. I converted some US dollars to Quetzales; we grabbed a bite to eat and walked to the airplane. We walked through a security check point, shortly thereafter turned right, and there it was, parked so that it faced the hangars and in such a position that it could see me when I came into view, almost as if it was waiting for me to show up. Antonov An-2, tail number N87AN, looked majestic as it welcomed me back. Was that my imagination, or did it really smile when it saw me? I know I smiled when I saw it.

It is of Russian design, built in Poland, and now owned by a couple of Americans. I never did like the Russian politics and the bad things they did to people and their rotten Commie philosophy, but I have to admit they know how to build a good airplane. I spent my military years in the Sixties silently fighting the Cold War, so I have it ingrained in my system. I even feel somewhat guilty about wanting to fly on a Russian airplane, but not any more than I did while visiting the Soviet launch complex in Baikonur in 1992 to see the launch of the

Soyuz TM-15 spacecraft. NASA is now in partnership with the Russians on the International Space Station. My cameras are made in Japan and have German designed lenses; I drove my parents Volkswagen to the New York World's Fair in 1964; Karoline drives a Honda Pilot. Times change, and old adversaries now have mutual business dealings, even if the trust between each other is not so mutual. So, while my loyalties are very strongly American, I appreciate good engineering, and the chance to have another good adventure flying in such a well-built plane like the An-2.

For three or four hours Douglas and I worked to make the plane ready to fly. I transferred oil from quart bottles into gallon jugs. I wiped up oil off the plane. I transferred oil from the plane and the gallon jugs to the shirt and jeans and boots and Mountain Lakes Seaplane Training hat that I wore. We stayed busy, and I know I did more things than transfer oil, but now I don't remember what they were, nor do I remember much of what Douglas did. Airplanes with names on their sides, such as United, Delta, Continental, COPA, TACA, and DHL, taxied by us. DHL uses older 727s that have ear-shattering jet engines. When the 757s taxied by, it looked as if their wingtips might strike the An-2's tail, for it was parked on the grass next to the taxiway. Several general aviation airplanes landed and took off; I liked seeing the DC-3s still in service. One pilot came up in a Cessna 206 or 210 that had a red cross painted on its tail. He said that the plane had been donated by "Wings of Hope" and he uses it to fly medical supplies to the remote villages in Guatemala. I'm sure he has a bunch of stories to tell. Bored young soldiers or policemen carrying 12-guage shotguns, spaced about 100 meters apart, guarded the airport, standing for hours on end, except when a plane needed to have access to or from the taxiway, when they would move orange safety cones.

Around 4 PM Douglas and I were given a ride in a minivan to the town of Antigua, approximately 50 miles away. The cost: $5.00 a piece. Douglas had made the arrangements, and the driver and his friend waited for us near the plane while we finished up for the day. It took a little while to leave the big city traffic, but the driver did a good job of dodging most of the black smoke clouds emitting from the diesel buses and trucks. Once we were on a major highway the traffic thinned; about an hour later the driver turned off the highway into the cobblestone streets of Antigua. We drove through several narrow streets, lined with multi-colored pastel stucco walls. Occasionally, I could see nice courtyards hiding behind some ornately carved doors. A huge conic volcano overlooks the town. The driver dropped us off near the Aurora Hotel, where we eventually caught up with Jeanne, and Nancy Johnson. Nancy is Douglas's sister and lives in Anchorage, where she works in the sales department of the KTUU TV station.

The two women had been out shopping. They weren't at the hotel, but the lady that works there told us that they had found another hotel because the Aurora didn't have reservations for them that night. We had an hour to wait, so Douglas and I went into a cantina, where we ordered a mixed drink: Papaya and pineapple juice. I generally don't care for pineapple, but the mixture was just right. I was a little concerned about this guy Montezuma, but during my stay in Central America I never had to endure his revenge. The water for the drink came out of a five gallon jug, so I just had to take it on faith that it was good drinking water. After the drink we went looking for a hardware store, and sure enough we found one. Douglas needed a wire brush; a lady tried to help us; we pointed to one on the wall about the time a man who spoke English walked up. He brought out a whole basket full, so Douglas paid the required 35 cents or so. Then we went into a small grocery store to buy some paper towels. The brush had to be worth more than the paper towels, but the three-roll package cost about the equivalent of $6.00. We figured out later the American brand name might have something to do with it.

Cathedral in Antigua

On one side of the city square there is a very wide white Catholic Church. It makes for some good night time photos. I guess Antigua has been discovered by retired Americans and the younger backpackers. I can see the why of the attraction, but at the same time, hope that the city can retain its charm and not turn into the box that has to be checked for the "You just gotta see it – It's Awesome!" type of places.

Douglas and I walked back to the Aurora Hotel and found Jeanne and Nancy waiting for us. We found a taxi and went to their new hotel to drop off luggage. It is located about three blocks from the town square, and I don't remember the name of it. It wasn't as nice as the Aurora, but it certainly was better than the place where Douglas, Neal, and I stayed. Nancy and Jeanne had a room that I think cost about $10 -12 a person, as opposed to the $4 per person that we guys paid. The four of us (Neal hadn't arrived yet) went out to dinner and I had fajitas, which were very similar to the ones I eat in Texas. Jeanne and Nancy talked about their visit to the church, and to a museum next door. They marveled how the priest had encouraged them to touch books that were over 400 years old. Jeanne speaks Spanish quite well, so I imagine that had something to do with the kindness of the priest. After a dinner that lasted about two hours, we all walked to the hotel where we men were staying. They were showing some movie on TV that I had no desire to see but Jeanne and Nancy and Douglas decided to watch, so I went to the room with three single beds, one lone ceiling light, and an open wall that looked down onto a veranda. And I do mean open, as in outside. I huddled on my bed wearing my light jacket that I almost left behind in my truck at the Houston airport, and started reading <u>Fate is the Hunter</u>. Earlier, Douglas showed me the shower down the hall, and told me not to touch the shower head, since the electric wire running near it from the electric water heater at the top of the shower carried 220 volts - enough said – I decided not to shower the next morning. He had stayed in the hotel the night before, and the room in which he had stayed was open, so he showed all of us the pillow he didn't sleep on – it felt like it had been packed with a bunch of wooden blocks. After I had gone to bed Douglas came into the room with Neal. He had flown in that night, having just arrived back in the States a couple days earlier after a two-week visit overseas. Antigua is at an elevation of about 8000 feet, there was no heat in the room, and the one thin blanket didn't do much to keep me warm that night. Neal and Douglas had sleeping bags and/or thermal pads on their beds, so I think they slept warmer than I did. At least I slept some of the time. Neal's bio-clock was still ticking in some other international time zone; the next morning he said he had been wide-awake since 2 AM.

January 27th

About 6:30 AM, the pastel colored walls that line the nearly empty streets glowed as the morning sun lit them up with that "sweet" light produced by low sun angles. Neal, Douglas, and I headed for a Bagel Bar, which obviously has some out-of-town influence. The bagel I ordered was actually better than most of the ones I have eaten in the States. The driver of the same van we had used the previous evening came during my second cup of very good coffee. The waitress gave me a paper cup and a lid that did little to keep the coffee contained while we drove on the cobblestones towards the highway.

Often, during the drive back to Guatemala City I saw Indian women walking with various cargo (pots and pans, baskets of fruit, five gallon pottery jugs, etc.) on top of their heads. Generally, they had their hands down by their sides, although there was one lady with a child under each arm and whatever she carried on her head. Always, these ladies walked with their backs straight, almost an advertisement for perfect posture. Sometimes they wore tennis shoes, sometimes they had sandals on, and often they were barefoot. Likewise, many wore hand-woven dresses of many colors and designs; others wore jeans. Most had a purposeful stride, looking very comfortable wearing their "hats". Sometimes they were alone and sometimes they had their families with them. A few even had smiles on their faces, faces that mirrored a hard-working life.

Vehicles of every description filled the streets of Guatemala City. Between the fog and the smog of bad smelling black diesel fumes and leaded gasoline, my eyes and my lungs burned slightly. Entire families of ten or twelve people would be huddled together in the back of small pickup trucks. Teenagers rode with one leg over the tailgates. Grandchildren rode in the laps of their grandparents. We passed or were passed by many trucks and buses. Every day people commute to work on the most colorful buses, but once again their faces and calloused hands and sun-wrinkled faces indicated that they work much harder than I do. Since I was riding shotgun I didn't have to concentrate on driving, so I had a chance to observe people. But what caught my attention most about these hardworking people were their smiles and laughs while talking to their friends or family members. This morning I didn't have my cameras with me, which is probably just as well, as each person is worthy of having his or her photograph taken, but there is not enough film available for me to take all of their photographs. Each has his or her own story; they all have their own dreams and wishes. All God's people.

Maybe the Antonov realized that this was the day to fly; maybe it was just tired of sitting on the grass. At any rate, after Neal removed and cleaned and reinserted all eighteen spark plugs on the 1000-hp 9 cylinder radial engine, added new oil, and I did odd jobs, including turning the prop several times to redistribute the oil that pools at the bottom of the lower cylinders, and Douglas made official visits to the Guatemala equivalent of the FAA, there came a time when we were all ready to start the engine. New batteries fully charged did their thing; Douglas and Neal did theirs, and the engine started after two or three turns of the prop, like it had last flown that same morning, and not ten months earlier. Oh, sure, there were some big puffs of white smoke, but nothing unexpected, as the radial engine roared back to life. As we taxied towards the end of the runway, I brought in the ladder and closed the door; the man in the tower gave us permission to take off. So we did! That day was extremely hazy; we turned left after leaving the runway and flew over the city heading roughly southwest. About eight miles out Douglas requested a termination of the flight plan and permission to return to the airport; this was planned in advance. It had been six or seven months since Douglas had last flown an An-2; his landing matched the plane's eagerness to fly – nearly perfect! We came back and put 100 gallons of fuel into the Antonov and then Douglas took it back over to the grass, only this time he parked it so it was facing the taxiway and runway, and not the hangars. That pleased the Antonov, for it could hardly conceal its anticipation of flying the next day. Happily, it watched the air traffic land and take-off, knowing that in less that 24 hours it too would be airborne.

Our van driver was back about 3:30 PM, so we all loaded up again and headed back to Antigua. He took us to the hotel where

Jeanne and Nancy were staying; I didn't mind paying the extra eight dollars for the room that Neal, Douglas, and I stayed in – especially by the next morning, because my bed had thicker blankets. The five of us walked back to the town square, stopping along the way to say hello to an elderly couple that Jeanne and Douglas knew. This couple owned a macadamia nut farm; I would have really liked to have gone there and enjoyed some free samples. Nancy and I walked by the big cathedral near the town square and I managed to take a couple of good photos, as dusk sought to obscure the magnificent looking Volcan Agua. By six PM the sun had disappeared and darkness had made its presence known. As we walked towards the place where we all agreed to eat dinner, I made the mistake of taking a photograph of three Indian women sitting on the street. It was more like swatting a hive of wasps. All three women wanted for me to buy necklaces and table cloths and other things they had made, and they followed Nancy and me to a restaurant that we were going to. I did end up buying a nice woven tablecloth for Karoline. Once inside the Middle-East restaurant we told Jeanne, Douglas, and Neal about the incident, and then I realized I wasn't going to have a chance to buy any souvenirs for my family. Nancy told me about a place we had just passed, so she showed me where it was and then went back to eat while I did a little shopping and bought wooden puzzle boxes shaped like birds. At the restaurant we only ate appetizers because we were told by somebody that the regular dinners didn't taste good; soon we departed and went to another one.

    We all made it back to the hotel; I walked out of my room and saw Jeanne and Douglas dancing under the moonlight – she was on her way to play scrabble with an American older woman who lived there. Nancy had a fire going in her room, so for awhile Douglas, Nancy, Neal, and I sat by the fire and they drank rum. Neal told stories about the tsunami that had recently hit Thailand. On one island, the chief recognized what was happening and ordered everyone to higher ground; nobody was lost. Apparently, no land animals died as a result of the storm, because they all left the beach areas. Neal told another story of elephants leaving, and one grabbed a person out of a river by his trunk and placed the person on his back and continued out of the storm's destructive path. By ten PM, everyone was tired and headed to their respective rooms and beds. All of us are near or over 50, and past the time of our lives where we waited until ten PM to start the evening.

I noticed near the shower of our room a big black spider with a body the size of a quarter, so I placed my boots on the mantle of the fireplace in my room.

January 28th

Early morning in Antigua is my favorite time to observe the town, before the workers fill the cobblestone streets, before merchants open their doors, before the buildings loose their soft glow from the sunrise, before the rush of everyday living.

Volcan Agua, as seen from one of the streets in Antigua

All of us - Jeanne, Douglas, Nancy, Neal, and me - ordered our bagels and coffee by 6:30 AM; just before our minivan driver arrived at 7 AM, Nathan Burke greeted us; as we climbed into the van I heard Anita Ibarguen say something about needing to pick up her passport. We drove to the hotel to pick up our gear and then we drove to Nathan's house to pick up his wife Annette. Nathan and Annette own their own chiropractic clinic and Anita works at the clinic as an acupuncture specialist. Douglas, Jeanne, and Neal had met these people in 2004. Jeanne had spent part of her life in Santa Fe, New Mexico, and it turns out that Anita had gone to school there. Nathan and Annette attended a chiropractic school in Dallas two years ago and bought the clinic after their graduation. They are two of the four licensed chiropractors in the entire country of Guatemala. I think Annette is about 29, and Nathan is about 33. Anita is in her mid-thirties, I think. I detected Annette having a slight accent and found out that she is from Holland. Anita grew up in Guatemala. The three of them were flying with the rest of us to El Salvador on this day.

Our drive into Guatemala City on this day seemed less hectic than the day before. This time I had my camera with me, so I opened the lens all the way and let the camera select the highest shutter speed for the available light. It is an auto-focus camera, so effectively I had a controllable point-and-shoot, which I found to be useful in the continuous subject and traffic changing conditions. Although not magazine quality, some of my photos came out reasonably well.

Once at the airport, Neal and I started preparing the Antonov for take off, and Nathan and I shared in turning the monstrous-sized prop several times. Douglas took off to file the flight plan and fill out the always present bureaucratic forms. An hour or so later he came back and asked for my pilot's license. He had listed me as part of the flight crew, with my title being the "Navigator"! This saved me from paying the $30 departure tax. During the flight I did monitor our flight path and watch it being plotted and displayed on the GPS receiver.

Anita's brother is a Guatemalan pilot and a member of the private aero club near where the Antonov was parked. She spoke to the person at the desk and he allowed us to go upstairs where members have their own dining area. We weren't there very long before Douglas came back ready to fly. Our flight plan called for us leaving either at 11 AM or at Noon, and we had to be airborne within one hour of the planned departure, or Douglas would have to re-file the flight plan.

It wasn't long before we were taxiing towards the end of the runway, and I had the duty of bringing in the ladder and closing the door. A few minutes after climbing out, Jeanne asked me to open the door. When Douglas gave the go-ahead, I opened it, and all of us in back managed to watch the landscape and local volcanoes go beneath us. I listened to the ground-to-air radio traffic at the headphone jack just aft of the co-pilot's bulkhead. Finally, after a year-and-a-half, the moment I had been waiting for came: Neal stepped out of the co-pilot's seat and let me sit there. Our flight to San Salvador only lasted a little over an hour, so my time in the cockpit only lasted about ten or fifteen minutes, because it was only fair to share that seat with the others. I have to admit (surprise! surprise!) that even with the five hours of previous time I have flying the Antonov, I would like to add some zeros after that number five. Although I actually had the controls when I flew the plane in Alaska, on this trip to El Salvador I only sat in the right seat but did not take the controls.

The An-2 on a grass field in El Salvador

We landed at a military airfield West of San Salvador, which is the same airfield where the air show had been held when Douglas, Jeanne, and Neal first visited last year. Clearing immigration and customs made me wish that the same tasks could be accomplished as easily in the United States. We ate our lunch and bought some liquid lunch for the big airplane and took off again, perhaps only spending one hour on the ground. Twenty minutes later, after heading west towards the coast and flying about 1500 feet, Douglas banked the plane left, landed on the best grass strip I have ever seen, and everyone but myself headed for the swimming pool of the private and exclusive Barillas Marina. I took photographs of some of the flowers and the local area; everyone told me to come on in, but I said Hermann Melville wrote a book about me, and Jeanne quickly responded, "You mean, the Great White Whale?"

A couple of hours later we all made our way back to the Antonov, where some of the people set up tents. Nancy had rented a bungalow for herself and Jeanne, and there was another one available this night that I rented for myself. As the dinnertime approached, we all lazily walked about a kilometer through a bunch of coconut, banana, and cocoa trees to the marina's open air dining area. Anchored perhaps two hundred meters away from the dock, a sailboat with twin masks pointing towards the full moon gently swayed back and forth. As I ate my steak in these peaceful surroundings, laughing with my friends, I thought that having Karoline eating dinner with me would add the finishing touch to this micro-vision of paradise.

Telephone cards could be purchased for $5.00, and it only cost ten cents a minute to call Karoline. While I talked to her, the others went back to the plane. By the time I arrived, Douglas had the Honda generator generating, the CD player playing, and Christmas tree lights strung around the plane. During the evening, I think Douglas and Jeanne danced in the moonlight again, as did Nathan and Annette. Bottles of very good smelling rum tempted me but it has been many years since I have indulged in alcohol beverages, and many more years since I drank that bottle of rum that turned me into Volcan Mateo, so I savored the smell and woke up the next morning with no headache or hangover and happy that I did not yield into the temptation.

Friday night party back at the Antonov. L-R: Nathan, Jeanne, Annette, and Douglas

At 11 PM, I walked from the plane to the marina with Nancy, Jeanne, and Annette. Annette said, "Imagine going to work on Monday morning like any other Monday and receiving a phone call that Jeanne, Douglas, and Neal are in town and want you to fly with them this weekend to El Salvador in the An-2", or words to that affect. So after careful but quick consideration, they closed the clinic and four days later traveled with us to El Salvador, then took the following Monday off as well. Nathan, Annette, and Anita are good traveling companions, and very likable people. For that matter, so are Jeanne, Douglas, Nancy, and Neal.

It looks like the girl is sitting on the prop's shadow.

January 29th

At the beach: L-R: Nancy, Anita, Neal, Jeanne, Douglas, Annette, and Nathan

Coconut trees, photos, breakfast at plane, hot coffee. Wander to concrete swimming hole, more photos, sit at round picnic tables, read, eat lunch, swap stories, make Kodak happy once again, talk to owners of twin-masted sailboat sailing from Oregon and dreaming of docking in Ireland and drinking at local pubs. Drink a cold coke, fill up water bottles from five-gallon bottle away from cantina to avoid one dollar charge for a new bottle from marina's store, watch others drink beverages stronger than my coke, living life of leisure today but bored, want to fly big Russian bi-plane, want to buy big Russian fly plane, stay that way until four o'clock when all eight of us board a motor boat for a ride to nearby island through channels cutting away at the roots of mangrove trees, walk down another grass runway towards the ocean while eating the mouth-drying and burning fruit that hides cashew nuts, stop at an abandoned resort that a hurricane proved mother nature has been around many more years than man and has the power to destroy what man builds, go two – three hundred meters to Pacific Ocean, and Nathan and Annette swim, we all watch sunset and drink fresh coconut milk chopped open by boat driver's machete, ride in back of wagon pulled by old tractor back to boat, full speed ahead back to marina, Neal remarks area is just like Thailand, dinner with owners of twin-masted sailboat, stories again, Jeanne and Douglas tell about rescuing fuel-soaked baby and the pilot with compound fracture and two other people out of a plane crash in Alaska on New Year's day – plane had hit power lines which sliced it open like sardine can – Douglas out in cold for three hours with no jacket but helping others live longer and all survived, giving real meaning to overused word "hero", we go to Antonov and entertained by sailboat owner playing Italian-made accordion, Douglas gives me an empty Mexican cigarette pack that has a bi-plane on the package, and afterwards I find a bunk house to sleep in.

January 30th

"PEDRO! MARIA" yelled the man at the end of the road, about a mile away from the plane, past the sugar cane fields, past the red ants nearly an inch long, past the cashew tree, past the glassy-water pond disturbed only by the ripples created by a cruising alligator (or croc) silently looking for breakfast. As we waited a moment while he gathered a half dozen bananas, his little girl and little boy snuck shy looks at us, the older kids ignored us, roosters wandered around his ramshackle house, and swinging out of the trees came the monkeys, Pedro and Maria and their family and friends. Perhaps there were ten all total, ranging from ten months to thirty-five years old. Two others monkeys wistfully looked at the free monkeys from their cages; we strangers gave the bananas to the other monkeys scampering over the branches above us, then we watched them and laughed at their antics of turning upside down, grabbing bananas, swinging from branch to branch, peeling the bananas and throwing the peelings to the ground as they held on to a branch with one hand and ate with the other. From Annette's bag, one gleefully stole an apple that she had brought as a snack for herself, and all of a sudden this monkey was like a five-year old kid going into a candy store for the first time. After I ran out of film, the fur of one of the monkeys sitting on a branch exploded into a halo of golden sunlight, each hair illuminated by the early morning sun, letting me witness perhaps the most beautiful view of a monkey I have ever seen in my life. To the many young men carrying machetes arriving in a pickup truck, we were just touristas, but they smiled anyway, as they prepared to cut tree branches to build a room near the owner's home, and after we started walking back to the Antonov, one of them showed us the track of the gator on the road near the pond and a couple of laughing girls in the ten-to-twelve age group cut sugar cane with their own machetes and loaded the stalks onto a handmade cart with wooden wheels. Their father told them to cut the sugar cane and they instantly complied with no back talk; while walking away from the house, they looked back and smiled at us.

Ten o'clock arrived all too soon, and I had to say goodbye to Nathan, Annette, Anita, Jeanne, and Neal. I threw my cell phone, some post cards, and my shaving kit behind the front seat of the van taking me to the airport, rode back to the plane to grab my suitcase, and hopped in the front seat for the ride to the airport. Nancy has friends living in San Salvador whom she made arrangements to visit; she and Douglas sat in the backseat of the van that Señor Salvador Bonilla drove. As I watched the traffic and road conditions, once again in my life the thoughts and dreams of driving my Ford F-250 4X4 diesel truck through Central and South America surfaced. Salvador used to live in Austin, Texas for a couple of years and spoke good English. He told me that it had taken him four days to drive between Austin and San Salvador. Drivers have to be alert for local conditions. He tells me to park at all night gas stations to avoid the banditos. Over there is a woman herding goats, watch out for the Mercedes that doesn't slow down to pass her; another woman carries her infant in one arm, holds the hand of her little boy, as she walks barefoot, head and shoulders erect so she can carry the large blue pot on top of her head. We pass some vendors selling American soft drinks and other vendors selling cashew nuts or coconuts. Horse drawn wagons and Toyota's park side-by-side at a small church.

At the airport I jump out of the van, shake hands with Señor Salvador and Douglas; Nancy gives me a sisterly hug. They drive off and soon afterwards I have my boarding pass and go upstairs to have a bite to eat. Oh, No! I left my cell phone, post cards, and shaving kit in the van, but I use the phone card to call Señor Heriberto Pineda, the manager at Barillas Marina, and ask that he check with Salvador about these things. Señor Pineda (I used to work with a Joe Pineda in Houston) tells me to call him back about 45-minutes later. What happened to my passport? The frantic button is hammered, how will I pass through security; how long will it take me to receive another passport? Where is it? Not in my camera case, not in my pockets, not in the restaurant, not by the telephone. Soon it's time to call Señor Pineda again. My stuff has been found, and I told him to give it all to Nancy, since she would be passing through Houston two days later. But where is my passport? At the Continental counter, the ticket agents help me look through my camera case, where I spot the passport hiding by itself in a side pocket. It's time to pass through the security checkpoint, run to the gate, and board the plane with about five minutes to spare. Whew!

Ten minutes after takeoff, the mountains and the coastline have been chomped up and swallowed by the clouds, which last all the way to Houston. Rain washes the plane as we disembark. Ever since my spur-of-the-moment weekend trip to Mexico City in 1988, without any luggage, I expect to be singled out by the customs personnel, and sure enough, they looked at their computer monitors and singled me out. Take my luggage into this room. (Not the search room, fortunately, but just the luggage inspection room). An agent that must have been fullback for the Dallas Cowboys in his previous life wanted to know where I have been, the purpose of my trip, if I have anything to declare. I told him about the wooden puzzle boxes. He expertly opened and looked into each one, sniffed the doll I brought for my granddaughter Camyrn, walked back to his computer machine, and told me to have a nice day. As I have mentioned before, I wish they would profile me as a guy that just likes to travel to off-the-wall places, but has absolutely no desire to do anything wrong because he is not smarter than trained custom agents nor is stupid enough to try sneaking anything illegal into the country.

To top off the day of loosing stuff and leaving my cell phone in El Salvador, I left my bank debit card in the pay phone that would not take coins, when I called Karoline to let her know I was back in the country. Still, I had a good trip!

La Porte, Texas 2005

Three weeks after I left the Antonov gang in El Salvador, I saw Jeanne, Douglas, and Neal again in the Houston area. They had flown the An-2 to have the FAA required annual inspection in La Porte, Texas, which is about 20 miles from my home. They arrived on a Friday night; briefly I saw them and picked up my cell phone and the post cards that I had left in El Salvador (It was easier for Nancy to leave them on the An-2 than meet me at the Houston airport). Since I went to Dallas for the weekend, I didn't see the An-2 people again until

Sunday evening, when they came to my house. They told me about one not-so-great experience they had when they landed their plane at a closed military airport in Mexico. From the air, the indications of the closed runway looked different than closed runways in the States. The younger guards packing all kinds of weapons were confused and handed the matter over to their supervisors. Jeanne and Douglas had five guards holding assault weapons on them while they rode in the back of a pickup to discuss the problem. Jeanne came through again with her excellent Spanish, so that probably helped. Everybody on the plane profusely apologized, but Douglas was worried that the plane was going to be confiscated. Finally, a grueling three hours later, they all flew the An-2 away from the airport. The previous year they had a passenger from California with them that stopped taking his medicine and became very erratic and angry. Finally, out of desperation, Douglas informed the guy he would have to leave. The man's wealth of many millions did not stop his wife from shooting him very dead four or five days later after he arrived home in California. Douglas, Jeanne, and Neal need to write their own book about their adventures in the Antonov!

The Stinson and the Antonov. Photo by Neal Oppen

During the next several days I showed several friends the plane, and we were just a few of the many people who stopped by after seeing the plane from the road adjacent to the airport. In the process, I met Bob Wagstaff, owner of K & W Aviation; in his hangar there is another big old An-2 being restored. The wings are off of this one, and it is far from the pristine condition of N87AN, but Bob hopes to have it flying in the next several months. What I found interesting about this plane is that Russian markings are still visible in several places, and one can vaguely see the old USSR flag and the letters "CCCP", the Russian letters for "USSR". Bob told me to come early on weekends and work late and help with that plane. I should have, but never did.

My Stinson was in between its hanging out at fix-it shops, so I flew it to La Porte. Neal took a bunch of photos of it and the An-2. A few days after the An-2 arrived in La Porte, I took Karoline to see it, and afterwards we took Neal, Douglas, and Jeanne to dinner at the Aquarium Restaurant in Kemah. Impressive as the restaurant is with sharks and stingrays and eels and tuna fish swimming around, Neal confirmed my suspicions that they had seen even more impressive restaurants with more sea life in other parts of the world, but everyone seemed to enjoy the meal anyway. The next day Douglas took Jeanne and Neal to the commercial airport – Jeanne headed out to Phoenix to pick up her motor home and Neal took off to go to other parts of the world. Douglas stayed at our house for the next several nights, until it came time for me to depart to Alaska on March 2nd to watch the Iditarod Race begin, something I had wanted to do for a long time. Douglas called me on March 21st from Beaumont, Texas. He had found a hangar to store the Antonov over the next several months, which means in the Fall I may have another chance to fly in it, and write another chapter in its history. The next day he planned of flying commercially to catch up with Jeanne; In July, I hope they have to chance to fly in my Stinson, either in Anchorage or in Valdez.

Flying the An-2 from La Porte, Texas to Phoenix, Arizona, March 2006

March 16th - La Porte, Texas

Wow! Has a year gone by already since I last saw Douglas Fulton and Neal Oppen, owners of the Antonov An-2 with whom I have previously flown on two other occasions? I last saw them at the La Porte, Texas Airport a year ago and now they are back again having another Annual Inspection done on the plane. And look at me, the sort-of designated historian for the adventures of the An-2 that has fallen down on my job of flying in that Russian-designed airplane and telling its story. OK, since I last saw it in 2005, it spent much of the year in a hangar at Beaumont, Texas, and only recently flew to Florida and the Bahamas without me, but I still have no new exotic photos of coconut trees like those in El Salvador or glad-to-be-back-on-the-ground stories after flying the windy passes of Alaska. Well, not so fast, because Texas has its own special winds.

Like hurricanes. Just a month after Hurricane Katrina devastated the Gulf Coast, along came Hurricane Rita, causing extensive damage to the Beaumont area. Although not as extensive or expensive as Katrina, Rita initially was categorized as a Class 5 hurricane, and without going into all the details, my own family evacuated, along with a bunch more people living in the Houston area. About a week after Rita chewed up the Texas eastern coast, my wife Karoline and I were enjoying the beauty of an early snowfall in Wyoming's Tetons, when my cell phone rang. Douglas called and asked if we sustained any storm damage. Then he told me that the An-2 came through the storm unscathed. I had forgotten that he left it in Beaumont last year. When I said those words to him, he said simply, "I didn't!" There is a guy that I know that has an aircraft maintenance shop in an old World War II hangar there, big enough to park the An-2 with its huge 60-foot wingspan. But the county airport manager wouldn't let Douglas store the plane in that hangar, but offered him the use of another WWII hangar. Great decision, because a Lear jet sitting in the first hangar was damaged when the roof collapsed during the storm and there was no damage to the hangar where the An-2 spent the summer. But hurricanes have a way of changing perspectives. Karoline said that if we lost our house we would not rebuild here, but go to Wyoming and put a cabin on our five acres on top of Casper Mountain. Since we are still in Texas, we obviously didn't suffer the fate of the straw house that the big bad wolf blew away with his huffing and a puffing. Neal and Douglas did not want to chance leaving the Antonov along the Texas coast again for another hurricane season. They found a place to store it in Blythe, California, and offered me a ride between Houston and Phoenix. Oh, well, I guess I will go, you know, it's a dirty job but someone has to do it! In all of my ancient life, I have never heard of hurricane damage in Blythe, California. Of course, this is near the Arizona border, and often it has been said that when the big earthquake strikes California, people along that border are going to have ocean front property. What is not heavily publicized and what most people don't realize is that the ocean front property along the California-Arizona border will be the Atlantic Ocean!

Shadow of An-2 on shallow ocean floor in Bahamas. Photo by Mavis Muller

Flying the Antonov back to Alaska through Canada is too expensive, so Douglas and Neal find a place to store it during the summer months. When the snow piles high enough in Valdez to walk up to the roof and the temperatures are cold enough to crystallize the bubbles that children blow and shatter like Christmas tree ornaments when they hit the ground, it's time to go south. Canadian geese are smarter than Neal and Douglas and his wife Jeanne, because they fly south before Winter sets in, not afterwards. None the less, the southern migration of these guys is an annual event for whom their happiness of hearing the cough and sputtering and roaring to life of the 1000-Hp round engine of the Antonov is only surpassed by the joy the plane feels of being liberated from a dark and dusty hangar by coughing and sputtering and roaring to life and then living, flying, enjoying its freedom, exhilarating in the beauty of flight to places not seen before or going back once again to the Bahamas where there's a hundred degree temperature difference from Valdez and the colors of the waters are blue and azure and dark blue and light blue and sky blue and blues only poets can describe where the shadow of the mighty airplane can be seen racing on the bottom of the shallow clear waters (I know because I saw this photo that their friend Mavis Muller took when she traveled with them – she was kind enough to send it to me and gave me permission to use it in this story).

Somewhere during the course of the trip to Phoenix I told Douglas that this was the first time I remember seeing him wearing shoes when he flew the An-2. Most of the time he is barefoot.

Different subject:

ANTONOVICH
ANTONOV – 2

Look at the symmetry of those two names. Antonovich is Karoline's maiden name. Maybe that's why I love this plane so much, because its name is 70% of Karoline's last name the first time around before she and I married Likewise, I can sort of symmetrically match my middle and last initial with the last part of the tail number of the An-2, and then match the first part of that number with my Stinson's tail number. Kinda neat!

Matthew A Nelson
N87 A N   (Antonov)
N8706 K   (Stinson)

It just so happened that this afternoon Douglas called me and told me that he and Neal were at Bob Wagstaff's hangar in La Porte working on the annual inspection on the An-2. The world-renowned multi-winner woman's aerobatics champion Debbie Rihn owns and runs Harvey & Rihn Aviation, which is based at the same airport. She often performs at air shows, and her performance alone is worth the price of the ticket. Speaking of air shows, Douglas and Neal flew the plane in Titusville, Florida, after their little jaunt to the Bahamas. They had stopped in Gainesville for oil for that big old radial engine – the plane has a 35-gallon tank just for oil, and it burns at least a quart an hour. Thirty-five gallons of oil! The useable fuel capacity on my Stinson is thirty-six gallons. Someone told them that if they flew in the air show they could have the Antonov's fuel tanks filled. Last January, I called Douglas from Titusville right after they had landed near Tampa. The New Horizons launch to Pluto had been scheduled on the same day, and I had gone to see it from the balcony of my friend's Ron Caswell's place. Ron later told me that he had seen the An-2 flying around during the air show and had wondered if it was the same one that I flew on.

Since Karoline had already assumed I would be going to the Houston rodeo today, she planned either lasagna or tuna fish sandwiches for supper, so I opted to go to the La Porte airport and see Douglas and Neal and eat dinner with them at the Runway Grill. The young waitress asked me come back on Friday evening and sing Karaoke but she is really lucky that she didn't have to listen to me.

When I arrived at the airport, Douglas and Neal were finishing up for the day. Jeanne had already left for Chicago. While I waited for them to go to dinner, I showed Bob the crankshaft out of my 1947 Stinson 108-1 that had broken in half last May while I was in flight. God and my Guardian Angel Jack Clodfelter kept me alive that day, and guided me safely onto the runway at Brazoria County airport in Angleton, Texas. Two days ago, on March 14th, I finally flew the Stinson for the first time in ten months.

March 18th - La Porte to Georgetown, Texas

Last night Douglas and I decided that I would fly with him and Neal on the Antonov, instead of me flying my Stinson in loose formation with the An-2. Although I was a little disappointed, the way things worked out we made the right decision. On the way to the airport I phoned my friend Harvey Ponder to tell him to hurry over to the La Porte Airport to see the An-2. Turns out he was on his way to see a doctor because he had injured his eye. Back in his Army days he had lived in Arizona, so knowing that he really doesn't have much of a desire to fly in the "Polack Airplane" that he calls the An-2, I told that we could give him a med-evac flight to Phoenix. He just laughed and told me to have a good time.

As I strapped myself in the seat just aft of the Antonov's cockpit, Douglas and Neal precisely followed the extensive start-up checklist. Once again in my An-2 adventures, I could hear the prop start its rotation; a couple of coughs and sputters later I heard that very distinctive sound of Puff the Magic Dragon rumbling to life. We departed at 11:20 AM, banked left and flew through the VFR corridor in Houston, which is between Houston Hobby and Houston Intercontinental Airports. We had a good view of downtown Houston on the south side, and could easily see the medical center, the astrodome, and Hobby Airport. Heading towards Burnet, we had a good tail wind, and our ground speed registered on the Garmin model 295 GPS receiver around 120 – 125 knots. Initially, we had low ceilings but not so bad that we couldn't fly. Nearer the Austin area our visibility decreased rapidly; at Round Rock Douglas said he had to land. Georgetown was just few miles away to the north, and clearly showed up on the GPS display, as well as the sectional chart that Neal and I closely watched. Georgetown Airport has two runways, so Douglas headed there. We flew at 1500 feet to avoid the 1300 foot towers in-line with our flight path, passing one whose top looked very close below the left wing. Had we been able to go higher we would have, and if the towers hadn't been so close we would have gone lower. About a mile out from the airport our visibility improved quite a bit and we were past those threatening radio towers. About 1 PM Douglas made a very good landing on runway 11, almost straight into the easterly wind of $100°$.

Even on rainy days the Antonov attracts the curious. The first guy we saw worked as an avionics technician and remembered meeting Ernie Neal nearly twenty years ago. Before I moved to Texas I had worked at Kings Avionics in Casper, Wyoming with Ernie; he and his wife Pam and their daughter had moved to Round Rock about the same time Karoline and I moved to the Houston area. Within minutes this guy still stuck in the Sixties started talking about the An-2, and then launched into a speech about how people need to keep Loran receivers in their planes, because in about five years the sun spot cycle will be peaking and modern day GPS receivers will be useless. He may be right – I'm certainly not going to forget that tidbit of information, and hopefully I will take his advice one of these days and buy a Loran unit off e-Bay while the price is still fairly low.

Inside the terminal sat three guys drinking coffee who started asking me questions about the An-2. We chatted a while. One of the guys often flew mentally handicapped children around in his Grumman Tiger. Another one had served as a C-5 load master for 29 years in USAF reserves and had gone all over world. With well-deserved pride in his voice, he told me that he had learned all the aircraft systems very well. Forgot what the third guy does. (Sorry) He did tell us about a 3000 ft. tower west of airport about 15 miles, direct on the flight path to Burnet. Good thing we stopped. I think he was the one who told me about the An-2 that had once been based at Georgetown Airport hitting a pole barn several years ago at a nearby airport. While I talked to these men Neal checked the weather then walked back to the plane and Douglas talked on his cell phone.

As we drove in the rain towards town in the airport courtesy car, Douglas asked if I had heard what happened. His father had just died that morning. We grabbed some lunch at a local cafeteria. Pretty somber mood for the rest of day. Back at the airport Neal camped on the weather computer. Not good. Their friend Ken Gray in Phoenix managed to find an airline ticket to Philadelphia for Douglas at a good price, with a schedule departure for Tuesday. We hung around the terminal until 7 PM, when it closed. Back in the plane Douglas heated a can of chili for me in the microwave, and Neal and I and Douglas read and chatted until 10 PM. It wasn't a good day for Douglas, and although he didn't talk much, Neal and I could both feel his pain, for we also remembered the pain when we lost our fathers. Douglas removed the table that sits across from the door of the plane and fixed up a bed from me using a cot and mattress he had bought from one of the discount stores. He sleeps in back of the plane on a bed that he constructed that is level when this tail-wheeled aircraft is on the ground, and Neal took his spot near the cockpit where I first slept three years ago by making a bed between the first two seats and the cockpit. As I lay in my sleeping bag I could see raindrops racing each other down the porthole on the door, and managed to sleep quite well.

March 19ᵗʰ – Georgetown, Texas

By 7 AM, we were all eager for Scott Stone, the man on duty that morning, to finish checking the fuel pumps and open the terminal building so we could go inside and have some coffee and look at the weather computer. Again, not good. Using the sink in the men's room, I managed to wash away the grungy. Photos on walls inside the terminal showed the early days at the airport. One corner had photos of four well-known women in aviation: Jeanna Yeager, Patty Wagstaff, Amelia Earhart, and Astronaut Eileen Collins. Another photo showed a plane augured into a runway nose first. Those things happen.

Inside the pilot lounge sits a display case for Tony Bingelis, one of the Experimental Aircraft Association's (EAA) well-known pilots. In the past there have been Tony Bingelis Memorial Air Races held at the Southwest Regional Fly-In (SWRFI) in Georgetown and New Braunfels, Texas. At the SWRFI held this year in Hondo, Texas, the winner of the Best of Show – Homebuilt, received the Tony Bingelis Memorial Award. On the EAA's webpage, referenced at the bottom of this page, I found an obituary and tribute to him. Below is a summary of what it says:

Tony Bingelis died at age 80 in 2001. His parents immigrated from Lithuanian [Seems sort of fitting for the An-2 with the name "Lithuanian Airlines" painted on its side to land here]. He was a World War II veteran pilot and an Air Force career officer. For almost 25 years he wrote his own column in the EAA magazine Sport Aviation called "Sportplane Builder" which was considered a premier guideline for the thousands of people who built their own airplanes. He built at least eight airplanes, "including two Emeraudes, a VP-1, a Flaglor Scooter, a Turner T-40, a Falco, an RV-6, and an RV-3. Many of these projects illustrate Tony's books, Sportplane Builder; Firewall Forward; Sportplane Construction Techniques; and Tony Bingelis on Engines."[1]

Walking around clockwise from the Bingelis display, there is a glass case filled with dozens of older aircraft radios and navigation equipment. One of the radios came out of a Stinson, but I forgot to take

---

[1] http://www.eaa.org/communications/eaanews/010330_bingelis.html

a photo of it. On another wall is mounted a propeller from an old Curtis aircraft, estimated vintage between 1910 and 1919. Underneath the prop is a 1943 San Antonio sectional chart that shows Georgetown and the surrounding area. Most of the artifacts in the room have been donated by Buz Landry.

Next to the newspaper notebook there was another piece of paper that I didn't read until after meeting Buz Landry, the man featured. He is Mr. Georgetown Airport as far as I am concerned. The paper that I photocopied has a photo of him standing in front of his Cessna-185, but the quality of the print isn't good enough to put into this story. In summary, the paper tells of Buz soloing an Aeronica 7AC on his 16th birthday, three days before he received his driver's license, and he had his commercial pilot's license before he graduated from high school. He flew as a crop duster for five years, and then flew for thirteen years as a corporate pilot for a Houston company. Besides the C-185 that he currently owns, he has owned several airplanes in the past, and all but one have been taildraggers. The paper closes with the comments that he raised his children as a single parent since they were pups, and that "Buz is a Christian, raised in the First Baptist Church in Georgetown." Unfortunately, I don't have the source of this write-up, but I hope the author doesn't mind. If I knew to whom to give credit, I would. Probably, there are very few days in any given year that Buz doesn't go to the airport.

When Buz started speaking, I went to the plane and picked up my tape recorder. When I asked him if I could record, he didn't say yes and he didn't say no, but he did say a couple of times that maybe more than fifty percent of what he said is true, grinning as he told me. But as of this writing, in May, 2006, the tapes haven't been transcribed yet, and I don't know when that will occur, so I'm writing the story anyway, and hope that I live up to the promise that I gave Buz that I would be inserting his words into this story. When the transcription is complete, I will go back and edit this story. When I started the recording he was talking to another man who has a large cattle and dairy business and flies several different aircraft, including helicopters. They talked about an old German man that made very good knives, and Buz told of giving the man his first airplane ride. Buz also talked about flying the crop dusters. After the other man left, Douglas walked in and Buz started talking about the different radios in the display case. With his Stetson, western clothes, and his trim build, Buz reminds me a lot of my Uncle Ed in Wyoming. Had the weather not encouraged us to land at the Georgetown Airport, I would have missed the opportunity and honor of meeting Buz and hearing some of his stories. I am not sure, but I think he may have been the third man who chatted with me the day before, giving the warning to avoid the 3000-ft. tower. Beneath the Curtis prop there is a loose-leaf notebook that has several copies of WWII and post-war newspaper front pages. One paper that caught my eye had the following two articles, and I use them in this story with the permission of the editor:

WILLIAMSON COUNTY SUN
Georgetown, Texas, Friday, February 8, 1946
Flying Ace To Appear at Southwestern
Col. Gregory "Pappy" Boyington,
Marine Corps Flying Ace, to Tell All

"[Appearing at the Southwestern University auditorium Wednesday, February 13, at 8:15 P. M., will be Lt. Col. Gregory "Pappy" Boyington, Marine Corps' top flying ace and Medal of Honor holder, who was held in a "special" prison by the Japanese for twenty months, learned about the Jap personality the hard way. He tells of his experiences and his program for Japanese rehabilitation in his talk, "Untold Truths About the Japanese."

"Pappy" met his first Japs in the skies over China as a member of the daredevil Flying Tigers. He became better acquainted with them when he led his famous Marine squadron, the "Black Sheep," in writing a blazing chapter of aerial combat history in the South Pacific. In January 1944, when he went down over Rabaul, he had Twenty-eight Japanese planes to his credit, making him the number one enemy airman of the people of Japan. Soon after he was picked up at sea by a Japanese submarine, his captors realized what a valuable prize they had.

He was flown to Japan and placed in as special "intimidation" camp. This meant he was given no medical care for his many wounds, he was not allowed to take shelter during the air raids, he received only a half of the regular food ration, he was not allowed to speak to fellow prisoners, and the United States Government was never notified of his capture. He was beaten, starved and humiliated. At one time he was hit forty-seven times with a baseball bat, but made no outcry. Fellow prisoners have since testified to "Pappy's" unflinching stoicism under torture as one of their greatest morale builders.

Colonel Boyington emerged from this experience with an unusually clear-sighted perspective of the Japanese, unhampered by hate or revenge. As one New York writer said, "He not only can take it, but he diagnoses it while getting it."

In his talk he gives new insight into the "little people" of Japan, and reveals incidents about the infamous Tojo and Prince Konoye. He tells of the Japanese reaction to the atomic bomb, and how he managed to outwit the Japs and lived to tell his story.]"

Famous Texas Ace To Stunt
Thirty 1946 Airplanes To Arrive Saturday

"[Sam N. Wilcox, Jr. president of the Georgetown Junior Chamber of Commerce, received a telephone call from Jack W. Bates, of Fort Worth, arrangement manager for the Southwestern Aviation Expedition,...stating that the aerocade flight consisting of thirty 1946 model airplanes will arrive at the Georgetown Airport Saturday afternoon, Feb. 9, at 2:55 o'clock.

Mr. Wilcox was told by Mr. Bates that among those coming will be Colonel John Landers, famous Texas Ace, who has thirty German and Japanese planes to his credit. Col. Landers will stunt a BT-13.]"

By noon vending machine and drizzle boredom overcame Neal, Douglas, and me. We grabbed the courtesy car and ate lunch at the Monument Inn. The name makes the place sound old, but it was opened in 1995, and the food was pretty good. We then drove around Georgetown. Near Southwestern University Douglas spotted some condominiums under construction, close to completion. Since he is a drywall contractor in Alaska, he wanted to see the walls. Neal and I took a quick look inside, and while we waited for Douglas to reappear, Neal walked around a bit and saw a sewer plate announcing the Georgetown Sesquicentennial (150th) year celebration. He said that he had never seen a personalized sewer plate before! Afterwards, we all attended the play, *"You Can't Take It With You"*, put on by a local stage company. And we were only charged $16 each, (which I thought was a little high) because they gave each of us the senior rate! Ha! Ha! Oh well, we weren't doing anything else and the performance was well done. Sounds like a steak!

Mike Gentry, the afternoon man working the airport terminal, and I started talking. He was a retired aircraft mechanic from the Air Force, so when I took him out by the Antonov, he made some comments about how well the landing gear was built. After I told him in our conversation that I worked at the Johnson Space Center, he asked me if I knew any astronauts. When I told him yes, he asked me if I knew "Vegas" Kelly. My answer was no, but then I realized "Vegas" had flown on STS-114 last year, the same space shuttle mission commanded by Eileen Collins, whose photo is on the wall. Mike worked on the planes that "Vegas" flew in the Air Force. It dawned on me that I just happened to have an STS-114 mission pin on my hat, so I gave it to him – the pin, not the hat! Immediately, the grinning Mike pinned it onto his denim jacket.

About dark-thirty Douglas and I went back to town to eat some authentic Mexican food at Taco Bell (well, sort of!). We could see the lights on the plane when we drove back to the airport, so we knew that Neal had the Honda generator fired up. When we opened the door, we saw two guys sitting in on the last row of seats. Simon Diver and Joshua greeted us. In years past, Simon had flown the same An-2 that had crashed a few miles away into the pole barn; only his father was the one flying that time. From what I remember, he was flying at night, and hit a ditch that he hadn't seen. The plane ground-looped into the barn, twisting the fuselage. His dad also owned several DC-3s and Convairs in Gainesville, Texas, which he used to fly cargo. Simon told us in his English accent that he was mentoring Joshua, a high school kid. Together, they had rebuilt another plane, and the reason they had come by was to pick up a Cherokee 150 that was parked next to the An-2. Joshua was taking ownership of the 150, due to all of his hard work helping Simon. Neal told him to learn to fly gliders and do aerobatic work. Good kid. After I came home I sent Simon a CD of some of my flying stories, and received this e-mail from him:

Matt,
Thanks for the great Disk of stories, it was good talking to you guys,

sorry for the late reply. Josh has passed his written and has started training. I don't know if you saw on the news but the Tornado that went through Gainesville last week knocked out my Dads DC3's and Convairs!! Moderate damage to some and not so much to others. Pretty wild what the weather can do.
Take care
Simon Diver

More rain, lightening and thunderstorms visited us that night. Listening to the rainfall on the plane reminded me of "The rain falls on the plane in Spain" or "The plane in Spain flies through the rain" or however that song goes. Actually, I found it rather soothing, and the winds didn't rock the plane all that much, so all in all, I once again slept fairly well.

March 20th – Georgetown to Pecos, Texas

Calm, clearing morning. Another sort of shower in the sink. Airborne by 7:40 AM. For my friend Hawks Abbott, make that 0740! Those guys weren't kidding when they warned us about the 3000-foot tower. Even on a day like today it looked menacing. Finally, we made it to Burnet for our fuel stop, after a short 15 or 20 minute flight and two days from Houston, making the five hour drive from Houston live up to the old axiom, "Go by air when you have time to spare!" While taking on 245 gallons to fill the 317 gallon tanks, I talked to Daniel Smith who was wearing a shirt with the name of D & D Avionics Services. When I asked if he knew Ernie Neal, no only did I have a "yes" answer, Dan used his cell phone to call Ernie, and then he handed the phone to me. Neither Ernie nor I were grandfathers the last time we talked! Even more of the small world talk, Dan had also worked for Kings Avionics in Salt Lake City, after one of the owners moved from Casper. While Dan and I visited, another guy talked to Douglas about flying Russian helicopters registered in South Africa from Florida to California.

Right after takeoff we flew over the pretty water of Lake Buchanan, where I've had a couple of floatplane lessons. This is a man-made lake with the water from the Colorado River flowing into it. No, not that big Colorado River, but the one that flows in Texas. Karoline and I have twice stayed at a lodge on the northern end of the lake and have taken dinner cruises on the river to see bald eagles, and I have landed a Cessna 172 on floats on the river. From the air Buchanan Dam looks quite impressive. It was built in the 1930s. During our climb out we had a good tailwind and a ground speed of 120 knots; soon we encountered 40-knot head winds.

After we flew over Lake Buchanan, Douglas moved to the back of the plane, Neal moved to the left seat, and I sat in the co-pilot's seat. Neal took the controls for a while, and later I took over. During that flight I flew 2.5 hours. On the pilot's side, most of the Russian instruments have been replaced with American instruments, but the original Russian instruments are still in place on the co-pilot's side. The airspeed is in kilometers per hour, so roughly 90 miles an hour equates to 150 kilometers per hour; likewise, the altimeter reads in meters, so 4500 feet is close enough to 1500 meters. It doesn't take long to adapt. For the backup radio, an American-built Collins is used, but the prime VHF radio is Russian made, and it is very clear. Despite ideological and political differences, I am still impressed with Russian engineering. I absolutely detest the politics of the former Soviet Union, but greatly respect their rocket and airplane manufacturing and design capabilities. One thing that the sticks out in my mind is the electric fuel pump on board the plane used to pump fuel out of 55-gallon (or whatever the liter equivalent is called) drums. They knew that the plane might not always land on an airport with fuel tanks available, but the drums can be transported fairly easily.

Soon, the green Texas hill country disappeared and the rugged-and-sparsely scattered mesquite trees spoke of the true nature of the tough men and women who settled this land. We passed south of the San Angelo Airport in clear sky but the tower personnel told incoming flights that the westerly winds were gusting between 36 and 42 knots. I have never been to San Angelo, but feel like I know it well, because my good friend and former co-worker Shirley Connally lived there for many years while growing up. We heard the same range of wind velocities from the Midland/Odessa tower. Our ground speed ranged from 47 to 87 knots, and the winds aloft were also reported to be between 35 to 45 knots all the way up to 9000 feet. Douglas didn't feel well in back of the plane. All I could do to try and keep it steady. Neal was patient with me as sometimes I drifted slightly off course and altitude. Bill Readdy, one of my astronaut friends, told me that he flew the An-2 over thirty years ago and it was like flying a tractor. Today I could relate. Just as I reported about flying through Windy Pass in Alaska in my first An-2 story, the An-2 Colt tried to live up to its name as it strived to grow up to become a bucking bronco. I felt like a tennis shoe in a tumbling dryer. Reminds me of the lines in the song, "Born and Raised in Black and White", written by Don Cook and John Jarvis, and sang by The Highwayman (Waylon Jennings, Willie Nelson, Kris Kristofferson, and Johnny Cash) that tells of people going insane from the West Texas winds.

From over Midland about thirty-five thousand feet, one can see thousands patches of light-colored dirt, usually square or rectangular in shape. Flying a couple of thousand feet above the ground, visible in each square are the rocker arms of oil pumpers. With those pumps constantly going up-and-down, one has to wonder about the oil shortages that are always being reported by the media and how high the price of gasoline will go. It seems strange to me that when oil goes up a dollar a barrel, there is a dime increase at the gasoline pumps that same day, but when oil falls a dollar a barrel, it takes a week to go down a nickel! Enough editorializing!

For the last thirty minutes of flying, a somewhat pale Douglas came back to the pilot's seat, Neal took over the co-pilot's position, and those nasty stomach gremlins did some of their nasty stuff to me almost as soon as I went to the back of the plane. The guys up front decided to land at Pecos. Just before we were to touch down Douglas added power and did a go-around, saying he didn't think he could land there, with the wind gusting between 30 and 45 knots. He came around again, and managed to do a perfect landing on runway 27, stopping at the junction of runways 27 and 32. When we stopped, I opened the door and placed the small ladder into position, while the plane gyrated as if were on center stage at a rock-and-roll concert. We had to move the plane off the active runway, and worried that the left wing was going to lift due to the high winds, Neal and I gave some ballast of over three hundred pounds when we walked on the lower wing to the outer strut between the left wings, and I sat on the hub centered around the strut on top of the bottom wing. With the 45-knot wind still howling, Douglas opened the throttle of that 1000-Hp engine and stepped on the right brake to rotate the plane. He backed off the power when the tail came up, causing the fuselage to go horizontal, making the airplane ready for take off and wanting to go. Little nervous on that one! Neal and Douglas said I had more material for my next story. A couple of times Douglas said that he was glad he hadn't bent any metal. Me too! In fact I was glad that he didn't bend any metal and didn't bend me either! When it comes to landing that plane in rough winds, Douglas and Neal are some of the best pilots to have in the cockpit. My skill level certainly does not match theirs.

  After we secured the plane as best we could with the chocks for the massive tires, Neal remained with the Antonov while Douglas and I walked towards the terminal. Dennis Blanchard, owner of the Pecos Air Center, gave us a ride in the fuel truck and told us to go in and have a soft drink and a burrito. We weren't the first ones to enjoy his hospitality and that of his wife Isabelle. The Navy had a T-34 trainer from Corpus Christi parked on the ramp. A Marine Captain and a young Navy Ensign said hello, but the Ensign didn't know Bryce Abbott, the son of my friend Hawks, no relation to the two Black Hawks that sat on the tarmac. On the wall and in display cases there were probably hundreds of military unit patches and/or decals; including a patch from VXE-6, one of the best Navy Squadrons with whom I flew most of my flights to and from Antarctica, and a decal from STS-69, one of the space shuttle missions that Ken Cockrell flew on. He was one of the four astronauts I served with when I was attached to the Naval Space Command reserve unit in the 1990s. On the wall there was a photo of Patty Wagstaff thanking Dennis and Isabelle for hospitality and burritos; a SR-71 crew had written the same kind of sentiments, as well as all kinds of helo and plane photos and their grinning pilots. I knew I should have jotted down some of the names of people who had stopped at this really good place. Free-and-great tasting burritos are probably why so many aircrews stop. After my photos were processed, I had one of the photos taken of the An-2 at this airport enlarged and sent two copies for Neal and Douglas to sign and send back to the Pecos Air Center and to the people at the Georgetown airport.

  Douglas and I took the courtesy car around this West Texan desert town filled with tumbling tumbleweeds and I had Douglas stop at a Motel 6 so I could have a room for that night that didn't rock and also had a shower. We went back and fueled the plane, taking on 239 gallons for today's flight of 270 miles. Neal and Douglas stayed in the plane this night, but didn't mind going back to the motel and taking their showers before we all ate dinner at a truck stop. I dropped them back at the airport and went back to the motel, fell asleep shortly after 9 PM, and slept until 4 AM when some guy called me on the phone. He said, "Hello, this is Tom Bodet giving you a wakeup call. Now, before you get mad at me, remember you are the one that requested the wakeup call!"

March 21st - Pecos to Phoenix and back to Houston

It was still dark when I drove the courtesy car to the plane. While Douglas and Neal took care of other preparations for the plane, I hand-turned the four-bladed prop through ten complete revolutions. Morning exercise. Take off occurred at 5:40 AM, still dark – Douglas barely had to turn the plane before we were lined up on runway 27. Checklist complete, give it power, and off we go, go West young Man! Initially it was calm, but then we encountered some light head winds, and we climbed to 8500 feet until the ground speed started going down, so we flew most of the trip near 6500 feet. Once again we had good tail winds, often giving us a ground speed between 110 to 120 knots. Could barely make out Guadalupe Peak, highest point in Texas, but shortly after we passed it the sky lightened up some, so looking back at it several miles later I could see it better as the sun lit it up. Saw several old volcano remnants to the north, but I was standing behind the pilots and didn't have the best visibility out of the side windows, so I didn't take any photos. Near daybreak we could see some of those windmills with their slowly rotating three blades that are as big as the guns on the Bismarck. Neal remarked how much they looked like an ancient prehistoric monster. Sure enough, those white blades clawing through the air reminded me of the scythe carried by the Grim Reaper. I didn't want to even think about how the An-2 would look if its four-bladed prop had waltzed too close to one of those three-bladed windmills. Not a good geometry solution, but could be one bad problem! As the sun illuminated the landscape, I thought how much of the land looks like the tanned weather-beaten and wrinkled leathery face of a hundred year-old woman. Each wrinkle could tell a story, each hill and arroyo and dried up stream could tell geological stories or may be able to intrigue an archeologist about some ancient Indian tribe sitting around stone fire circles or tipi rings chipping flint arrowheads. About 8:30 AM we flew north of El Paso through the clear fly zone between the city and the Military Operation Areas (MOAs) that go all the way to Albuquerque. The songs of Marty Robbins entered my mind, but I didn't feel the same calling of El Paso that he did when flying over the city at 30,000 feet. But indeed, we were "Out in the West Texas town of El Paso…" Around Deming New Mexico I took the controls, and flew for the next two hours, until just out of Chandler, AZ. The GPS shows state lines on it; near the state line we had to go over some 8000-ft. peaks, and Douglas had me fly close to them to gain more mountain flying experience. Actually, I guess I could have been a lot closer, but I just need to build up the old confidence. In Arizona I flew along a spectacular canyon with yellow walls. Maybe they call it Yellowstone! The territory east of Phoenix is much better scenic wise than near the city. A few minutes out of Chandler I switched seats with Neal, and soon afterwards, Douglas did a routine, but after the one in Pecos, a slightly boring landing. The people in the tower told us to park near its base, which is where we secured the plane. About 30 minutes after we landed, Ken Gray picked us up. He has been a friend of Neal and Douglas for several years, had flown with them in the Bahamas a few years ago, and took the airborne photos of the An-2 flying in the Bahamas and in Alaska that Douglas and Neal use on their business card, shown below. He makes his living as a photographer, and there is no doubt by the quality of his work that he is a professional. Mavis Muller, another friend of Neal and Douglas, was waiting for them when we showed up at Ken's place. She lives in Homer, Alaska, but had also been on the recent trip to the Bahamas. She showed some photos that she had taken of the trip; I was also very much impressed with her photography, so I asked to her if I could use some of prints. She had been in Austin as a member of one of the 1400 bands that played there the previous week. We were twenty-five miles away when we were in Georgetown. Douglas and Neal have some very interesting and colorful friends.

Douglas's and Neal's business card. Photos by Ken Gray

Neal drove Ken's car to take Douglas and me to the Phoenix airport. My Southwest flight to Houston stopped in El Paso six hours after I flew near the same airport in the An-2. My friend Bob Simle met me at Houston Airport and drove me back to the La Porte airport to pick up my truck. Today is my granddaughter's Camyrn's 3rd birthday. I stopped by to see her but she had just gone to bed a few minutes earlier and was already sound asleep. Quite a trip! Had Harvey Ponder decided to fly with us to Phoenix on a med-evac flight, he would have had three days to enjoy the journey. Thanks, Douglas and Neal for inviting me on another adventure. Thanks to all the people that we met along the way for your hospitality. Thanks to God again for keeping us safe.

Casa Grande, Arizona, March 3-4, 2007

It had been nearly a year since I flew from Houston to Phoenix in the An-2. Douglas, Jeanne, and Neal were back in Arizona. On the weekend of March 3rd and 4th, they had the An-2 at the Cactus Fly-In, hosted by the Arizona Antique Aircraft Association, Inc., about fifty miles south of Phoenix. Douglas and I had talked a few times on the phone, and I was hoping that I could fly with them across the Grand Canyon. His schedule, if you can call it that, became a victim of his shoulder surgery, so the idea of flying with them across the canyon was put on hold for this year, but there was no reason for me not to take a Southwest Airlines flight out to Phoenix and meet up with them at the air show, and then fly across the Grand Canyon anyway. Actually, I looked into flying the Stinson out, but when I figured it would probably cost a couple of thousand dollars in fuel and living expenses, I decided that it would much cheaper to take Southwest to Arizona. Or so I thought when I purchased my ticket. At any rate, on the afternoon of the 3rd I sat in the An-2 again. Only on this trip I didn't fly it or in it, but that doesn't mean that I didn't have a chance to visit with Douglas, Jeanne, and Neal, and also Ken Gray, whom I met in Phoenix last year. And seeing the colorful planes at the air show didn't hurt my feelings, either. Although the visit was rather short, it was still good seeing my friends again.

Matt, Jeanne Passin, and Douglas Fulton

Through the looking glass (of the An-2)

Chandler to Douglas, Arizona, 2008

April 17th

Waking up at 4:45 AM (make that 0445 CAPT Hawksorius Oozic) usually is not something I care to do, but when I did it today, it didn't bother me at all. Of course, my social-security-eligible-raggedy-old body still thought it was Houston time, and not Phoenix time. No problem – 6:45AM is close enough to when it's my normal stop-dreaming-about-airplanes-and-hit-the-snooze alarm time. Besides, I had a better reason for waking up that early than just going to work. I had a plane to fly. Not just any plane, but that big old bi-wing aeroplane with the 60-foot wingspan, a 1000-hp radial engine, and has the words *"Lithuania Airlines"* painted on it's sides, you know the one that I have written more about than my Stinson, the plane I flew around Alaska in 2003, Guatemala and El Salvador in 2005, Houston-to-Phoenix in 2006, and saw but did not fly in Casa Grande, Arizona in 2007. Now, is it coming back to you? Yep, none other than the Antonov An-2, tail number N87AN.

Douglas knocked on my motel room door about 5:22 AM; an hour later he started the engine that roars like a lion. He and Neal Oppen had slept in their flying RV, or at least that's where they spent the cold night. Neal said he hadn't slept at all. Douglas has his own sleeping compartment built into the back of the plane, aft of the door, and Neal has any the rest of the fuselage to use, between the cockpit and the door. The plane's interior looked pretty much like it always has, or at least since I first saw it in 2003. Not so for the outside. It looked as if it had spent the last bunch of years rotting and hiding out in the jungles of Peru – in fact no longer could you see the words *"Lithuania Airlines"* but there was a name I had never seen before – *"PANAGRA"*. Even the golden light of dawn didn't help this derelict relic look any better. When Douglas and I drove to the airport, I couldn't believe how badly the Antonov looked. It reminded me of the bucket of bolts starship that Harrison Ford piloted in Star Wars back in the last century, not the greatest looking one but one of the greatest to fly. That An-2 fit in that category. You could close your eyes and visualize Harrison Ford flying that plane in an Indiana Jones movie. Or, you can open you eyes and see him fly it in *"Indian Jones and the*

Kingdom of the Crystal Skull". That's why it was painted to look like it had been rescued from the jungles of Peru. It's kind of neat, knowing that this same An-2 that I flew today appears in that movie, and Harrison is telling his friends that he had the chance to fly the same airplane that Matthew A. Nelson, Esq., STS-144, has flown!

For take-off, I sat in the passenger cabin, in first class just behind the cockpit, listening with my headset to Douglas and Neal chattering in pilot talk. The engine of an F-16 sounds like the whine of a mosquito in comparison to the deep roar of the two engines on an F-4; likewise, when a thousand thundering horses living inside the An-2's mighty engine decide in unison to stampede out through the 4-inch exhaust pipes, Cessnas and Pipers look over with envy, and well, your can "hearalize" (kind of like visualize!) what I'm talking about. Douglas keyed his mike and asked me something like, "Matt, isn't that a sweet sound?" Naturally, I eagerly agreed. As we waited for the engine to warm up, a bright yellow Beech Staggerwing taxied by to the fuel pumps. A few minutes later the Antonov lifted off, probably within 500-feet from beginning the take-off roll of runway 17 at the Chandler Stellar Airpark. I had a good view of the Staggerwing out of my window.

**An-2, still partially painted as it was in the movie,
"*Indian Jones and the Kingdom of the Crystal Skull*"**

When I arrived in Phoenix the night before, I gave Douglas a call on my cell phone; he answered, "Lithuanian Airlines!" I told him that I had just arrived and want to apply for the co-pilot's job. A few minutes after we were airborne, Neal came back from the co-pilot's seat and I started my new job. It only lasted an hour-and-a-half, but that's an hour-and-a-half longer than I flew the plane in 2007. It had been two years since I had last flown this plane, and I have to admit that my skills have rusted. Guess the only way to regain proficiency is to fly it a bunch more hours! When I sat down we were at 3000-feet; Douglas had me bring it up to 5500-feet. The co-pilot's altimeter and airspeed are in meters and kilometers, respectively; during the climb I had to maintain (or tried to maintain) an indicated airspeed of 152 kilometers/hour (83 mph) and then leveled off at 1600 meters. This isn't exactly 5500 feet, but I had adjusted the altimeter to give me an easy reference point. Once, I had inadvertently climbed to 1700 meters and Douglas cheerfully chided me for busting airspace. That would have put me over 5800 feet. We were on a course of 120 degrees, and there were some good-sized hills along our flight path. When I move to Montana I will have to improve my proficiency of flying near-and-around mountains. But Douglas flies in Alaska all the time. To me, we were flying sort of close to the hills, but he gave me some good pointers and the flight went smoothly. We did encounter a couple of downdrafts, and although I thought I was handling the plane OK, when he came back up front, Douglas grinned and remarked that it sure was bumpy in the back! Sorry guys!

A few miles northwest of Tucson we flew by the Bio Sphere facility, which is quite impressive from the air. I had my camera in my pocket and should have taken it out. I like my job at the space center, but most of the time I'm in a room with no windows, and quite often the high population, high traffic, heat and humidity of Houston is depressing. Looking at Arizona from the cockpit of the An-2, with the side windows open, and flying with friends in the early daylight hours over the sparsely populated desert does a lot to improve one's mood. Just before we landed Douglas the pilot took over to bring the An-2 into Douglas International Airport (KDGL), which is right by the Mexican border. (Douglas-Bisbee Airport is located about 10 miles north.) On the way down I told him if his name were Bill, he would have to keep his plane at Billings. He just grinned.

Douglas taxied the Antonov to a large World War II type of hangar and shut her down. It was 8:10 AM and nobody was around. We didn't have to wait for long before Les and Richard showed up. A bit later the massive hangar doors were opened, and Neal started power washing the right side of the plane. They are going to leave the left side painted as it was in the Indiana Jones movie, but wanted to bring the right side back to the normal paint job of *Lithuanian Airlines*. The water-soluble paint that had been applied for the movie had baked in the sun while the plane was in Baja over the Winter, and had been attacked by the wind, so it was cracked and peeling quite badly. Neal asked me to take photos with his digital camera while he cleaned the plane.

The An-2 at Douglas International Airport, Arizona

Douglas and me at his international airport, Douglas, Arizona

While Neal washed the plane, Les and Ginny talked to Douglas about flying the plane in August during a planned air show at the airport. They want to sell raffle tickets so that the winner and a few family members and/or friends can fly in the same plane that was used in the Indiana Jones movie. Richard was going to give me a ride into town, but Douglas asked me if I would like to go with Ginny and Les as they were ready to leave, so I hopped a ride with them. As we drove in, I was given a tour of the town and they told me about some of its interesting history. They took me to a bus station so I could go back to Phoenix. A few hours later, after four hours of listening to nothing but Spanish on the radio, the bus driver dropped me off at the motel where I had stayed the night before. Once more, I had had a good trip to Arizona, seeing Douglas and Neal, and flying the An-2 again. I anticipate flying and writing about it many more times.

Another flight on Southwest Airlines and I was home by 1:15 AM, in time to go back to work in the room with no windows to support the American space program, working with the same space shuttle Ku-band antenna that we had installed on Tuesday of this week, one that has flown several times in space. Maybe, this will be the same Ku-Band antenna that will be on-board the space shuttle that takes me to space during my self-designated flight of STS-144! Just wish NASA would see the merits of my twenty-five years of handling space flight equipment and select me for the next round of astronaut training. If that is the case, my mountain flying in Montana might just have to wait a few more years. NOTE: The newly painted Antonov is pictured at the bottom of the first page of this story on An-2s.

Other An-2s

Whoa, is that the An-2 colt sitting in front of Bob Wagstaff's hangar in La Porte, Texas? Sure thing – it is the one he and Reggie and some other people were working on two years ago when Douglas and Neal had their Antonov here. Look at that beautiful paint job! Two years ago there were no wings attached to the poorly painted fuselage that still had a red hammer and sickle on it. These photos were taken about April, 2008.

Bob Wagstaff's An-2 at La Porte Airport

Look at that old antique. Nice An-2, though! Photo courtesy of Lance Borden

September 15, 2008

Hurricane Ike struck Galveston and Houston on Saturday, Sept. 13th. Besides doing billions of dollars of damage, and destroying many thousands of homes, it wiped out the Lone Star Flight Museum in Galveston, and Bob Wagstaff's An-2 at the La Porte airport. My Stinson was OK and safe at the same airport. I had just picked it up a week before the storm, after it had been in Galveston all summer for an extended annual. Michelle and I weathered out the storm together – both Karoline and Keith had to work. I thank God that we were all safe, and that we had very little damage to our house. Several times since that time I have flown over some of the areas hit by the storm. Even after seeing the news coverage, it is still almost unbelievable.

Bob Wagstaff's An-2 at La Porte Airport after Hurricane Ike

October 2007 and September 2006

I know, I'm backing up a bit. Every October there is a Fly-In at Reklaw, Texas. The old Stinson Flying Machine and I wandered over; somebody from Texas had his An-2 there. My friend Dave Moore took this photo of me taking off and the An-2 taxiing. In September of 2006 my friend Dana Van Burgh sent the photo of the one in Casper, Wyo.

That's my Stinson taking off with a Texas-based An-2 taxiing, Reklaw, TX, Oct. 2007.
Photo by David Moore

My friend Dana Van Burgh sent me this photo of the An-2 in Casper, Wyoming.
Somebody flying with it said, "It is ugly but it is really slow!"

Flying Safari in South Africa, Namibia, Botswana, and Zambia, and Kenya, August 2008

Flying Safari in South Africa, Namibia, Botswana, and Zambia, and Kenya, August 2008

Introduction

Five years ago I wanted to go to South Africa and fly around in a Cessna 182 owned by Hanks Aero Adventures, but my Stinson flying machine was jealous of me flying another airplane and refused to go airborne until I spent my African flying money on it. This year I kept my African flying plans secret, but the Stinson still found out, and decided to show me who was boss by pouting for three months while its annual inspection was being performed. Only it chose the wrong time, because I went anyway, while it was looking at other planes having the freedom to fly while it sat in a dusty hangar in Galveston. As a side note, a week before Hurricane Ike destroyed much of Galveston, the Stinson decided it was time to leave Dodge, and by doing so, extended its own lifespan. By the time Hurricane Ike came ashore, I had been back from South Africa for two weeks. Not just South Africa, but Namibia, Botswana, Victoria Falls in Zambia, and Kenya. Roger "Mzungu" Moore, my friend from Dallas, met me in Johannesburg (Jo'Burg) on August 8th; he flew right seat in the 182 while I piloted the airplane in a circular route that began on August 11th and ended on August 21st at the Lanseria airport in Jo'Burg. We traveled together in all the countries mentioned but Kenya; he has led many photographic expeditions to Kenya, so while we did not go there with each other, he was there with me in spirit. His web page is www.rogermoorephotography.com. This is the story of the three weeks I was fortunate to spend flying around Africa and having the opportunity to photograph many of the animals that call Africa home

August 5th – August 10th

Finally, the day came for me to depart Houston. Only Tropical Storm Edouard caused extensive flight delays, and the Air France flight to Paris was cancelled. An airlines representative phoned me early on Tuesday morning and told me that instead of the afternoon flight, I could probably be on a flight leaving at 2 AM the next day, but they would still have to wait to see what the storm was doing. By late evening, it looked like I would be able to go, so I went to the airport early and was told I could make a midnight flight. Instead of arriving in Paris around 8 AM, I arrived there about 3 PM on August 6th, so my biggest regret was not having enough time to go to the Louvre. I made up for it by taking a train to see the Eiffel Tower. Forty-two years had passed since I had last seen it. When I made the Air France flight reservations last October using my Continental Airlines frequent flyer miles to go to Jo'Burg, I arranged to stay overnight in Paris because I knew it would be a very long flight if I just went straight through to Jo'Burg.

On Thursday, the 7th, I boarded the flight to Jo'Burg; ten hours later after flying over the Sahara desert, Nick and Chris Hanks met me at the airport. Many times had I looked at their website (http://www.seflflysafari.com/), talked to them on the phone, and exchanged bunches of emails. By the time we finally met, I felt like I was meeting old friends. Not old as in elderly. I have that distinction.

They drove me to the very nice Zulu Nyala Lodge located in Randburg (part of Jo'Burg), and there Nick gave me a very detailed notebook covered with bull hide that had each of the twelve flight legs separated into their own individual envelopes, and each of these envelopes contained runway information, frequencies, points of interest along the way, sample flight plans, contact information, and charts. The next day, I was told by Andre Kemp that somebody could be given the keys to the airplane and fly the route just with the information that Nick and Chris provided. They are very thorough in providing their clients this information, and in making arrangements for flight clearances and lodging arrangements. I can't give them enough praise for their efforts.

The next morning a driver named Ephraim (I think) picked me up at the Zulu Nyala and drove me to Lanseria Airport. Chris met me and walked me over to the tower, where air traffic controller Andre Kemp gave me a very good briefing about flying in Johannesburg and South African airspace. While Andre and I were talking, Nick took my logbook and pilot's license and other data to have my license validated in South Africa. He said he dropped it off at the office on 0808080808 (8:08 AM on the 8th of August, 2008). Sounded good to me. After receiving my briefing from Andre, I met up with Nick, who took me to see the plane and introduced me to Johan and his son Pierre, who are two very good mechanics. Nick also showed me his Helio Courier, which he and Chris had flown from the United States several years ago. That plane has an endurance of eight hours; it took them five hours to fly across the Atlantic and five months to make their way to South Africa. During the course of their journey, they realized that other pilots could learn from them, and they decided to start Hanks Aero Adventures to facilitate pilots with flight clearances, lodging, etc. OK, Nick, I have given you a CD with stories I have written, and now you are reading this. I am still waiting to receive your stories about those five months (and any others you have written) of flying through Africa. Hint, Hint! I hope this message goes directly to the "Oh, yeah, I promised Matt some stories" part of your brain and goes to Chris's brain to tell Nick that it is time you send them! I'm still waiting eagerly to read them.

While I was with Andre and Nick, Chris had gone back to the big airport to pick up Roger, or "Mzungu", as he likes to be called. Mzungu is Swahili for white man. After we all hooked up, he and I followed Nick and Chris to their home in the rental car that they had arranged for us to have. Of course, I had to become familiar again of driving a car where the gear-shifting lever is operated with my left hand and my right elbow hangs out the right side of the car. Chris prepared a good lunch, and then Nick and I had a couple hours of briefings and flight planning.

On Saturday, Lynn, a lady that works for the Hanks, drove Mzungu around Jo'Burg. That night he had some eye-opening stories to tell me about life in South Africa. While we were eating, we were kidding each other about something or another, and he asked me if I wanted to arm wrestle. So I said, "OK", and impromptu and without warning, instead of trying to push his arm backwards, all of a sudden I pushed his hand the other direction, causing him to spill his glass of wine all over the table. I bought him another glass of wine, but I don't think our waitress was as amused as I was.

That same morning I met Amy Shaw, a young flight instructor who worked for the Lanseria Flight Centre. Nick had arranged for her to be the instructor who would validate my American pilot's license to be legal to fly in South Africa and surrounding countries. Prior to flying Nick's 182, Amy gave me another briefing about flying in South African airspace and the proper words to say over the radio and the sequence to say them. We then flew for about an hour over the general practice area, going through the radio calls and reporting points, while she pointed out the local landmarks such as the satellite tracking station and a lake called the Hartesbeespoort Dam. After I had sent the initial deposit to Nick and Chris a few months earlier, they had sent me a cockpit trip kit, which included local charts, an audio CD made from actual conversations between air traffic controllers and pilots, a homework assignment, etc. to prepare me. By the time I flew with Amy, I had a good mental image of the local area, and in fact, had even studied some satellite photos obtained on GoogleMaps.com. I had flown also several hours with Carl Nepute in a rented 182 at a local airport, so I could be more familiar with the handling characteristics of a 182. It all paid off. On Sunday, Amy and I flew the course that I had plotted out on the homework assignment; altogether, I flew slightly over three hours with her. I was a little worried that I would blow my check ride, but I didn't, and now I have this adventure to write about.

While flying with Amy, I told her of some of my adventures picking up my float plane rating, and mentioned about having flown in Alaska. She told me that flying floats in Alaska is one of her dreams, so I gave her Don Lee's name, owner of Alaska Floats and Skis, whom I have flown with. He hires lady instructors. Since I left Africa, Amy has been in contact with Don, and it looks like she may be going to work for him in 2010. She no longer works for Lanseria Flight Centre, but is now having the time of her life flying twin-engine aircraft on UN missions around the Congo. I received some emails from her after I returned home, and I'm printing them here because her story is so interesting and she is such a dynamic person:

"I have been with this company since beginning of September now, was busy working out my notice at Lanseria when I flew with you. I am based in the Republic of the Congo in Brazzaville at the moment (we work 2 months at base, one month off back in south Africa); we fly for the United Nations world food Program into The democratic Republic of the Congo (DRC-formerly Zaire), Central African Republic and occasionally Cameroon. On the 15th November I will be flying over to Uganda where the plane goes for maintenance (super excited about that cause I hear it is beautiful there!). It is really beautiful in this part of the world as it is proper jungle, we go fishing down on the Congo River on our off days and the other day in Bangui in central African Republic we paid a local to Row us up the river in this little

boat they use here- basically a hollowed out tree trunk - right into the jungle- was actually kind of creepy cause its so unstable and the crocs in the river next to us where HUGE!!

My aircraft is a Let410, Czech Aircraft; it holds 21 people including the 2 crew. Its a nice bush flying aircraft because its "hot and high" short field take off and landing performance is incredible so we get to see the really tiny villages and remote areas that the 1900 and Kingair pilots don't get to see because the strips we go into are sometimes as short as 600m which the 1900's just won't get into! I am enjoying every minute of it! We mostly fly UN workers in and out of their bases, and occasionally refugees which is sometimes sad- had to fly 11 orphans from Central African republic back to the DRC which was the country they had left to take refuge from (there is big fighting in Eastern DRC at the moment- the UN is actually pulling their people out of there cause its getting too dangerous).. was horrible to be the one who had to send these poor kids back to a place like that-all because of politics! But it is often very rewarding, as is the nature of this work! Sometimes its ridiculous- We flew across 2 countries the other day to deliver a flat screen TV to some UN official!! Gives you an idea of where all the grant money goes!

We have had a quiet couple of days here in the Congo- most of our flights are into the DRC and there was a DRC public holiday today, so the whole country comes to a standstill, so organizing fuel posed a problem! Today's task for the crew (for which I am project manager) involved planning our Bar we are wanting to build onto the front porch of our crew house. It will be a proper coconut bar made with the local (very rustic!) wood which will give it loads of character. It will be called the "Brazza-Bar-Balaas" .... and to fill you in, a hangover in South Africa is commonly called a "babalaas"..:)

Hey!
Thought you'd appreciate this- (photo of An-2) *it is sitting, apparently, abandoned at Bangui Airfield in Central African Republic. We're busy contemplating the feasibility of our engineer getting it serviceable and then me and one of the captains (who is rated on the thing) quietly removing it to finer pastures of South Africa... Also whether it counts as aircraft theft if one removes an aircraft that appears to have no owner...Ha!*

Hope you're well. Amy

Flying the 1940 Tiger Moth in Krogersdorp, South Africa

August 10th

On Sunday afternoon, after I received my license validation, Mzungu and I drove to Krogersdorp to fly a 1940 Tiger Moth. This fine airplane is owned by Christopher Kyle and Martiens Steyn; their sons Merrick and Mitch Kyle and Peter and Rowan Steyn greeted us at the airport. I wanted to fly that plane because of the thrill of flying such a beautiful and historic biplane, and Mzungu wanted to fly it for photographic opportunities, and we both had our wish granted. Chris is an instructor, so now I have an hour's time in a Tiger Moth written in my logbook. What fun! He and I flew over to the same practice area I had flown the 182 with Amy. Stick and rudder and open cockpit bugs in your teeth kind of flying. I like flying Stearmans, and I certainly liked flying the Tiger Moth. It responded well to my movements on the stick and rudder pedals, and Chris demonstrated a couple of stalls when I asked him to. An hour is simply not enough time to fly a plane such as the Tiger Moth, but then again, it is an hour well remembered. Mzungu was only airborne about thirty minutes, but he stepped out of the plane with a big grin on his face as well. After the flight ended, I didn't want the evening to end without spending more time with these fine people, so I invited all of them and Tammy and Wendy, the wives of Chris and Martiens, to dinner. I am glad they accepted. Since that time, I have had several emails from Chris, and Merrick and Mitch sent me a thank you email after I sent them post cards of Wyoming elk and moose. I have also sent them emails with photos I took on the African trip. Chris has a way of making me feel good, and we both have a love of aviation. I have taken the liberty of including some of his emails:

Hello Matt,

Hope all is well with you! How's your Stinson doing? The S108 is a fine airplane, has some very fine aerodynamic designs built in. You see we are the privileged few of all the aviators in the world to have flown and still fly such great classics! The old Tiger is doing just fine and I enjoyed the honour of flying her for 2.5 hrs on Sunday. After some 37 years of flying all kinds of airplanes including Jets and Turbines, I tell you what, for me the purity of the oldies is absolutely unmatched for the sheer joy of flight!
Kind regards,
Chris Kyle.

Chris,
I know what you mean about the old airplanes. I haven't flown anything fancy like you have, but that's OK, too. The USAF F-16 Thunderbirds performed at an air show yesterday, but on Saturday I had to make the Stinson flap its wings, too.
Matt

Hi Matt,
You know what, it's meeting people like you that makes life really worth it! The pic of N8706K on the apron below Stinson Tower is great. You are feeling of being part of aviation and the joy of flying whatever it is, that counts and bonds us together as a band of brothers who simply enjoy the same things in life. Flapping the Stinson's wings is more important than the might of the Thunderbirds, I think.
Kind regards,
Chris Kyle.

Hi Matt,
Some brilliant shots! I kind of get the feeling that you really enjoyed your visit to this part of the planet. I think Africa in it's pure form, has a way of really bringing us back to where we should be, that of course, if you take politics and human perversion out of the equation. I've lived here all my life but still find much peace and equilibrium in experiencing things as God intended them to be.
Kind regards,
Chris Kyle.

Chris Kyle and me

Chris and Roger
(both of these are his photos)

Great fun flying this Tiger Moth

Lanseria to Upington, South Africa

Photo courtesy of Roger "Mzungu" Moore

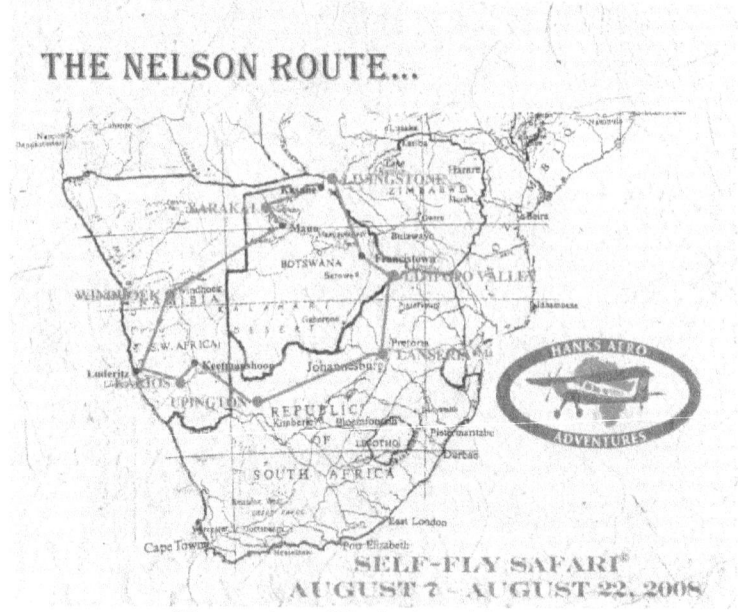

Map courtesy of Hanks Aero Adventures

August 11th

"India Whiskey Papa, you are cleared for take off on Zero Six Left with a left turn out", or words to that affect, resonated through my headphones. "Lanseria Tower, India Whiskey Papa is cleared for take off on Zero Six Left with a left turn out", I repeated, as I looked over at Mzungu. He smiled and shook my hand, and I lined up India Whiskey Papa onto the runway and gave it full throttle. "God, please keep us safe", I said in a silent prayer that I knew He heard. I didn't have Amy Shaw along side to guide me through the slightly confusing and intimidating proper radio communications I needed to make to the different controllers in South Africa, nor did I have my long time Stateside flight instructor Carl Nepute along to help me fine tune my flying skills in a Cessna 182. As the pilot-in-command, I was on my own. Mzungu had flown for a couple of hours in a Cessna 172 to learn how to land a plane in case something happened to me, but now I was the guy strictly responsible for piloting the plane around for the next ten or eleven days in totally new airspace on a new continent through four different countries. Yesterday's cross-country check ride in the 182 and wonderful flight in the yellow Tiger Moth were now fond memories and notations in my logbook. Today, I had to act like a pilot who knew what he was doing.

Our morning started off with a good breakfast at the Zulu Nyala Lodge (http://www.zulunyala.com/accomcm.htm), a quick drive to the airport, and some last minute briefings by Nick. Johan and Pierre were there to double check that the plane was in top mechanical shape, we had some last minute photos, and just before Mzungu and I entered the plane, I said to all there that I wanted to say a prayer. I asked God for a safe flight, gave thanks for the opportunity of making it, and forgot to give Him thanks for the expert mechanics that had prepared the plane and for Nick's efforts in making this trip available to me. Shortly after 10 AM, I hollered out the window, "Clear Prop!", watched the prop turn until the two blades disappeared into a clear transparent circle, checked the oil pressure, and heard that mighty engine roar. Glance out to the right side of the plane, see a thumbs up from Nick and a grin from Mzungu, make a radio call to Lanseria Ground for taxi instructions, give a final goodbye wave to Nick, Johan, and Pierre, take a deep breath, say one more silent prayer, release the brakes and advance the throttle, hold the yoke back, start the taxi roll, and hope that the guys walking near the end of the hangars will move out of the way by the time we arrive there. They do.

The charted course marked with the pink magic marker line on it that Nick and I had made had us flying West towards the satellite ground station and then turning Southwest towards Upington, located on the Western side of South Africa. Once airborne, we sort of zigged and zagged along the pink line. I had not yet programmed my own GPS receiver, and didn't follow the one that Nick had loaned us close enough. Our zigging and zagging and looking at South Africa caused us to be an hour late arriving Upington. On this day, and on the other days of our trip, it was fairly hazy outside, which was kind of a disappointment. But we verified our GPS coordinates with the charts, and by the end of the trip, Mzungu would nudge me if I tended to drift off course. In fact, by the end of the trip he was a pretty good navigator, and although I could have flown the entire route without his help, I was glad that he took on this task so eagerly. His efforts certainly made my job easier.

Augrabies Falls. Photo by Roger "Mzungu" Moore

At Upington we refueled, paying cash in South African Rands. Usually, I can easily determine exchange rates in my head, but for some reason on this trip I could never keep up. It wasn't until later that I realized how much we paid in US dollars. Ouch! We still had several hours of daylight left, and we thought we wanted to fly to Augrabies Falls. While it was good to see the falls, it probably wasn't worth the extra 1.8 hours of flight time to go there. But even though I would not probably repeat this section of our trip, I must admit that the view of the countryside around the falls is much prettier than flying over much of Botswana.

Upington is a pleasant town near the Namibian border. Our lodging was at the Bain's House, a B & B with very nice accommodations (http://www.bainshouse.com.). The man who picked us up at the airport told us about some beautiful fields of flowers, but Mzungu and I realized that we didn't want to spend a couple of extra flight hours to fly there. A young lady about twenty-five greeted us, and offered to cook us dinner, but told us if we wanted we could go to a restaurant. We could tell that she wanted to cook (actually, I think she had already been cooking it), and we definitely made the right choice by eating there. All of the places we stayed had two beds in the room; in the Bain's House we each had our own rooms. After a wonderful breakfast the next morning, the owner took us back to the airport and we paid the first of our landing, parking, navigation, and customs fees. Chris and Nick gave us a packet of money before we departed Lanseria to cover these fees. The lady customs officer was very polite and official acting, but then when everything was settled, she walked with me out to the parking lot and gave me her personal business card and address, so I could send some NASA decals to her son. She told me that she and her husband are Christians and they would pray for Mzungu and me to have a safe journey.

Cañon Lodge and Fish River Canyon, on to Windhoek, Namibia

August 12th – 13th

For the first time in my life, I crossed an international border flying as pilot in command. We had a straight out departure for Keetmanshoop, Namibia. An hour or so into the flight, I noticed that the mixture control was almost full rich, even though I had previously leaned it out. The vernier knob had come loose, and I was more ignorant about how it worked at the time then I am now – all I had to do was screw it in! But I didn't realize that until we landed back in Lanseria several days later. But we all have a little of MacGyver blood running through us – we measured the length of the mixture control shaft required to lean the engine properly, and Mzungu tore off a strip a paper the same width, and folded it up over the shaft like a tent and it worked fine for the rest of the trip. After that, for the rest of the trip, that piece of paper was part of our checklist.

Enroute, we had a strong head wind that caused us another hour of unexpected fuel consumption and delay. All those crosswind landings that Carl had me go through paid off when I landed at Keetmanshoop. Within minutes, we had cleared customs and were on our way to Karios Airport, located near Cañon Lodge. Here is a website for them: http://www.namibian.org/travel/lodging/private/canon.htm. Nick Hanks told me to fly over the lodge and the lodge personnel would send a driver for us at the dirt strip. Mervin drove up in a Land Rover as we were securing the plane.

Cañon Lodge

The lodge itself is located in an outcrop of rocks, and the architects made use of the rocks to form walls of the cabins. Our cabin had a big old rock that stuck out about three feet. About an hour or two after arriving, Mervin took us on a scenic game drive. We saw some kudos, oryx, jackals, a couple of Texas looking windmills, and quiver trees similar to Joshua trees. These are so named because the tree contains hollow tubes, which the original dwellers used to hold their arrows. For dinner that night oryx meat was served, and this tastes every bit as good as elk meat. Mzungu and I took a couple extra pieces, which we ate as a snack the next morning as John drove us out to Fish River Canyon. It is much smaller than the Grand Canyon, but has often been compared to it. What I saw is every bit as beautiful.

Onyx

Quiver Tree

Fish Canyon. Photo by Roger "Mzungu" Moore

We had planned on flying over the canyon, but when we departed on Thursday we were uncomfortably low on fuel. Keetmanshoop doesn't sell fuel anymore, but I was able to buy 60 liters (about 15 gallons) from Cañon Lodge. The plan was for us to buy fuel at Luderitz, located on the coast, but they were fogged in. Fortunately, we met Freddie von Seydlitz, a Namibian pilot and owner of Immenhof Air Safaris (http://www.immenhofnamibia.com/air-safaris.html) who helped arrange fuel for us at Sossusvlei (http://www.sossusvleilodge.com/). This is a resort area that caters to Italians. It took us 2½ hours to fly there from Karios, and I was watching for every potential landing sight, especially during the last hour. We took off with 45 gallons of fuel, I leaned it out as best as I could, kept the manifold pressure slightly low because I had heard that Charles Lindbergh taught General Jimmy Doolittle's pilots that technique when they were training for their Tokyo raid in the B-25s. When we landed at Sossusvlei, I checked the fuel in the tanks and found we had 25 gallons left. Flying for 2½ hours in a Cessna 182 and only using 20 gallons of fuel surprised me. After lunch we were on our way to Windhoek, the capital city of Namibia. This was the most intense flying day we had during the entire trip. Mzungu had remarked during our flight that Freddie was an angel. I know who sent him. It was a little disappointing not to fly to Luderitz and up the Namibian coast, but we certainly came through safely.

If I ever go back to Namibia, I plan on going back to Cañon Lodge and to Immenhof Lodge, Freddie's place. Next time, I plan on flying over the Fish River Canyon, too. The area may not have a high abundance of animals, but it certainly doesn't lack for beautiful scenery.

Mapula Lodge – Okavango Delta, Botswana

August 15th - 17th

File a flight plan. Wait for the fuel truck. Pay the parking, landing, and navigation fees. Come on, let's go before the El Presidente shows up and the airport closes. I think the South African president was departing Windhoek, Namibia, or the Namibian president was going to depart to South Africa. I can't imagine just freely walking around the ramp between the plane and the refueling office at our nation's airport, even if is not the main airport, when our president is departing within an hour's time. But that's what we did. Mzungu and I departed Windhoek's Eros airport and trimmed our sails and GPSs to Maun, Botswana. Of course, we had a little help from the air traffic controllers in Windhoek telling us to stay out of the main airport's airspace.

Our flight to Maun was over some of the most boring and unappealing country I have ever seen. And it was hazy and bumpy. Ask Mzungu. We left Windhoek a little later than anticipated, and lost an hour due to the time change. By the time we landed at Maun, it was 4 PM. Fuel the plane, grab the gear, clear customs, pay landing and navigation fees, file another flight plan, go through the metal detector, walk slowly so as not to leave the pregnant lady police officer in the dust so she and another woman police officer can look into the plane and justify how their rice bowls are filled. Come on, lady, will you hurry up! Finally, wheels up at 5:25 PM, sunset is about 6:15, and we have once chance only to make Xarakai airport before sunset. The dirt strip was visible three miles out, exactly where my good old GPS indicated it should be. We couldn't see much of the Okavango Delta, or at least I couldn't, because the sun was in my eyes and reflecting over the water. But at 6:10 PM, I flew over the runway, set up for a left downwind and a short field landing, touched down with full flaps, making my best landing on the entire trip. Had I misjudged at all, or made any major mistakes, we probably would have had to return to Maun, because it was dark within about 15 minutes after landing, and there was no such thing as runway lights. On final, I could see a Land Rover and a few people at the end of the strip.

Our guide Josiah and game spotter John met us with broad grins and offered us snacks and a cold drink. I was ready for the water. We also met a couple from France, and Robert, Pat, and Rachael, their eleven-year old daughter, all from England. Everybody had stopped for a Sundowner, waiting for Mzungu and me to land, while they were on their evening game drive. Earlier in the day, a lioness and her two cubs were observed near where we tied the plane to a couple buckets filled with sand. We spent about an hour making our way back to Mapula Lodge; I remember seeing a couple of hippos at a distance, and driving over this rickety old log bridge.

What a delightful place, is this Mapula Lodge (http://www.mapulalodge.com). All the staff we met were very nice, and seemed genuinely happy to see us. I felt like I have known Joseph, the camp manager, for years. While we were sitting around a campfire waiting for dinner to be served, another man came up. He said something like, "Matt no?", and it dawned on me his name is Matt, and he was asking me if my name is also Matt. I immediately said, "I am Matt Yes, so you must be Matt No!" From that moment on I called him "Matt No", and he called me "Matt Yes". He is one of the guides, but most of the time I didn't see him, because Josiah was our guide while we were there.

When dinner was served, all eighteen guests sat down at a long table, there was wine for those who wanted it, bunches of forks and knives surrounded each plate and it was up to me to decide which one I should use, the food was delicious, and the service was fantastic! Often after our meals, Mzungu passed gas as if he were playing the trumpet loud enough to knock down the walls of Jericho, and I started joking, "The lion does not sleep tonight!" Naturally, I never had that problem, because I am a nice guy and nice guys don't do things like that!

After dinner Josiah led us to our bungalow or cabin or room or whatever it is called. From the outside it doesn't look like much, but the inside has a rugged elegance and the porch overlooks a marshy area larger than a football field. During the night we could hear hippos snorting. This was the only place Mzungu and I stayed where the mosquito netting was rolled downward over the beds. I used Mzungu's night vision scope and thought I saw a zebra laying down; in the morning it was still there, only disguised as a white tree branch. There was a bathtub inside the place, but the outside shower only has three walls; the open wall looks out over the swamp. I must say having a bright yellow full moon and a green swamp and a white tree branch that thinks it is a zebra makes a most unusual shower curtain! Near the lodge's main area, there is a place to sit down and look out at the swamp, as you contemplate what you will do for the day or what kind of day you already had enjoyed. Anybody wandering around in the swamp in a canoe, or any curious hippos, can see you go about your business. Mzungu made a couple of photos!

Spooky hippo eyes
Left: Baboon

During the morning game drive we saw zebras that think they are zebras, a few elephants that don't care what the zebras think, bunches of birds, impalas, baboons, giraffes, and some wild dogs. In the afternoon, we went on a Mokoro canoe ride through the swamp where I managed to photograph some of the water lilies, some very dangerous hippos staring at us with eyes the size of plums, and Rachael and her family. She is mature for her age, a delight to be around, and has been traveling the world with her parents since she was four.

Shortly after dinner on the second night, four elephants came wondering though the camp, very close to where we ate. They were eating trees nearby, when someone snapped a photo using a camera with a flash. That spooked the elephants, and one started to charge us from about fifteen feet way, or at least it looked like that to me. Later, I was told that an elephant would do a mock charge when his or her ears are flat, but it's a real charge when she folds here ears back. This was a mock charge, but enough to make my heart pump a little faster. Josiah took us in the Land Rover back to the cabin, because the elephants went down the path towards the cabins. Mzungu had already left and missed seeing them. There was one straggler, standing near a tree, looking at us from about twenty feet away, ears trimmed for fight, fully illuminated by the full moon. Beautiful sight, one I won't forget. Great camp, one I won't forget! The next morning it was discovered that the elephants left their marks in front of each of the cabins. After breakfast we were driven back the airstrip for our flight to Victoria Falls.

Think we all know what these animals are!

Victoria Falls, Livingston, Zambia

August 17th

After a short game drive back to the Xarakai airstrip, Roger and I made sure that the wings of the plane were not damaged, since there was evidence elephants had gone to the bank and made a deposit. But I realized what I saw had been there when we tied up the plane a couple of days earlier. We were airborne by 9 AM, and had a fairly short flight to Kasane, located in the Northeast corner of Botswana, near the border of Namibia, Botswana, Zambia, and Zimbabwe, along the Chobe River. After the customs and fuel stop, we flew to Livingston, Zambia, and received flight clearance to over fly Victoria Falls. General aviation aircraft are required to be at 6000-feet over the falls, and have their own assigned radio frequency. Although I announced our position several times, the radio remained quiet. Roger and I were the only ones flying; we didn't even see any of the numerous helicopters that fly tourists over the falls. Although we did not officially have permission to enter Zimbabwe airspace, which is located on the other side of the falls, minor incursions are allowed. Roger used my camera and it didn't look like any photos would turn out because of the haze, but I managed to make some of them look good. I contacted Livingston Tower when we departed from the falls for landing instructions, but had a hard time understanding the lady controller. After I asked her to repeat a couple of times, a man spoke in a clear but slightly agitated voice: "India Whiskey Papa, you are cleared to land Runway one zero." Thank you sir, that's all I wanted to know.

The Zambezi Sun hotel is within walking distance to the falls, is fancy, expensive, and caters to visitors from all over the world. While it is a nice place, Roger and I both agreed that we liked the Mapula Lodge much better. But Victoria Falls is not located in the Okavango Delta, and neither were we. Had I known better, we would have spent two nights in Livingston and two at Tuli Safari Lodge, instead of one and three, respectively. Gives me a reason to go back. By the time we walked to the falls, we only had two hours to spend before sunset. I have heard it said that the view is better from the Zimbabwe side, but I was pretty impressed with what I saw and heard from the Zambia side. Two hours is simply not enough time to spend there. And when one considers that Americans are charged a $135 visa fee, our night there turns out to have been very expensive. If I ever go back to Africa, I certainly plan on spending more time at Victoria Falls (and would obviously have to plan on spending more money!). What a fantastic place! It is expensive, but I am not sorry I went there. Known by the natives as Mosi-oa-Thunya, the "smoke that thunders", the first European to see the falls was Scottish explorer Dr. Stanley Livingston.

Near the falls, there is a statue of Dr. Livingston, with this inscription:

> *"16 November 1865 The most wonderful sight I had witnessed in Africa, no one can imagine the beauty of the view from anything witnessed in England. It has never been seen by European eyes, but seems so lovely must have been gazed upon by angels in their flight."*

The aerial photos of Victoria Falls on this page and the previous one were made with my camera, but Mzungu was the photographer

Tuli Safari Lodge, Botswana

August 18th – 21st

Prior to flying over Victoria Falls on Sunday, Mzungu and I discussed whether or not to wait until Monday to do so. It was a good thing that we decided to fly over the falls on Sunday, because the visibility was absolutely rotten on Monday. Our next leg of our odyssey took us to the Tuli Safari Lodge (http://www.tulilodge.com/) located in the Limpopo Valley in Botswana. A more direct route would have been to go straight from Livingston to Tuli, flying over Zimbabwe, but it is difficult to obtain permission to fly through Zimbabwean airspace, and the current political situation and stories of airplane seizures were enough to convince us that we didn't need the hassle. We flew back towards Kasane, Botswana, sort of following the Zambezi River, crossing back into Botswana near the area where the borders of Botswana, Namibia, Zambia, and Zimbabwe all merge. I had filed a flight plan at the Livingston airport, which allowed us to enter Botswana near Kasane, but to keep flying south to Francistown to clear customs.

It took a couple of hours of flying before we arrived in Francistown. Our flight path took us near, but not over Zimbabwe, and we kept a close eye on our chart and two GPS receivers to ensure we did not violate Zimbabwean airspace. By this time, we were quite adept in our navigation techniques, and Mzungu let me know if I started drifting off course. As I mentioned before, I could have flown the course without his assistance or without using GPS receivers, but my task was much easier using both. Flying over Botswana is like flying over West Texas, and often just a boring. Of all the airports where we landed, I had the most difficulty finding Francistown. Once on the ground, we had the most difficulty with all the people whom we had to deal with. What should have been about a thirty-minute stop ended up taking an hour-and-a-half. Although Nick and Chris Hanks took care of the money issue after we came back home, we had to pay extra money to the lady that handled the landing fees. Our plane, "India Whiskey Papa", had been at the airport in June, and the pilot had failed to pay the landing fee. I was worried that if I didn't pay, something bad might happen, such as the plane being confiscated. But there was no bribery involved, and I was given an official receipt from the lady. Mzungu and I were both ready for lunch, but we had encountered so much rudeness and bureaucracy that once the officials took our money and I filed a new flight plan, we left "Fleecetown" as fast as we could, figuring we could survive on the snacks we had in the plane. Besides, it had started to rain.

About an hour later we landed at the Limpopo Valley Airport, where we were met by Rudy, a driver from the Tuli Safari Lodge. Shortly after securing the plane and paying the required landing fees, we happily sat in the back of the Land Rover and bounced along the dirt road to the lodge area. While Brinny Tshabalala, the manager, was welcoming us with some tropical fruit drinks, we received a warm singing and dancing greeting from the staff ladies. Each place we stayed had its own charm; the Elephant Room at the Tuli Safari Lodge is by far the most fancy place we stayed on the entire trip.

Moscow, our driver and guide, and now friend, actually had spent six or seven years working in the Okavango Delta prior to going to work at Tuli. We had arrived to late to go on that evening's game drive, but on Tuesday morning, he expertly drove us around the area. The very first animals we saw were a small pack of hyenas; after that we encountered a bunch of elephants. Although in Kenya I saw many more animals than in the countries Mzungu and I traveled, I actually saw more elephants in Botswana than I did in Kenya. Over the next couple of days we saw jackals, giraffes, a multitude of birds, impalas, kudos, etc. The surrounding area is arid, and has some nice landscapes similar to the Southwestern United States.

Our time at Tuli was relaxing. One night Moscow and I stayed at a Hide, a building set up to watch the animals come to a nearby pond, but the season was the wrong time of year for game viewing. We didn't leave the lodge until about 10 PM, and except for a couple of flashlights, which we hardly used, our only light was from the illumination of the Milky Way. We heard hyenas off in the distance, but I couldn't tell for sure if they were laughing at me or not. The next morning we had to change a flat tire!

Jackal

On the last day we were at Tuli, Mzungu and I went on an evening/night game drive. Moscow drove; a young man by the name of John strapped himself to the spotter chair located in the front of the vehicle and operated the spotlight. Prior to darkness setting in, we all stopped for a sundowner, which is another word for picnic. After dark, Mzungu captured a very good image of a hyena trapped in the glare of the spotlight. My photos were just a blur.

Hyena captured by Roger "Mzungu" Moore

Photo by Roger "Mzungu" Moore

South African Airlines DC-3

    Prior to leaving on Thursday morning, we were given special treat. The night before we saw some airline pilots arrive; the next day we found out that they were the crew for a South African Airlines DC-3

flying tourists around the country. Not only did the crew consist of the two pilots, they had their own stewardess, who dressed like the stewardess's of the 1940s era. We started talking; when we went to the airport the pilots accompanied us, and showed us the inside of their beautiful airplane. I became a make-believe DC-3 pilot when I sat in the left seat. The plane is owned by a museum, and the two pilots fly it for fun.

Had we not already exceeded our contractual amount of flight hours in the Cessna 182, I would have liked to spend more time flying around the hills between Tuli and Lanseria. Yep, Lanseria, as in Johannesburg, South Africa. Our flying safari was coming to an end. Two hours after departing the Limpopo Valley Airport, we were landing back at our starting point. By that time, I was in communication with the Lanseria Tower and flying my final approach for Runway 06 Right. I could see another lumbering-along DC-3 landing, but had not been cleared to land yet. Meanwhile, the ground seemed to be rising rather rapidly towards us. The DC-3 turned off the active runway, I was given the clearance, and shortly afterwards we touched down for the first time. Runway 06R slopes downward. I went airborne a little, and thought, "Oh Great! I have managed to fly the entire trip without an incident and now I might just crash on my final landing." So I pushed the throttle in a bit, said another prayer, regained my composure and control of the plane, and successfully landed the second time. I had landed twice each day Mzungu and I had flown, so I guess I just had to keep that number constant. Two landings for the price of one!

I taxied the plane to the Customs area, paid the landing fees, and left Mzungu in the terminal with Lynn, who was there to greet us since Nick and Chris were off flying with another group of aviators seeking fun, travel, and adventure. I fueled the airplane, and taxied back to the hangar. Pierre' helped me push the plane back into the hangar. Lynn bought us lunch, we visited for a while, and she drove us to our hotel. Mzungu's and my African bush-flying safari was over. What an adventure! I have already mapped out my next route with Hanks Aero Adventures even if I may not go back to Africa again. But my South African validation on my pilot's license is valid for five years!

East African Aero Club, Masai Mara, and Amboseli, Kenya

August 22nd – 26th

In October 2007, when I made my reservations to go to Africa, in order to use my frequent flyer miles, I had very little choice of dates. Since my return flight was scheduled on August 26th, and my flight with Hanks Aero Adventures ended on the 21st, I decided to go to Kenya for a few days. Following a four-hour flight on South African Airlines from Johannesburg and a window seat that allowed me to see the top of Kilimanjaro, and a not-so-quick taxi ride through rush-hour traffic, I walked through the front door of the Aero Club of East Africa (ACEA) – (http://www.aeroclubea.net/). Several months ago, while searching the Internet to see if I could do any flying in Nairobi, I came across a club newsletter with an article in it about Joachim Pfeffer, Peter Boeheim, Matthias Koehler, Daniel Szlapak, and Jonathan Somen going to Alaska last year and picking up their seaplane ratings from Don Lee, the same man Amy Shaw wants to fly for. Ultimately, that led me to making contact with Joachim. It turns out that he and Peter own a game camp on the northern end of the Masai Mara called the Mara-Siria Camp (http://mara-siria-camp.com/en/index.html). Daniel put me in touch with Peter, who is also the owner of Phoenix-Safaris (http://www.phoenix-safaris.de/), and Peter was very instrumental in making my arrangements with Joachim. My thanks to all.

Since the ACEA also offers temporary membership to foreign pilots and has some guest rooms, I opted to stay there instead of at some hotel in Nairobi. When I went into the pilot's briefing room to check email, Wellington Kuria warmly greeted me. He has the fire in his eyes to become a pilot, and I think one of these days he will make it. Located at Wilson Airport in Nairobi, the club's history is about as long as the history of airplanes. Famed aviatrix Beryl Markham received her commercial pilot's license when she was a club member, and most certainly Denis Finch-Hatton downed a beer or two at the pub. Visiting the club, even as a transient pilot, and spending time looking at the historic photos and artifacts on the wall, gave me a very similar feeling of awe that I experience when I visit The Explorers Club's building in New York City. It wasn't on the same level that I felt when I was in Jerusalem in 1966 and saw where Jesus walked and lived, but it was still exhilarating to see a glimpse of African aviation history.

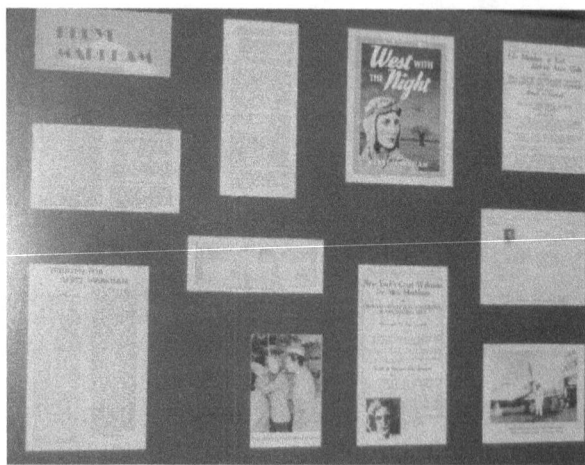

Inside the Aero Club of East Africa

On Saturday, the 23rd, Joachim met me at 7:30 AM and within a few minutes we were airborne in his Cessna 206 to the Mara-Siria game camp. After flying through a lot of haze, and over the Rift Valley, about an hour after take-off we flew over the camp and shortly landed at the Kichie Mara airport. Before we had the plane secured, Jacob, the camp manager, drove up in a Land Rover. During the twenty-minute ride from the airport to the camp, I saw more wild game, especially zebras, than I had in the previous ten days combined. Now I had an idea what Roger meant about the abundance of game in the Mara.

Jacob and Jacahim with his Cessna 206

After a welcoming glass of juice, and a quick visit to my new home of a luxurious tent, complete with running water, I took a hike with Leshau, a young Masai man, to the Mara River to look at hippos do what hippos do. It took us about one hour to hike downhill to the river – it would have been take less time had I not been wearing my cowboy boots with slick soles. Leshau gave me his walking stick to use, and often I was glad to have it. Along the way he told me of Masai life, and of their diet of meat, milk, and blood. Once a week they tap into a vein on a cow's throat and drink a liter or two of it. Sometimes they drain the blood and cook and eat it like a scrambled egg. They eat no vegetables or fruits, with the exception of berries. Their clothing is red, and the old way of dyeing clothes is to rub some type of grass with their fingers. Leshau demonstrated the technique, and sure enough, his hands turned a reddish-orange. Before we reached the river, Leshau communicated with Jacob on a cell phone, which seemed ironic and a mixture of old and new cultures. Two fat ladies once wanted to hike with Leshau to see the hippos. It took them seven hours. He told me that he could be in Nairobi in seven hours! At Mapula Lodge I never saw anything more than the eyes of hippos. When we reached the Mara River, I saw several of the not so cuddly creatures, and managed to capture with my camera one of them yawning.

Masai women

    We then drove to a Masai village, which is where Leshau lives when he is not staying at Mara-Siria Camp. Nine ladies welcomed me with melodious songs, and I was given a tour of the village. Very primitive! I have no regrets that I was not raised there. Leshau showed me the ear rings his mother wore, with holes the size of eggs in the ear lobes. A young man gave me a demonstration of starting fire by twirling a hardwood stick, and when the spark burst into flame, Leshau grabbed an elephant dung ball in his hands and held it until it too started burning. The village was only about three months old – every seven years new camps are built, because the cow dung plaster on the huts made of thorn bush branches finally becomes to heavy. After a rain, the walls and ceilings are re-plastered. The small village has two rings of thorn bush branches, with the inner ring forming the corral that is used to keep the cattle safe at night from lion attacks. The huts are located between the two rings of the branches, and a thorn gate is closed nightly. However, that still didn't stop lions from killing two cows the second day I was at Maria Siria. Leshau said that his father has six wives and twenty-two children, and they all seem to enjoy the company of the others. The first wife always has the first hut on the right when entering the camp; the second wife has the next hut in the circle, going counter-clockwise.

Masai men

    In the afternoon I then went on a game drive. Joachim drove the Land Rover, and besides viewing the usual amount of zebras, elephants, giraffes, seeing lions was the highlight of the drive. I'll let the photos do the talking of the game drives at the Masai Mara. Our dinner that night at the Mara-Siria Camp was made for kings and queens. The next day Abraham drove the Land Rover on a all day game drive, and did quite well in spotting cheetahs, a couple of rhinos, and took us to the Mara River where we were able to see the migration of the wildebeest. Fantastic! My best photo of the entire trip is the one of the two wildebeests jumping over the croc to enter the river. On the next several pages, I'm only going to name the animals that aren't known to every school kid.

Baboons

Cape Buffalo

Impala

Cape Buffalo

Hyenas

Jackal

Vultures

Warthogs

Mongoose

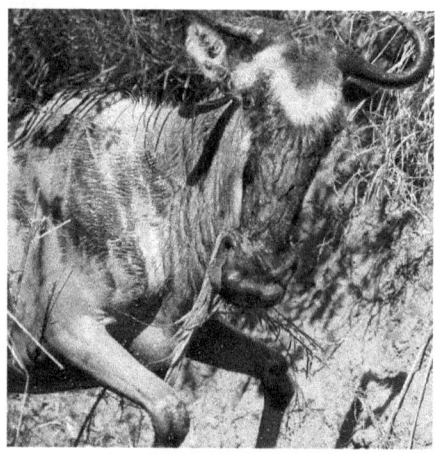

Look at that wildebeest jumping over the croc at the Mara River!

Mt. Kilimanjaro

On Monday, Joachim flew me in the Cessna to Amboseli. Rachael from the Ol Tukai Lodge (http://www.oltukailodge.com/) met me at the airport, and set me up to go on an afternoon game drive. Mt. Kilimanjaro was covered over with clouds all day, until about the time the game drive started. Another favorite photo of mine is of the giraffe standing in front of the Mountain, which is located in Tanzania, sixty miles / one hundred kilometers away.

Mt. Kilimanjaro and my last photo of a giraffe

Tuesday morning I took an Air Kenya flight to Nairobi; from there I left that afternoon back to Johannesburg, and then about midnight I boarded my Air France flight to Paris. By Wednesday night, I was back in Texas. Thanks go to God for giving me this opportunity to see more of His wonderful creation, and for keeping Roger and me safe. (Good old Jack Clodfelter make his way over to Africa). Roger "Mzungu" Moore is a great travel companion! Thanks go to Karoline for encouraging me to go on this trip. Hopefully, I will make it back to Africa again. Whether I do or not, I still have very fond memories of this magnificent continent.

Gen. 1:25 *And God made the beast of the earth after his kind, and cattle after their kind, and every thing that creepeth upon the earth after his kind: and God saw that it was good.*

Airplanes My Friends Fly

Mike Ferguson's Bonanza, Montana

One of these two planes is "Brand X", the other one is "The MiG Killer"!
One is owned by Russ Voorhees and the other one by Ernie Carlson, both in Montana.

Steve Palinkos's C-180, Montana

Bob Hamm's J-3 Cub, Montana

Chuck Carver's PA-140, Montana

Lance Borden's Luscombe 8F, Texas

Carl Nepute's J-3 Cub, Texas

Jim Gardner's 1946 C-120, Texas

Al Irvin's PA-140. His wife Joyce is in the Montana plane. Courtesy of Al

Bob Kraemer's Stearman "Alice" with him standing by the "Round Engine" in Missouri

Brian Carroll's brand new RV-7 that he built himself in Montana

Gideon Jones owns both the 1946 Ercoupe and the Legend Cub, Texas

Norm Kalat's Champ in Alaska. Courtesy of Norm

Chris Maxey's STOL King in Montana. Photo by Russ Voorhees

Chuck Thomas's Super Cub, Alaska. Photo courtesy of Chuck.

Eric Weaver's Twin Bee seaplane, Florida

While the majority of my flying has been in commercial or military aircraft as a passenger, sometimes I was lucky enough to have been the pilot myself, or as in the case of the flying on the EA-3B, a crewmember. Flying in a floatplane as a tourist is not the same as controlling the plane from the left seat. Likewise, it's more memorable to have flown across the Grand Canyon in my own plane than at 30,000 feet in an airliner. Most pilots don't have a chance to fly the An-2, nor fly around Africa. While I may not have had the flight experiences of many thousands of pilots who regularly fly the bush, military jets, commercial airlines, or space shuttles, I still cherish the memories I have made; I thank God for giving me the opportunity to fly and for always keeping me safe, and for the friends I have made who also share my passion of "slipping the surly bonds of earth". Once again, I am thankful that Karoline recognizes that I have the Travelitis Disease - a wanderlust that she doesn't fully understand, yet she still encourages me to pilot those magic carpets, to fly more "Flights of (as) The Voyager".

"We contrive to make the invisible air support us, we relinquish the security of feet on the ground because flying is demanding, delightful, beautiful: because we love it. Very few of us are actually crazy, and nearly all of us manage the risks as well as we can, but we all willingly trade some of our security for the immeasurable beauty of the sky." - Paul J. Sampson

Psalm 8: 1-5, 9 **"Oh LORD our Lord, how excellent is thy name in all the earth! who has set thy glory above the heavens. When I consider thy heavens, the work of thy fingers, the moon and the stars, which thou hast ordained; What is man, that thou art mindful of him? And the son of man, that thou visitest him? For thou hast made him a little lower than angles, and hast crowned him with glory and honour. O LORD our Lord, how excellent is thy name in all the earth!"**

Psalm 55: 6-8 **"And I said, Oh that I had wings like a dove! for then I would fly away, and be at rest. Lo, then would I wander far off, and remain in the wilderness. I would hasten my escape from the windy storm and tempest."**

www.ingramcontent.com/pod-product-compliance
Lightning Source LLC
Chambersburg PA
CBHW070634160426
43194CB00009B/1457